DESTROYERS,
FRIGATES
AND
CORVETTES

DESTROYERS, FRIGATES
AND
CORVETTES

ROBERT JACKSON

BARNES
&NOBLE
BOOKS
NEW YORK

This edition published by Barnes & Noble, Inc.,
by arrangement with Amber Books Ltd
2000 Barnes & Noble Books

M 10 9 8 7 6 5 4 3 2 1

ISBN: 0-7607-1995-0

Editorial and design by
Amber Books Ltd
Bradley's Close
74–77 White Lion Street
London N1 9PF

Design: Keren Harragan

Printed in Singapore

PICTURE CREDITS:
TRH Pictures

ARTWORK CREDITS
All artworks Istituto Geografico De Agostini S.p.A. except the following:
Mainline Design (Guy Smith) 14, 15, 19, 20, 21, 22, 25, 32, 43, 46, 50, 63, 65, 73, 76, 125, 140,
149, 155, 156, 163, 184, 190, 216, 220, 222, 226, 228, 231, 232, 234, 235, 239, 241, 242, 248,
249, 250, 258, 259, 262, 264, 265, 271, 273, 277, 286, 287, 296, 298

CONTENTS

Introduction

At the end of the nineteenth century, the political strength of the major powers was measured by the size of their navies, and in particular, the power of their battleship fleets. Yet it was the invention of a much smaller instrument of war – the torpedo – that lead to the creation of the first destroyers, vessels purpose-built to combat this new weapon.

All the major navies had adopted the self-propelled torpedo by the 1880s, the latest models having a range of about 500m (1640ft) at a speed of 18 knots. The original compressed-air method of propulsion gradually gave way to electric motors. Capital ships and specially designed torpedo boats – HMS *Lightning* was the first – both deployed torpedoes from tubes or launch cradles at close range, making torpedo boats extremely vulnerable to defensive fire. An exercise conducted by the British Royal Navy in 1885 showed that although all the attacking craft were 'sunk', some of their practice torpedoes got through. The solution was to counter the torpedo boats with gun-armed 'catchers' deployed from capital ships. By the 1890s, these had evolved into larger, independent vessels called 'torpedo boat destroyers', designed to accompany larger units. Between 1892 and 1893, the first six ships, later called simply 'destroyers', were ordered for service with the Royal Navy.

Above: HMS Boxer, one of the improved Batch II Broadswords which, among other modifications, were lengthened to accommodate the Type 2031Z towed array sonar.

7

Above: HMS Inconstant, which was launched on 12 November 1868 and, when completed, proved to be the fastest warship afloat.

By 1895, 36 destroyers, led by HMS *Gossamer* and HMS *Rattlesnake*, had been launched. They were capable of 27 knots, but the torpedo boats then being built could reach 24, giving a slender speed margin. They were succeeded by an improved class, the first being HMS *Havoc* and HMS *Hornet*, which made in excess of 30 knots and were armed with two torpedo tubes mounted on the centreline, one 12-pounder and five 6-pounder guns. Sixty-eight were built, their displacement gradually increasing from 285 to 365 tonnes (280 to 360 tons).

The other major naval powers, in particular Italy, were quick to follow Britain's lead. In Germany, the architect of destroyer development was Admiral von Tirpitz, who had been a torpedo specialist and who placed great emphasis in building up the German destroyer and torpedo boat forces in the years leading up to World War I. German destroyer tactics envisaged delivering massed attacks on capital ships, and so the German vessels generally carried a larger torpedo armament than their British contemporaries. There was also less distinction between torpedo boats and destroyers; in fact, the latter were termed Grosse Torpedoboote (Large Torpedo Boats). The term Zerstörer (Destroyer) was not adopted until the B97 class was laid down between 1914 and 1915. At the other end of the scale, the boats of the 'S113' class, designed as flotilla leaders, were the largest destroyers built during World War I, and were armed with four 150mm (5.9in) guns.

In the years between the two World Wars, destroyers were key participants in the maritime arms race that developed when international events overturned the terms of the various naval treaties which restricted warships' numbers, tonnage and armament. In order to keep pace with worldwide destroyer developments, Britain laid down 16 big Tribal-class vessels of 1900 tonnes (1870 tons), followed by the 1717-tonne (1690-ton) J and K classes. An entirely new design of small, fast destroyer (915 tonnes/900 tons and 32 knots) was also introduced: the Hunt class, 20 of which were on the stocks at the outbreak of war. Although of limited endurance, they were to provide excellent service in home waters.

To bolster trade protection, the Admiralty ordered more sloops, which displaced between 1106 and 1270 tonnes (1000 and 1250 tons) and which, although slow, had a good endurance. By 1939, 53 were in service. Finally, a completely new type of small long-endurance vessel called a corvette, based on the whale-catcher, was introduced from 1939.

One of the German Navy's most important and versatile classes of ship of World War II was the torpedo boat, the groundwork for its operational use having been done by Admiral von Tirpitz long before World War I. The first 12 torpedo boats built between the wars were laid down in 1924 and completed between 1926 and 1929. They were the ships of the Wolf class and the Möwe class. With a displacement of around 945 tonnes (930 tons), the vessels were powered by two-shaft geared turbines and were capable of 61km/h (33 knots). Twenty-one torpedo boats were ordered and launched between 1939 and 1942, of similar displacement, but with the emphasis on armament, especially anti-aircraft weaponry.

The German Navy began World War II with two classes of destroyer; the Diether von Roeder class, comprising six ships, and the Leberecht Maass class of 16. The two classes were similar in size and displacement, although the von Roeder class, the last of the pre-war destroyers, had a superior speed and range. Both classes carried an armament of five 127mm (5in) guns, four or six 37mm AA guns, eight or 12 20mm AA guns, eight 533mm

(21in) torpedo tubes, and 60 mines. Many of these vessels became early casualties during the Norwegian campaign of April 1940, leaving the German destroyer force sadly depleted, but destroyer production had suffered because of the emphasis on U-boats. Although Germany laid down more advanced destroyers, with a heavier armament (particularly AA) and a longer radius of action after the outbreak of war, they came too late and were expended in action either in the Arctic or in French coastal waters.

The French Navy had a large number of very fine destroyers in 1939, but never had a chance to use them effectively before the Armistice. Many were deliberately scuttled when the Germans occupied the French Mediterranean ports; others went on to give valuable service in the Allied cause. France's pre-war destroyer development was closely linked to Italy's, as the two countries strove to maintain naval parity. Italy's destroyers were fine, well-designed ships, but suffered very heavily during the war. As many as 74 were lost in action against British forces and some 30 more scuttled or captured by the Germans as a consequence of the Armistice. Fifty new destroyers were laid down after Italy's entry into the war, but by the Armistice in September 1943, only six were completed.

Japan, whose destroyer designs had always reflected British influence, produced vessels of indigenous design in the 1920s. The first of these, the Momi class, proved excellent vessels in coastal waters and in support of amphibious landings. Japan's destroyer forces suffered horrendous casualties in World War II, few vessels surviving to the final surrender.

In the construction of destroyers, it was the United States that surpassed all other combatants. The Craven and Sims classes were completed before Pearl Harbor, and larger, better-armed ships like the Benson-Livermore and Fletcher classes followed swiftly. The USA ended the war with the massive total of 850 destroyers, and another 105 on the stocks.

The modern destroyer would hardly be recognisable to one familiar with the classic gun-and torpedo-armed vessels of World War II. Even the term 'destroyer' is somewhat loose, covering as it does vessels ranging from the small, gun-armed Kotlin class of the former Soviet Navy up to the Russian Sovremenny and American Spruance and Kidd classes, each as large as light cruisers of the 1940s.

Since World War II, the destroyer has evolved from a torpedo-armed, all-gun surface warfare vessel into a specialist anti-air or anti-submarine

Above: British and American seamen swap notes in front of three destroyer escorts provided for Britain under the Lend-Lease scheme of World War II.

ship, capable either of independent operations for a short time or of operating as an escort in a task force. The losses suffered by the Royal Navy's destroyers during the Falklands war proved to NATO that the UK's minimally armed warships, which had been so constructed to satisfy restraints imposed by the UK Treasury, were extremely vulnerable in a conventional war, let alone the nuclear scenarios proposed for any future conflict in the North Atlantic theatre of operations. Short-term action was taken to rectify some of their faults, and plans made to update them as they became due for refit, with the installation of close-range weapons a high priority.

Probably the most capable modern destroyer design is the Spruance class, optimised for ASW. Modifying the design for the anti-air role produced the Kidd class, which at the time of commissioning were the most powerfully-armed general-purpose destroyers in the world. Some of the Spruance-class vessels were retrofitted with the Tomahawk cruise missile, discharged from vertical launchers, but not all the 31 ships received the necessary modifications, as it was deemed too expensive.

FRIGATES

Ever since the frigate was conceived in the eighteenth century – when it was used mainly for reconnaissance and commerce raiding – it has formed a very important element in the world's navies. Today, the name is applied to a wide variety of vessels, ranging from very expensive and highly specialised anti-submarine warfare ships like the Royal Navy's Type 22, to cheaper ships like the US Navy's Knox class, designed to escort convoys and amphibious warfare task groups.

The frigate was an important part of the warship inventories of both east and west during the Cold War. The British Leander class of general purpose frigate, for example, which entered service in the 1960s, served the Royal Navy well for many years: 26 were built. They were to have been succeeded by 26 examples of the Type 22 Broadsword class, conceived as ASW ships for the Greenland-Iceland-UK gap against Soviet high-performance nuclear submarines; 14 were built. The other principal British frigate was the Type 21 Amazon class, of which eight were built.

To counter the modern nuclear-powered submarine, with its high underwater speed, most modern frigates are fitted with twin-shaft gas-turbine engines with controllable-pitch propellers. They must be at the cutting edge of naval technology, making their design and construction prohibitively costly for smaller navies, which usually prefer to buy them 'off the shelf' from the principal maritime powers.

France rates her frigates as sloops, and uses them mainly as 'gunboats' to protect her interests overseas, particularly guarding the approaches to the French nuclear test centre at Mururoa Atoll in the Pacific.

During the Cold War, some European nations – the Netherlands and the former Federal German Republic, for example – cooperated in frigate design and construction, producing vessels to satisfy a common requirement. At the turn of the twentieth century, Britain, France and Italy were studying a joint proposal for an anti-aircraft frigate, the Horizon class.

Although optimised for anti-submarine warfare in the world's leading navies, frigates tend to be used as general purpose 'workhorse' vessels in smaller navies. Only those that serve wealthier countries are customised for that nation's particular needs. Saudi Arabia, for example, purchased French Type F2000 class frigates in the 1980s, and in terms of capability and state-of-the-art electronic equipment, at the time of delivery these vessels could out-perform many of the frigates in service with NATO and the Warsaw Pact.

Some smaller navies however, opt for small, light frigates armed with missiles. Since the end of the Cold War, the former Soviet Union, specialising in this type of ship, has offered many vessels for sale on the international arms market. Although Russian maritime technology in many areas is less sophisticated than the latest Western equipment, it is adequate for those Third World nations keen to secure naval superiority in their particular spheres of influence.

Above: USS McFaul, one of the very latest ships of the Arleigh Burke class of fleet escorts (destroyers).

GUNBOATS

This type of warship has been included here because in many ways, the nineteenth-century gunboat was the ancestor of the destroyers, corvettes, sloops and frigates, the 'small ships' that have formed such an important part of twentieth-century maritime history. Throughout Victorian times, the gunboat was a principal instrument in policing the empire. They carried a crew of 30 or 40, commanded by a lieutenant, an ideal first command for an ambitious young officer in a navy where chances of promotion had hitherto often depended on the death of someone more senior. Instead of gunboats, the ships that police the trouble spots of today's world are the destroyers and frigates, their officers and men of much the same mould as their forebears of a century and a half ago.

Abukuma

The original *Abukuma* of this class was a World War II Japanese cruiser which was sunk during the Battle of Leyte Gulf in October 1944. Her namesake is classed as a destroyer escort (DE) by the Japanese Maritime Self-Defence Force, but is more properly classed as a frigate. There are five other vessels in the class: the *Jintsu*, *Ohyodo*, *Sendai*, *Chikuma* and *Tone*. The first pair of the class was approved in the 1986 defence estimates whereas the last couple were approved in the 1989 estimates. Their main gun has an elevation of 85 degrees and can fire a 6kg (13.2lb) projectile over a distance of 16km (8.6nm) in the surface engagement role, or 12km (6.5nm) in the anti-aircraft role. The torpedoes used are the Honeywell Mk46 Mod 5 Neartip anti-submarine type, which have a range of 11km (5.9nm) at 40 knots.

Country of origin:	Japan
Type:	Frigate (destroyer escort)
Launch date:	21 December 1988
Crew:	120
Displacement:	2591 tonnes (2550 tons)
Dimensions:	109m x 13.4m x 4m (357ft 4in x 44ft x 13ft)
Endurance:	6485km (3500nm)
Main armament:	One 76mm (3in) gun; Phalanx CIWS; ASROC A/S system; six 324mm (12.75in) torpedo tubes
Powerplant:	Two shafts, two gas turbines, two diesels
Performance:	27 knots

Adelaide

HMAS *Adelaide* and her sisters (*Canberra*, *Sydney*, *Darwin*, *Melbourne* and *Newcastle*) are the Royal Australian Navy's variants of the Oliver Hazard Perry class of guided-missile frigate. All six ships have been modernised and are equipped to carry the Sikorsky Seahawk ASW helicopter. The weapons system is being upgraded, with various options being considered. These include the installation of a short-range missile system – probably Evolved Sea Sparrow – as well as the fitting of enhanced electronic, mine avoidance and torpedo countermeasures. HMAS *Adelaide*, *Darwin* and *Canberra* are at Fleet Base West, with the remainder at Fleet Base East. For operational tasks, the vessels are fitted with enhanced communications and other equipment such as electro-optical sights. All the ships can operate in the fighter direction role.

Country of origin:	Australia
Type:	Guided-missile frigate
Launch date:	21 June 1978
Crew:	184
Displacement:	4165 tonnes (4100 tons)
Dimensions:	138.1m x 13.7m x 7.5m (453ft x 45ft x 24ft 6in)
Endurance:	7783km (4200nm)
Main armament:	One 76mm (3in) gun; Phalanx CIWS; Harpoon SSMs and Standard SAMs; six 324mm (12.75in) torpedo tubes
Powerplant:	Single shaft, two gas turbines
Performance:	29 knots

Akitsuki

By far the largest destroyers built in series by the Japanese, the Akitsuki-class ships were originally conceived as anti-aircraft escorts. They were the only eight-gun destroyers in the Japanese fleet, and it would seem that the quadruple torpedo tube mounting was a later addition. Anti-aircraft armament was progressively strengthened during the war. The most distinctive feature of the class was the complex casing of the single stack. Extensive trunking enabled the funnel to be sited far enough abaft the bridge both to reduce the smoke problem and aid visibility, while placing it sufficiently far back to permit extra anti-aircraft platforms to be installed where the afterstack would normally have been. Twelve ships of this class were built, of which six were sunk. The *Akitsuki* herself was lost on 25 October 1944.

Country of origin:	Japan
Type:	Destroyer
Launch date:	2 July 1941
Crew:	285
Displacement:	2743 tonnes (2700 tons)
Dimensions:	134.1m x 11.6m x 4.11m (440ft x 38ft 1in x 13ft 6in)
Endurance:	14,797km (7990nm)
Main armament:	Four twin 100mm (3.94in) and two twin 25mm AA guns; one quadruple 610mm (24in) torpedo tube mounting
Powerplant:	Two sets of geared steam turbines
Performance:	33 knots

Alecto

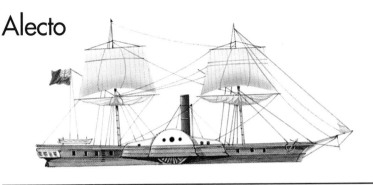

In the 1840s, the engineer Isambard Kingdom Brunel wrote a lengthy report on the screw propeller. It was examined by Admiralty officials, who realised that the use of a propeller would eliminate one of the principal objections to steam-powered warships, which was that a paddle wheel would get in the way of a ship's broadside gun arrangement. With advice from Brunel, the Admiralty authorised the building of a small, screw-driven steam sloop, the *Rattler*, for use as a trials ship. In 1845 she was matched against a paddle steamer of similar size, the *Alecto*, and won easily, ending the test by towing the paddle steamer backwards. After that, new warships were designed with engines and propellers, and some older vessels were retrofitted, but the engines were for auxiliary power only. It would be some time before steam won the day completely.

Country of Origin:	Britain
Type:	Paddlewheel Frigate
Launch date:	not available
Crew:	66
Displacement:	816 tonnes (803 tons)
Dimensions:	Not known
Endurance:	Not known
Main armament:	Two 6-pounder guns
Powerplant:	One 200 hp engine driving two paddles
Performance:	Not known

Almirante class

The Chilean Navy has traditionally operated a mixture of British and American warships since its inception. The Chilean Navy's two Almirante-class destroyers – *Riveros* and *Williams* – are among the oldest in service anywhere in the world. Built by Vickers-Armstrong Ltd of Barrow, they were completed in 1960. The vessels were fitted with twin rudders, affording exceptional manoeuvrability, and the ventilation and heating systems were designed to suit the Chilean climate, which varies greatly along the country's lengthy coastline, which extends from the tropics to Cape Horn. Each ship is armed with four Exocet SSM launchers and with Seacat quadruple SAM launchers. The main armament is disposed in four single mountings, two superimposed forward and two aft. The guns are entirely automatic, with a range of 11,430m (12,500yds) and an elevation of 75 degrees.

Country of origin:	Chile
Type:	Destroyer
Launch date:	12 December 1958 (Riveros, first unit)
Crew:	266
Displacement:	3353 tonnes (3300 tons)
Dimensions:	122.5m x 13.1m x 4.0m (402ft x 43ft x 13ft 4in)
Endurance:	9650km (5208nm)
Main armament:	Four 102mm (4in) guns; four 40mm(1.5in); six 324mm (12.75in) torpedo tubes; Squid A/S mortars
Powerplant:	Two shafts, geared turbines
Performance:	34.5 knots

Almirante Brown

Originally to have been a class of six, with four to have been built in Argentina, the Meko 360H2 Almirante Brown-class design is based on the modularised systems concept, whereby each of the weapons and sensor systems carried form a separate modular unit and can be interchanged with a replacement or newer system without the usual reconstruction that otherwise accompanies the modernisation of a ship. The four ships (*Almirante Brown*, *La Argentina*, *Heroina* and *Sarandi*) were all built by the German firms of Thyssen Rheinstahl and Blohm und Voss, and were commissioned between 1983 and 1984. *Almirante Brown* took part in the allied Gulf operations in 1990. Fennec helicopters were delivered in 1996 to improve ASW capability and provide over-the-horizon targeting for SSMs. All units were operational at Puerto Belgrano in 1999.

Country of origin:	Argentina
Type:	Destroyer
Launch date:	28 March 1981
Crew:	200
Displacement:	3414 tonnes (3360 tons)
Dimensions:	125.9m x 14m x 5.8m (413ft 1in x 46ft x 19ft)
Endurance:	7783km (4200nm)
Main armament:	Four twin Exocet launchers; one octuple SAM launcher; one 127mm (5in) DP gun; two triple 324mm (12.75in) torpedo tubes
Powerplant:	Twin shafts, four gas turbines
Performance:	30.5 knots

Almirante Padillo

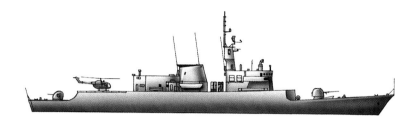

Prior to the *Padillo* entering service, the most powerful unit in the Colombian Navy was a Halland-type destroyer, also German-built. Commissioned in 1983, the *Almirante Padillo* and her three sister ships, commissioned a year later, gives the Colombian Navy a considerable surface attack capability, although the ships of this class are now overdue for modernisation. A refit programme, which would include the fitting of surface-to-air missiles, remains top priority, but the required funding is not available. The ships were built by Howaldtswerke, Kiel. Each carries an MBB 105 helicopter for anti-submarine warfare, and is fitted with a Thomson-CSF Sea Tiger search radar with a range of 110km (60nm). The ships carry the Atlas Elektronik ASO 4-2 hull-mounted active attack sonar. A similar class of vessel was built for the Malaysian Navy.

Country of origin:	Colombia
Type:	Corvette
Launch date:	6 January 1982
Crew:	94
Displacement:	2134 tonnes (2100 tons)
Dimensions:	99m x 11.3m x 3.7m (325ft 1in x 37ft 1in x 12ft 1in)
Endurance:	11,112km (6000nm)
Main armament:	One 76mm (3in) gun; one Oerlikon 30mm (1.1in); eight Exocet SSMs; six 324mm (12.75in) torpedo tubes
Powerplant:	Two shafts, four diesels
Performance:	27 knots

Alvand

On 25 August 1966, it was announced that Vosper Ltd of Portsmouth had received an order for four 'destroyers' for the Iranian Navy. They were in fact of the small *Vosper* Mk5 frigate type, with one main gun forward, two secondary guns aft, anti-aircraft and anti-submarine weapons. Each vessel was fitted with gas turbines for high speed and diesels for long-range cruising. Originally known as the Saam class, the vessels all received new identities after the Iranian revolution and became the Alvand class. One of the boats, the *Sahand*, was sunk by the US Navy during a confrontation in the Persian Gulf on 18 April 1988. Another vessel, the *Sabalan*, had her back broken by a laser-guided bomb in the same skirmish, but was repaired and was operational again by the end of 1991. The other two vessels are the *Alvand* and *Alborz*.

Country of origin:	Iran
Type:	Frigate
Launch date:	25 July 1968
Crew:	125
Displacement:	1372 tonnes (1350 tons)
Dimensions:	94.5m x 11.1m x 4.3m (310ft x 36ft 5in x 14ft 1in)
Endurance:	6485km (3500nm)
Main armament:	One 114mm (4.5in) and two 35mm guns; 5 SSMs; AS mortars
Powerplant:	Two shafts, two gas turbines, two diesels
Performance:	39 knots

Amazon

The Type 21 Amazon-class general-purpose frigate was a private shipbuilder's design to replace the obsolete Type 41 Leopard- and Type 61 Salisbury-class frigates. Because of numerous bureaucratic problems, private and official ship designers were not brought together on the project, resulting in a class which handled well and was well liked by its crews, but lacked sufficient growth potential to take the new generation of sensor and weapon fits. Completed in May 1974, HMS *Amazon* was the only Type 21 not to see action in the 1982 South Atlantic campaign. A serious fire aboard the vessel in 1977 brought to light the dangers inherent in all aluminium superstructures. However, it was not until after the Falklands conflict (in which the Type 21s *Ardent* and *Antelope* were lost) that the Royal Navy reverted to using steel.

Country of origin:	Britain
Type:	Frigate
Launch date:	26 April 1971
Crew:	177
Displacement:	3404 tonnes (3350 tons)
Dimensions:	117m x 12.7m x 5.9m (384ft x 41ft 8in x 19ft 6in)
Endurance:	9265km (5000nm)
Main armament:	One single 14mm (4.5in) DP gun; four single 20mm AA guns; two triple 324mm (12.75in) ASW torpedo tubes
Powerplant:	Twin shafts, four gas turbines
Performance:	32 knots

Amberto di Giussano

One of a class of four units built to counter the powerful French Lion-class destroyers, *Amberto di Giussano* represented an extremely efficient class of ship. Lightly armoured, she was one of the fastest destroyers in the world at the time of her launch; one of her class achieved a speed of 42 knots during trials and maintained a steady 40 knots for eight hours. Classified as a light cruiser before the outbreak of World War II, the *di Giussano* became part of the Italian Navy's 4th Division at Italy's entry into the war in June 1940, and undertook many minelaying operations. They were very cramped and uncomfortable ships which proved to be wet and lacking in stability. Together with a sister ship, *Alberico da Barbiano*, she was sunk by the British destroyers *Legion* and *Maori* on 13 December 1941, 900 lives being lost in the two ships.

Country of origin:	Italy
Type:	Destroyer
Launch date:	27 April 1930
Crew:	220
Displacement:	5170 tonnes (5089 tons)
Dimensions:	169.4m x 15.2m x 4.3m (555ft 9in x 49ft 10in x 14ft 1in)
Endurance:	7037km (3800nm)
Main armament:	Eight 152mm (6in) guns
Powerplant:	Two sets of geared steam turbines
Performance:	40 knots

Andromeda

F 57

HMS *Andromeda* was a Batch 3 ship of the Leander class of frigate. From the 17th Leander, the design was amended by increasing the beam. HMS *Andromeda* was the first of five broadbeamed Leanders to be fitted with Sea Wolf short-range surface-to-air missiles and with the sea-skimming Exocet anti-ship missile, recommissioning in 1980. After refitting, HMS *Andromeda* and the other four Batch 3 vessels were the most powerful of their class. A successful design, the Leander class sold well to overseas navies, the ships in foreign service being generally better armed than those serving in the Royal Navy. India's Leanders, known as the Godavari class, were fitted with a mixture of western and Russian systems. Leander-class vessels were also sold to Australia and the Netherlands, and all had better armament and sensor fits than their Royal Navy counterparts.

Country of origin:	Britain
Type:	Frigate
Launch date:	24 May 1967
Crew:	260
Displacement:	3009 tonnes (2962 tons)
Dimensions:	113.4m x 13.1m x 4.5m (372ft x 43ft x 14ft 10in)
Endurance:	8894km (4800nm)
Main armament:	Twin 114mm (4.5in) guns; two single 20mm (0.7in) AA guns; two triple 324mm (12.75in) ASW torpedo tubes; Exocet, Sea Wolf
Powerplant:	Two shaft geared steam turbines
Performance:	27 knots

Annapolis

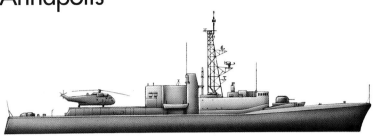

Completed in 1964, the *Annapolis* and her sister ship, *Nipigon*, were developed from the original St Laurent class and served in the destroyer escort role alongside two other groups, the Mackenzie and Restigouche classes. As originally built, the ship's armament included a Mk10 Limbo three-barrelled ASW mortar. As they were fitted with a hangar and armed with a Sea King ASW helicopter each, the *Annapolis* and *Nipigon* were designated DDH. The two ships underwent a full Destroyer Life Extension (Delex) programme between 1982 and 1985, being fitted with new air radar, sonar, communications and electronic warfare equipment. *Annapolis* is based in the Pacific Fleet in a readiness condition; *Nipigon* is in reserve. The latter's main armament and radars were removed in 1994 but replaced in 1995. Both ships are scheduled to pay off between 2001 and 2002.

Country of origin:	Canada
Type:	Frigate
Launch date:	27 April 1963
Crew:	246
Displacement:	2946 tonnes (2900 tons)
Dimensions:	111.5m x 12.8m x 4.1m (366ft x 42ft x 13ft 6in)
Endurance:	7970km (4300nm)
Main armament:	Two 76mm (3in) guns; six 324mm (12.75in) torpedo tubes
Powerplant:	Two shafts, turbines
Performance:	28 knots

Araguaya

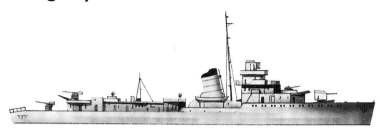

A<i>raguaya</i> and her five sisters were built to replace six British H-class destroyers which, under construction for Brazil, were taken over by the Royal Navy at the outbreak of World War II. They followed the same design but used American equipment. All were built between 1943 and 1946 at the Ilha des Cobras Navy Yard. *Araguaya* was launched in 1946 and discarded in 1974. All the ships of this class were named after rivers, the others being the *Acre, Amazonas, Araguari, Apa* and *Ajuricaba*. The original H-class destroyers destined for Brazil were to have been named *Jurua, Javary, Jutahy, Juruena, Jaguaribe* and *Japarua*. They saw war service with the Royal Navy as *Handy, Havant, Havelock, Hearty, Highlander* and *Hurricane*. The H class destroyers were efficient, capable ships. Two of those taken over by the RN, *Handy* and *Hurricane,* were lost in action.

Country of origin:	Brazil
Type:	Destroyer
Launch date:	20 November 1943
Crew:	190
Displacement:	1829 tonnes (1800 tons)
Dimensions:	98.5m x 10.7m x 2.6m (323ft x 35ft x 8ft 6in)
Endurance:	9265km (5000nm)
Main armament:	Four 127mm (5in); two 40mm (1.6in) guns
Powerplant:	Two shaft geared turbines
Performance:	35.5 knots

Ardent

Ardent was one of a class of eight units with which the Royal Navy began a new era of destroyer construction, after a lapse of eight years from the end of World War I. The class introduced quadruple torpedo tubes and had full shields for their 11.9cm (4.7in) guns. *Ardent* and her sister ship *Acasta* were sunk in June 1940 by the German battlecruisers *Scharnhorst* and *Gneisenau* while escorting the aircraft carrier *Glorious*, which also fell victim to the German guns. Apart from the above-named, the ships of this class were the *Achates* (lost 31 December 1942), *Acheron* (lost 17 December 1940), *Active*, *Antelope*, *Anthony* and *Arrow*. Two more ships of this design served with the Royal Canadian Navy as the *Saguenay* and *Skeena*. The former was damaged in a collision off Newfoundland in November 1942 and the latter ran aground on the coast of Iceland in 1944.

Country of origin:	Britain
Type:	Destroyer
Launch date:	1929
Crew:	138
Displacement:	2022 tonnes (1990 tons)
Dimensions:	95.1m x 9.8m x 3.7m (312ft x 32ft 3in x 12ft 3in)
Endurance:	4630km (2500nm)
Main armament:	Four 120mm (4.7in) guns; eight 533mm (21in) torpedo tubes
Powerplant:	Twin shaft geared turbines
Performance:	35 knots

Ariete

The Ariete-class ships were improved versions of the Spica class of 1936–8. The vessels of this class were not laid down until 1942 and 1943, by which time the Italians had the benefit of much combat experience. Over 40 units were planned in an extended programme but, although construction was spread over three yards, only 16 were laid down. These were the *Alabarda*, *Ariete*, *Arturo*, *Auriga*, *Balestra*, *Daga*, *Dragone*, *Eridano*, *Fionda*, *Gladio*, *Lancia*, *Pugnale*, *Rigel*, *Spada*, *Spica* and *Stella Polare*. Only the *Ariete* served with the Italian navy, a month before the armistice. The remainder, in various stages of construction, fell into German hands, and 13 saw sea service. Only two, the *Ariete* and *Balustra*, survived the war. The reason so many Italian warships were captured by the Germans was that they were being built in northern Italy, and were readily accessible.

Country of origin:	Italy
Type:	Torpedo boat
Launch date:	6 March 1943
Crew:	155
Displacement:	813 tonnes (800 tons)
Dimensions:	82.85m x 8.6m x 2.8m (269ft 9in x 28ft 2in x 9ft 2in)
Endurance:	1852km (1000nm)
Main armament:	Two single 100mm (3.94in) and two single 37mm (1.45in) AA guns; two triple 540mm (17.72in) torpedo tubes; up to 28 mines
Powerplant:	Two sets of geared steam turbines
Performance:	31 knots

Arleigh Burke

This large class of guided-missile destroyer was designed to replace the ageing Adams- and Coontz-class destroyers which entered service in the early 1960s. The principal mission of the Arleigh Burk class is to provide effective anti-aircraft cover, for which they have the SPY 1D version of the Aegis area defence system. The Arleigh Burkes are the first US warships to be fully equipped for warfare in a nuclear, chemical or biological environment, the crew being confined in a citadel located within the hull and superstructure. The ships are heavily protected; plastic Kevlar armour is fitted over all vital machinery and operations room spaces for this purpose. Armament includes one 127mm (5in) DP gun and two 20mm Phalanx CIWS mountings, and the ships are fitted with a platform for an ASW helicopter. There is also a laser designator for the guidance of the DP gun's Deadeye shells.

Country of origin:	USA
Type:	Guided missile destroyer
Launch date:	16 September 1989
Crew:	303
Displacement:	8534 tonnes (8400 tons)
Dimensions:	81m x 18.3m x 9.1m (266ft 3in x 60ft x 30ft)
Endurance:	11,118km (6000nm)
Main armament:	Harpoon and Tomahawk anti-ship and land attack cruise missiles; one 127mm (5in) gun.
Powerplant:	Twin shaft gas turbine
Performance:	32 knots

Armando Diaz

Armando Diaz and her sister ship *Luigi Cadorna* were part of the Italian Navy's building programme of between 1929 and 1930, and were originally classified as light cruisers. They bore a strong resemblance to the previous group of fast cruisers, but they had more internal space, which in turn permitted reduced upperworks and a smaller bridge. These improvements helped to enhance the vessels' stability in heavy seas. Both ships had a seaplane catapult on the rear superstructure. They could carry up to 138 mines, depending on the type. Both ships, reclassified as destroyers, operated extensively in the Mediterranean during World War II, but *Armando Diaz* was sunk in February 1941 when the British submarine HMS *Upright* torpedoed her while she was in the process of escorting a convoy.

Country of origin:	Italy
Type:	Destroyer
Launch date:	10 October 1932
Crew:	220
Displacement:	5406 tonnes (5321 tons)
Dimensions:	169.3m x 15.5m x 5.5m (555ft 6in x 50ft 10in x 18ft)
Endurance:	5185km (2800nm)
Main armament:	Eight 152mm (6in) guns
Powerplant:	Twin shaft geared turbines
Performance:	36.5 knots

Artigliere

By 1936, Italy had developed a successful destroyer design, and in 1937 was ready to lay down the first batch of what eventually formed the largest single class of destroyer built for the Italian Navy. Twenty-one units were built, all of which saw extensive war service as effective escorts. They were capable of taking a great deal of punishment, although as with all pre-war destroyers, the anti-aircraft armament proved ineffective and was soon improved. During the night of 11–12 October 1940, the *Artigliere*, serving with the 12th DD Flotilla, was engaged in a night action with the British cruiser HMS *Ajax* and received heavy hits. She was taken under tow, but the next day, following reports that the British cruiser HMS *York* was approaching, her crew were taken off and the vessel herself was cast adrift and sunk.

Country of origin:	Italy
Type:	Destroyer
Launch date:	12 December 1937
Crew:	230
Displacement:	2540 tonnes (2500 tons)
Dimensions:	106.7m x 10.2m x 3.5m (350ft x 33ft 4in x 11ft 6in)
Endurance:	4447km (2400nm)
Main armament:	Four 120mm (4.7in) guns
Powerplant:	Twin screw geared turbines
Performance:	38 knots

Asagiri

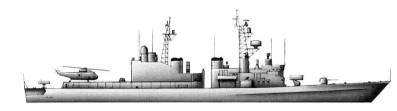

The fast guided-missile destroyer *Asagiri* and her seven sister ships (*Yamagiri*, *Yuugiri*, *Amagiri*, *Hamagiri*, *Setogiri*, *Sawagiri* and *Umigiri*) were all laid down between 1985 and 1988 and commissioned between 1989 and 1991. The last four named above were fitted during building with an improved air search radar, undated fire control radars, and a helicopter datalink. All eight vessels are now equipped with a towed sonar array. In service, the first ships were found to have a high infrared signature, and modifications were subsequently carried out to the mainmast and forward funnel to reduce the problem. The funnel is slightly offset to port and the after funnel to the starboard side of the fuselage. The large hangar structure is asymmetrical, extending to the after funnel on the starboard side but only as far as the mainmast on the port.

Country of origin:	Japan
Type:	Destroyer
Launch date:	19 September 1966
Crew:	220
Displacement:	3556 tonnes (3500 tons)
Dimensions:	137m x 14.6m x 4.5m (449ft 4in x 48ft x 14ft 6in)
Endurance:	8153 km (4400nm)
Main armament:	One 76mm (3in) gun; Harpoon SSMs; Sea Sparrow SAMs; six 324mm (12.75in) torpedo tubes
Powerplant:	Two shafts, four gas turbines
Performance:	30+ knots

Asagumo

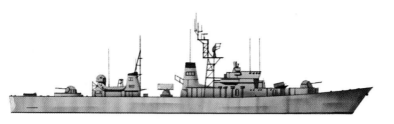

The *Asagumo* and her six sister ships – *Makigumo, Minegumo, Murakumo, Natsugumo, Yamagumo* and *Aokumo* – were part of a Japanese Navy modernization programme initiated in the early 1960s. *Yamagumo* was ordered under the 1962 fiscal year new construction programme, *Makigumo* under the 1963 programme, and *Asagumo* under the 1964 programme. The ships all have the word 'cloud' in their names: *Makigumo*, for example, means 'Rolling Cloud', while *Yamagumo* means 'Mountain Cloud'. *Asagumo* was the second Japanese destroyer to bear the name; the first was sunk by the American cruiser *Denver* in Surigao Strait during the Battle of Leyte on 25 October 1944. The Japanese tend to name their warships after natural features and the elements; for example, there were the Moon, Rain and Cloud classes in service alongside the Asagumos.

Country of origin:	Japan
Type:	Destroyer
Launch date:	25 November 1966
Crew:	210
Displacement:	2083 tonnes (2050 tons)
Dimensions:	114m x 11.8m x 4m (374ft x 38ft 9in x 13ft)
Endurance:	11,380km (6145nm)
Main armament:	Four 76mm (3in) guns; six torpedo tubes
Powerplant:	Twin shaft diesel engines
Performance:	28 knots

Asashio

The Asashio class of 10 units were larger versions of the two preceding classes of destroyer. Their arrival marked Japan's abandonment of any restrictions imposed by pre-World War II treaties. The new steam turbines proved unreliable at first, and problems with the steering gear were not corrected until December 1941. In due course, however, this design overcame most of the faults inherent in previous classes, and became the basic plan for the next two classes of destroyer, Kagero and Yugumo. During the war, the Asashi class was used extensively in the protection of the Japanese Combined Fleet. *Asashio* and *Arashio* were sunk in 1943, when a transport force they were escorting was annihilated by air attack in the Bismarck Sea. Three more vessels – *Michishio*, *Asagumo* and *Yamagumo* – were sunk in the Battle of Leyte.

Country of origin:	Japan
Type:	Destroyer
Launch date:	16 December 1936
Crew:	200
Displacement:	2367 tonnes (2330 tons)
Dimensions:	118.2m x 10.4m x 3.7m (388ft x 34ft x 12ft)
Endurance:	7408km (4000nm)
Main armament:	Six 127 mm (5in) guns
Powerplant:	Twin shaft geared turbines
Performance:	35 knots

Astore

Launched in June 1907, *Astore* was one of a group of six torpedo boats completed between 1907 and 1909 as a follow-on design to the eight-strong Cigno class. She was classified as a high seas torpedo boat, and was intended for service in the Atlantic. Apart from her three torpedo tubes, she was lightly armed, and her radius of action was reduced to 590km (318nm) at full speed. The Italian Navy had 19 such vessels in service, all laid down from 1905 onwards. They all had distinguished active careers during World War I. *Astore* and her five sister ships served mostly in the Atlantic, where their main task was convoy escort. Two of the ships were later converted into fast minesweepers, but the remainder stayed substantially in the same configuration throughout. All ships in the class survived the war and were discarded in 1923.

Country of origin:	Italy
Type:	Torpedo boat
Launch date:	22 June 1907
Crew:	150
Displacement:	220 tonnes (216 tons)
Dimensions:	50.3m x 5.3m x 1.75m (160ft 2in x 17ft 5in x 5ft 9in)
Endurance:	3335km (1800nm)
Main armament:	Three 47mm (1.8in) guns; three 450mm (17.7in) torpedo tubes
Powerplant:	Twin screw triple expansion engines
Performance:	25.8 knots

Athabaskan

Launched between 1970 and 1971, *Athabaskan* and her three sisters (*Algonquin*, *Huron* and *Iroquois*) were designed specifically for anti-submarine warfare operations. They have the same hull design, dimensions and basic characteristics as an earlier class of large, general-purpose frigates, cancelled in the early 1960s. Properly designated Destroyer Helicopter Escorts (DDH), they carry two Sea King ASW helicopters. They are equipped with anti-rolling tanks to stabilise them at low speed, a pre-wetting system to counter radioactive fallout, and an enclosed citadel from which control of all machinery is exercised. A comprehensive electronics system includes an effective long-range radar warning device. The Athabaskan class ships, optimised as they were for operations in the extremely rough waters of the Arctic, formed a valuable contribution to NATO's ASW forces during the Cold War.

Country of origin:	Canada
Type:	Destroyer
Launch date:	27 November 1970
Crew:	246
Displacement:	4267 tonnes (4200 tons)
Dimensions:	129.8m x 15.5m x 4.5m (426ft x 51ft x 15ft)
Endurance:	8334km (4500nm)
Main Armament:	One 127mm (5in) gun; one triple A/S mortar
Powerplant:	Twin screw, gas turbines
Performance:	30 knots

Audace

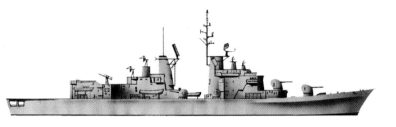

Ordered from Yarrow shipbuilders by the Imperial Japanese Navy as the destroyer *Kawakaze*, and laid down in 1913, this vessel was transferred from Japan to Italy while still under construction and initially named *Intrepido*. Launched in 1916 and completed the following year, in 1929 she was reclassed from destroyer to torpedo boat. During World War II she was used for minelaying duties, mostly in the Adriatic. On 9 September 1943, following Italy's armistice with the Allies, she was seized by the Germans in Venice and designated TA20. She continued with minelaying operations, narrowly escaping attack by the large Free French destroyers *Le Terrible* and *Le Fantasque* on 18 March 1944. Her luck finally ran out on 1 November 1944, when she was sunk in action with the corvettes *UJ202* and *UJ208* by the British escort destroyers *Avon Vale* and *Wheatland*.

Country of origin:	Italy
Type:	Torpedo boat
Launch date:	4 May 1913
Crew:	120
Displacement:	1016 tonnes (1000 tons)
Dimensions:	86m x 8.3m x 2.8m (283ft x 27ft 6in x 9ft 6in)
Endurance:	2779km (1500nm)
Main armament:	Seven 102mm (4in) guns
Powerplant:	Twin screw geared turbines
Performance:	27 knots

Audace

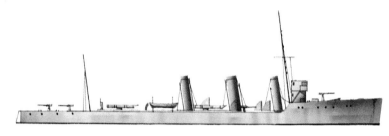

Essentially enlarged versions of the earlier Impavido class, *Audace* and her sister *Ardito* are good examples of multi-function fleet escorts with the primary role of destroying enemy submarines. Two helicopters with a comprehensive weapons kit and sensors are carried by each vessel. *Audace* has a flush-decked hull of high freeboard and an uncluttered superstructure, but some of her weapons have a poor arc of fire due to the height of the superstructure. The double hangar is housed aft, while the fore bridge houses the communications and sensor equipment. The embarked helicopters (two AB212s or one Sea King) carry both Mk44 and Mk46 torpedoes, Mk54 depth bombs and anti-ship missiles. The two Audace-class ships proved to be such excellent vessels that two units of an improved Audace design were ordered to replace the Impavido-class destroyers.

Country of origin:	Italy
Type:	Destroyer
Launch date:	2 October 1971
Crew:	381
Displacement:	4470 tonnes (4400 tons)
Dimensions:	135.9m x 14.6m x 4.5m (446ft x 48ft x 15ft)
Endurance:	6482km (3500nm)
Main Armament:	Two 127mm (5in) guns; one SAM launcher
Powerplant:	Two shaft geared turbines
Performance:	33 knots

Augusto Riboty

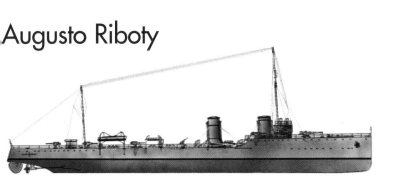

Augusto Riboty and her two sister ships were originally planned to be lightly armoured light cruisers to be laid down in 1913. However, they emerged as flotilla leaders with heavy armament. *Carlo Alberto Racchia* and *Carlo Mirabello* were both sunk by mines, but *Augusto Riboty* survived World War II. She was allocated to the Soviet Union under the terms of the peace treaty, but remained in Italy and was scrapped in 1951. Minelaying was Riboty's principal occupation during the conflict, although in October 1940 she was engaged in transporting Italian troops to Albania as part of the invasion support force. Early in 1943 she was also involved in transporting troops and supplies to the Axis forces fighting in Tunisia. As their surface vessels and aircraft had suffered unacceptable losses by 1943, the Axis were forced to rely more on submarines for supplying their forces.

Country of origin:	Italy
Type:	Flotilla Leader
Launch date:	24 September 1916
Crew:	150
Displacement:	2003 tonnes (1972 tons)
Dimensions:	103.7m x 9.7m x 3.6m (340ft x 32ft x 12ft)
Endurance:	4259km (2300nm)
Main Armament:	Eight 102mm (4in) guns
Powerplant:	Twin shaft turbines
Performance:	22 knots

Avon

Before World War II, measures had been put in hand by the Royal Navy to build vessels – frigates – that were suitable for escorting Britain's vital ocean convoys. *Avon* was one of over 90 ships of the River class laid down between 1941 and 1943 and completed between 1942 and 1944. They were ocean-going anti-submarine escorts and proved better adapted to that role than the smaller Flower-class corvettes. Two sets of engines were installed and in later vessels the fuel capacity was increased from 447 to 656 tonnes (440 to 646 tonnes). The original light armament was also increased. After World War II many ships of this class were passed to other navies, where they continued to give good service until the 1960s. *Avon*, which was launched in June 1943, went to the Portuguese Navy in 1949 as the *Nuno Tristao*. HMS *Awe* was also transferred to Portugal at the same time.

Country of origin:	Britain:
Type:	Frigate
Launch date:	19 June 1943
Crew:	140
Displacement:	2133 tonnes (2100 tons)
Dimensions:	91.8m x 11m x 3.8m (301ft 4in x 36ft 8in x 12ft 9in)
Endurance:	5556kn (3000nm)
Main Armament:	Two 102mm (4in) guns
Powerplant:	Twin screw vertical triple expansion engines
Performance:	20 knots

Avvoltoio

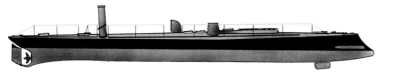

*A*vvoltoio was rated as a second-class torpedo boat; commissioned in 1881, she was designated 2Y from 1886, the 'Y' signifying that she had been built in Yarrow. Launched in 1879, *Avvoltoio* was typical of the torpedo boats of her day. Since surprise was the principal weapon of such craft, early types were fast and small, lightly built, and unprotected, their sole purpose being to get close enough to enemy capital ships to use their torpedoes effectively. *Avvoltoio* was the second such type adopted by the Italians; she was discarded in 1904. During the period when *Avvoltoio* came into service, Italy was still smarting over the war with Austria which ended with the disastrous battle of Lissa just over a decade earlier, when two Italian ironclads were sunk and another damaged. Italian naval leaders were determined to build a maritime force that would dominate the Adriatic.

Country of origin:	Italy
Type:	Torpedo boat
Launch date:	1879
Crew:	20
Displacement:	25 tonnes (25 tons)
Dimensions:	26m x 3.3m x 1.3m (86 ft x 11ft x 4ft 6in)
Endurance:	Not known
Main armament:	Two 356mm (14in) torpedo tubes; one 1-pounder revolving cannon
Powerplant:	Single screw vertical triple expansion engine
Performance:	21.3 knots

Avvoltoio

By the mid-1880s the small torpedo craft of the previous decade had evolved into large, ocean-going vessels. This class was originally rigged as three-maasted schooners. The *Avvoltoio* and her four sister ships – *Falco, Sparviero, Aquila* and *Nibbio* – were first-class boats able to keep up with the fastest ships in the fleet and possessed an adequate radius of action. They were operational in the Dardanelles against the inferior Turkish Navy during the Balkan wars of 1911–12, but as far as it is known, they did not register any successes. The concept of the torpedo boat was vindicated during the conflict, however, when the Greek torpedo craft *No 11* sank the Turkish central battery ship *Feth-i-Bulend* (*Great Conqueror*) at Salonika on 31 October 1912. All ships of the Avvoltoio class were discarded between 1912 and 1914.

Country of origin:	Italy
Type:	Torpedo boat
Launch date:	1889
Crew:	65
Displacement:	132 tonnes (130 tons)
Dimensions:	46.3m x 5.2m x 2.3m (152ft x 17ft 2in x 7ft 9in)
Endurance:	2222km (1200nm)
Main armament:	Three 356mm (14in) torpedo tubes; two three-pounder guns
Powerplant:	Twin screw vertical triple expansion engine
Performance:	26.6 knots

Badr

Although better described as a Fast Attack Craft (Missile), *Badr* is really a small frigate, carrying much the same armament as larger vessels; the intention is to double the SSM capability in due course with the installation of eight lightweight Otomat or Harpoon. She is one of six Ramadan-class boats in service with the Egyptian Navy, all commissioned between 1981 and 1982. The craft were built at the Portchester yard of Vosper Thorneycroft Ltd, some of the hulls being manufactured at Portsmouth Old Yard and towed to Portchester for fitting out. The boats underwent an electronic warfare systems upgrade between 1995 and 1996. They are fitted with the Marconi Sapphire Weapons Control System, with two radar/TV and two optical directors. *Badr*'s British origins keep with a tradition that has seen the Egyptian Navy equipped mostly with British warships since its earliest days.

Country of origin:	Egypt
Type:	Frigate
Launch date:	25 November 1980
Crew:	30
Displacement:	312 tonnes (307 tons)
Dimensions:	52m x 7.6m x 2.3m (170ft 7in x 25ft x 7ft 6in
Endurance:	2570km (1388nm)
Main armament:	One 76mm (3in) gun; two 40mm (1.5in) gun; OTO Melara SSM; portable SA-N-5 SAM
Powerplant:	Four shafts, four diesel engines
Performance:	40 knots

Baleno

Baleno was one of a class of four fast destroyers – the Folgore class – built for the Italian Navy in the early 1930s. They saw hard service in the Mediterranean, being progressively fitted with heavier anti-aircraft armament, and none survived the war, all being sunk in action. On 16 April 1941, *Baleno* and another destroyer, *Luca Tarigo*, were escorting five merchant ships from Sicily to Tripoli. The convoy was sighted by four British destroyers, which attacked immediately. In spite of a gallant fight, the *Luca Tarigo* and the merchantmen were sunk with heavy loss of life. *Baleno* managed to limp away with a severe list, heavily damaged and taking on water. Her crew were unable to carry out enough repairs to keep her afloat, and she capsized and sank the next day. The other vessels in the class – *Folgore, Fulmine* and *Lampo* – were all sunk in action with British surface ships.

Country of origin:	Italy
Type:	Destroyer
Launch date:	22 March 1931
Crew:	450
Displacement	10,156 tonnes (9996 tons)
Dimensions:	105m x 21m x 7.6m (344ft 6in x 69ft x 25ft)
Endurance	3200km (2000 miles)
Main armament:	Four 254mm (10in) guns; eight 152mm (6in) guns
Powerplant:	One Ford GAA V-8 petrol engine developing 335.6 or 373 kW (450 0r 500 hp)
Performance:	18 knots

Balny

Balny, launched in 1886, was one of a group of 10 ocean-going torpedo boats designed by Normand as a development of existing launches; in particular *Balny* was based upon the design of *Poti,* which that shipyard had built for the Imperial Russian Navy. However, the ships were not really big enough for their task and rolled badly in heavy seas. This meant that they were clearly not suited to working in their main operational area, which was the Bay of Biscay. All French torpedo craft at this time were designed with offensive operations against Italian naval bases in mind, and possibly against British bases too, as relations between France and Britain in the latter years of the nineteenth century were often tense. All that was to change in just a few more years, when Germany emerged as the principal threat.

Country of origin:	France
Type:	Torpedo boat
Launch date:	January 1886
Crew:	22
Displacement:	66 tonnes (65 tons)
Dimensions:	40.8m x 3.4m x 1m (134ft x 11ft x 3ft 3in)
Endurance:	Not known
Main armament:	Two 355mm (14in) torpedo tubes in the bow
Powerplant:	Single screw compound engine
Performance:	19 knots

Baptista de Andrade

The *Baptista de Andrade* and her three sister ships (*Joao Roby, Afonso Cerquiera* and *Oliveiro E Carmo*) have been in service with the Portuguese Navy since the mid-1970s, and a planned modernisation programme, which was to include surface-to-surface missiles and SAMs, has been postponed several times. Originally intended for South Africa, the ships were all built by Empresa Nacional Bazan at Cartagena. Their main Creusot-Loire 100mm (3.9in) gun has a rate of fire of 80 rounds per minute and has a range of 17km (9nm) in the surface engagement role or 8km (4.4nm) in the anti-aircraft role, for which it can be elevated to an angle of 80 degrees. The torpedoes carried are the Honeywell Mk46 lightweight anti-submarine variety, which have a speed of 40 knots and are effective up to 11km (5.9nm).

Country of origin:	Portugal
Type:	Frigate
Launch date:	March 1973
Crew:	122
Displacement:	1402 tonnes (1380 tons)
Dimensions:	84.6m x 10.3m x 3.1m (277ft 6in x 33ft 9in x 10ft 2in)
Endurance:	1019km (5500nm)
Main armament:	One 100mm (3.9in) gun; two Bofors 40mm(1.5in); six 324mm (12.75in torpedoes
Powerplant:	Two shafts, two diesels
Performance:	22 knots

Battle class

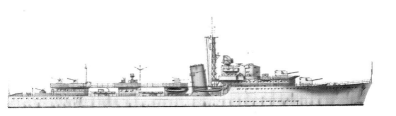

The Battle-class destroyers had their genesis about the time of Matapan, when the Royal Navy was still desperately seeking ways of countering the aerial threat that had been so badly underestimated in the 1930s. Bitter experience had shown that the dive-bomber needed to be countered by plenty of metal, but although the 'pom-pom' was an excellent weapon, main battery guns were capable of only 40 degrees or 55 degrees maximum elevation. The specification for the new destroyer called for 85 degrees and a high rate of fire. The overall result was a very large ship with considerable endurance and twinned gun houses, both sited forward. Only five units were completed before the end of hostilities in Europe, and were deployed to the Pacific in 1945. In that theatre they served in the British Task Force 57, which formed part of the US Fifth Fleet and was based on Ulithi Atoll.

Country of origin:	Britain
Type:	Destroyer
Launch date:	December 1943 (first unit)
Crew:	232
Displacement:	2418 tonnes (2380 tons)
Dimensions:	115.52m x 12.26m x 3.28m (379ft x 40ft 3in x 10ft 9in)
Endurance:	8032km (4337nm)
Main armament:	Two twin and one single 114mm (4.5in) DP plus two twin and two single 40mm (1.5in) AA guns; two quintuple 533mm (21in) TT
Powerplant:	Two sets of geared steam turbines
Performance:	35.5 knots

Benson

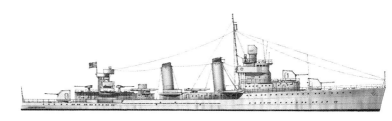

The Benson-Livermore class of destroyers used the same hull and machinery as the earlier Sims class, but had the boiler spaces divided for improved damage control, necessitating a return to two funnels. Only the first 24 hulls were completed with the full designed armament. Ninety-six Bensons were built between 1939 and 1943, and though the last 64 were officially the separate Livermore class, there were only marginal differences, leading to the latter type having a slightly greater displacement. On 10 April 1941, one of the Benson class, the USS *Niblack*, became the first US destroyer in World War II to carry out a depth charge attack on a suspected submarine contact off Iceland. This occurred while she and others of her class were operating the 'Neutrality Patrol', with orders to attack any U-boat that threatened American shipping.

Country of origin:	USA
Type:	Destroyer
Launch date:	15 November 1939
Crew:	250
Displacement:	1646 tonnes (1620 tons)
Dimensions:	106m x 11m x 3m (347ft 9in x 36ft 4in x 10ft 4in)
Endurance:	9265km (5000nm)
Main armament:	Five single 127mm (5in) DP guns; two quintuple 533mm (21in) torpedo tubes
Powerplant:	Two sets of geared steam turbines
Performance:	37 knots

Berlin

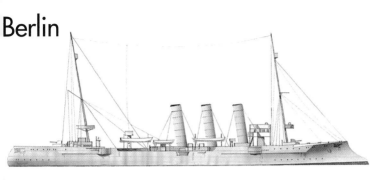

Berlin was a Brandenburg frigate of medium size developed from the larger and slower ships of the line. They were built as a consequence of the growing need for a special vessel to carry out fast scouting work, with sufficient speed to outrun the sloops that were usually deployed as lookouts for a main battle fleet. Frigates were never intended to fight the standard ships of the line, but were employed in cruising the world's oceans, protecting the commercial trade of their own country and attacking that of the enemy. *Berlin* was a good sea boat, and the experience gained from her performance led other countries to develop their own frigates along similar lines. These vessels grew from ships carrying around 20 cannon to larger types mounting over 40 guns on a single deck. The term 'frigate' lapsed from naval terminology in the 19th century, and did not reappear until World War II.

Country of origin:	Germany
Type:	Frigate
Launch date:	22 September 1903
Crew:	375
Displacement:	1016 tonnes (1000 tons)
Dimensions:	48.7m x 11.5m (160ft x 38ft)
Endurance:	Unlimited, depending on provisions
Main Armament:	Twenty 24-pounder guns
Powerplant:	Sail
Performance:	4 knots

Beskytteren

The Royal Danish Navy, though small, has always prided itself on maintaining an effective force of warships, and is very experienced at operating in northern waters. Used by the Royal Danish Navy for fishery protection duties, the *Beskytteren* is a modified Hvidbjornen-class frigate with a strengthened structure for ice operations. The vessel carries a Westland Lynx Mk 91 helicopter for reconnaissance and is fitted with two Thorn-EMI Sea Gnat six-barrelled chaff launchers. The small Danish Navy has several frigates, but is equipped mainly with fast attack craft armed with either missiles or torpedoes, and small patrol boats. *Beskytteren* was built in Denmark by the Aalborg Vaerft; she was laid down in December 1974 and commissioned in February 1976. Denmark also uses a more modern group of frigates, the Thetis class, in the fishery protection role.

Country of origin:	Denmark
Type:	Frigate
Launch date:	27 May 1975
Crew:	56
Displacement:	2002 tonnes (1970 tons)
Dimensions:	74.7m x 12.2m x 5.3m (245ft x 40ft x 17ft 5in)
Endurance:	7222km (3900nm)
Main armament:	One 76mm (3in) DP gun
Powerplant:	Single shaft, 3 diesels
Performance:	18 knots

Bettino Ricasoli

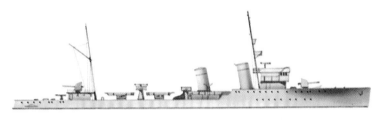

The *Bettino Ricasoli* was one of a group of four vessels built to update the World War I Palestro class. The armament was unusual in that there were two guns mounted aft on a platform with the third on the forecastle. The normal crew of 120 could be increased to 152 in time of war. *Bettino Ricasoli*'s machinery proved unreliable in service, and even at her best she could barely reach 33 knots. She was sold to Sweden and renamed *Puke* (*Pike*), but her engines continued to give trouble and she was stricken in 1947. The sale to Sweden was unusual in that the majority of Sweden's warships were Swedish-built, and probably came about as a result of the need to strengthen the neutral country's coastal defences with the onset of World War II. Sweden, however, was never under threat of invasion by Germany; for commercial and political reasons she was far more useful as a neutral.

Country of origin:	Italy
Type:	Destroyer
Launch date:	29 January 1926
Crew:	120
Displacement:	1480 tonnes (1457 tons)
Dimensions:	85m x 8.5m x 2.8m (278ft 6in x 28ft 2in x 8ft 10in)
Endurance:	3704km (2000nm)
Main Armament:	Three 120mm (4.7in) guns
Powerplant:	Twin screw geared turbines
Performance:	33 knots

Blitz

B*litz* and her sister ship *Komet* were designed to combat the much-improved type of torpedo boats that were then entering service with the world's navies. Normal gunboats were too slow to keep up with the fleet, so the torpedo gunboat, with its high speed and large number of light guns, seemed to be the answer. The ships were, in effect, prototype destroyers. Torpedo tubes were positioned with one in the bow, one firing aft and two on a turntable amidships. Apart from *Komet*, the other ships in the Blitz class were *Meteor*, *Planet*, *Trabant*, *Satellit*, *Magnet* and *Huszar*. The latter sank in December 1908 and the rest were ceded to Italy after World War I with the exception of *Satellit*, which went to France. They were broken up in 1920. All the destroyers except *Blitz* and *Komet* were built to different designs for evaluation purposes, so that one could be selected for standardisation.

Country of origin:	Austria
Type:	Destroyer
Launch date:	7 July 1888
Crew:	56
Displacement:	433 tonnes (426 tons)
Dimensions:	59m x 7m x 2m (193ft 6in x 22ft 11in x 6ft 6in)
Endurance:	Not known
Main armament:	Nine 3-pounder guns; four 355mm (14in) torpedo tubes
Powerplant:	Single screw, triple expansion engines
Performance:	26 knots

Bodryi

In the early 1930s the weakness of the Russian destroyer force was obvious and, as a result, in 1932 a new type of destroyer was designed with the help of Italy. However, it was not until 1935 that the first vessel of the new class, known as the Type 7, was laid down. *Bodryi* was among the first group of 28 ships, which were found to lack seaworthiness under the often severe conditions of the Arctic and northern Pacific areas in which they were intended to serve. In fact, *Bodryi*'s area of operations was the Black Sea where she served in the Soviet Navy's 2nd Destroyer Division. In the winter of 1941–42 she was heavily involved in transporting troops and supplies to the besieged fortress of Sevastopol. Damaged beyond repair in an air attack in July 1942, she was eventually broken up in 1958. In all, 20 ships of this class were lost in World War II.

Country of origin:	Russia
Type:	Destroyer
Launch date:	1936
Crew:	180
Displacement:	2072 tonnes (2039 tons)
Dimensions:	113m x 10m x 4m (370ft 3in x 33ft 6in x 12ft 6in)
Endurance:	4630km (2500nm)
Main Armament:	Four 127mm (5.1in) guns
Powerplant:	Twin screw geared engines
Performance:	32 knots

Bombarda

Bombarda was one of 59 Gabbiano-class escorts built under a wartime specification that called for a cheap, quick-to-build anti-submarine vessel for service in the Mediterranean. Two auxiliary electric motors of 150hp each were fitted to allow silent AS search at 6 knots, although these were not incorporated in *Bombarda*. Most of the class were seized by the Germans shortly after Italy's armistice with the Allies; *Bombarda* was captured on the slip on 11 September 1943 and numbered *UJ206*. She was severely damaged in an air attack at Venice on 25 April 1944 and scuttled there by the Germans a year afterwards. Later refloated and rebuilt for post-war service with the Italian Navy, she was not withdrawn from use until 1975. Other long-serving ships of the class were *Baionetta*, *Chimera*, *Cormorano*, *Crisalide*, *Farfalla*, *Gabbiano*, *Ibis*, *Scimitarra*, *Sibilla* and *Urania*.

Country of origin:	Italy
Type:	Corvette
Launch date:	31 August 1942
Crew:	109
Displacement:	740 tonnes (728 tons)
Dimensions:	64.3m x 8.7m x 2.5m (211ft x 28ft 7in x 8ft 4in)
Endurance:	5556km (3000nm)
Main armament:	One 102mm (4in) gun; depth charges
Powerplant:	Twin screw diesel engines
Performance:	18 knots

Bombardiere

Launched in March 1942, *Bombardiere* was one of the second group of Soldati-class destroyers that eventually formed the largest class of destroyer built for the Italian Navy. Their anti-aircraft armament, inadequate at first, was progressively improved. On 21 November 1942, she was in company with the destroyers *Legionario* and *Velite*, escorting a small convoy in the Bay of Naples, when she was attacked by the British submarine HMS *Splendid*; she evaded the torpedoes, which destroyed the *Velite*. On 17 January 1943, while engaged in a reinforcement operation to Tunisia, she was sunk by the submarine HMS *United* (Lt Roxburgh) off Marettimo. Three vessels of this class, *Legionario, Mitragliere* and *Velite*, were transferred to France under the terms of the Peace Treaty and renamed *Duchaffault, Jurien de la Graviäre* and *Duperre*.

Country of origin:	Italy
Type:	Destroyer
Launch date:	23 March 1942
Crew:	250
Displacement:	2540 tonnes (2500 tons)
Dimensions:	107m x 10m x 3.5m (350ft x 33ft 7in x 11ft 6in)
Endurance:	6300km (3400nm)
Main Armament:	Five 120mm (4.7in) guns
Powerplant:	Twin screw turbines
Performance:	38 knots

Bombe

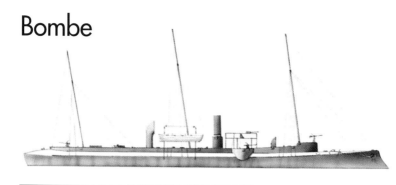

Bombe and her seven sister vessels of this class were distinguished by their three light raking masts, originally with a fore and aft rig, and a single raking funnel abaft the foremast. The boilers fitted in this class gave a great deal of trouble, and completion was delayed as a result. The bow was slightly ram-shaped; the stern had an overhang and the sides curved in to a narrow upper deck. The ships had 12.7mm (0.5in) of armour plate to protect their conning towers, and the main guns were mounted forward and aft and in sponsons on either beam, with the torpedo tubes further aft. One ship in the class, *Dragonne*, was fitted for experimental trials with howitzers in 1896. All eight vessels – *Bombe*, *Couleuvrine*, *Dague*, *Dragonne*, *Fleche*, *Lance*, *Sainte-Barbe* and *Salve* – were completed between 1887 and 1890, and were stricken between 1906 and 1914.

Country of origin:	France
Type:	Torpedo gunboat
Launch date:	April 1885
Crew:	70
Displacement:	375 tonnes (369 tons)
Dimensions:	59.2m x 6m x 3.1m (194ft 3in x 19ft 7in x 10ft 5in)
Endurance:	Not known
Main armament:	Two 355mm (14in) torpedo tubes; four 3-pounder guns; three 1-pounder revolvers
Powerplant:	Twin screw vertical compound engines
Performance:	18–19 knots

Bonhomme Richard

Launched in 1765, the *Bonhomme Richard* was originally the *Duc de Duras*, built for the East India Company for service between France and the Far East. She had a crew of 375 and, as well as the 12-pounder cannon, carried six 18-pounders and eight nine-pounders. In 1779 the *Duc de Duras* was placed at the disposal of the legendary American naval officer John Paul Jones and renamed *Bonhomme Richard*. Under his command she first escorted French troop convoys, then began a raiding cruise against British commerce in the Bay of Biscay. On 23 September 1779 she encountered a Baltic convoy, escorted by HMS *Serapis*. In the ensuing fierce fight, off Flamborough Head, she sank the *Serapis*, but was herself so severely damaged that she was abandoned and sank two days later. In total, 150 of her crew had been lost in the battle.

Country of origin:	USA
Type:	Frigate
Launch date:	1765
Crew:	375
Displacement:	1014 tonnes (998 tons)
Dimensions:	46m x 2m x 5.7m (152ft x 40ft x 19ft)
Endurance:	Unlimited, depending on stores
Main Armament:	Twenty-eight 12-pounder cannon
Powerplant:	Sail
Performance:	5 knots

Borea

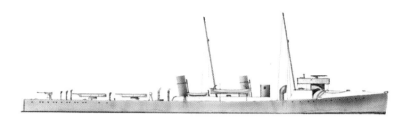

Borea and her five sisters formed the first major class of torpedo craft to be built in Italy. All ships were later reboilered, and their armament was modified. In 1915, minelaying equipment was added. *Nembo* was sunk in 1916 by the Austrian submarine *U16* which, in turn, was sunk by the exploding depth charges on the sinking ship. *Borea* was sunk by the Austrian destroyers *Csepel* and *Balaton* on 14 May 1917. Much of the Italian Navy's destroyer activity in World War I was centred in the Adriatic, where priority was given by both sides to mining the approaches to one another's harbours. The Italians had the more difficult task, for the Dalmatian coastline was riddled with natural harbours and inlets that gave shelter to Austrian shipping. Two more vessels of the Nembo class, to which *Borea* belonged, were lost in action with Austro-Hungarian naval forces.

Country of origin:	Italy
Type:	Destroyer
Launch date:	12 December 1902
Crew:	90
Displacement:	386 tonnes (380 tons)
Dimensions:	64m x 6m x 2.3m (210ft x 19ft 6in x 7ft 6in)
Endurance:	1850km (1000nm)
Main Armament:	Five 76mm (3in) guns; four 355mm (14in) torpedo tubes
Powerplant:	Twin screw triple expansion engine
Performance:	26 knots

Borea

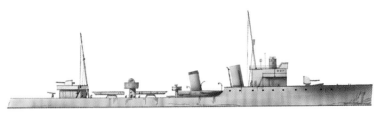

This class of eight fast destroyers were improved versions of the earlier Sauro class, being slightly longer and having more powerful machinery. In sea trials, the design speed of 36 knots was often exceeded. One of the class, *Turbine*, managed to maintain 40 knots for over four hours, although 33 knots was an average figure under operational conditions. Afer a few years of operational use, *Borea* was modified to carry anti-shipping mines; she could hold up to 52 of these weapons depending on type and size. All these ships served in the Italian Navy in World War II, although none survived the conflict. The *Borea* was sunk by Swordfish aircraft from the carrier HMS *Illustrious* off Benghazi on 17 September 1940. One of the class, *Euro*, was sunk by German bombers on 1 October 1943, a few weeks after Italy surrendered to the Allies.

Country of origin:	Italy
Type:	Destroyer
Launch date:	28 January 1927
Crew:	105
Displacement:	1697 tonnes (1670 tons)
Dimensions:	93m x 9m x 4m (305ft 9in x 30ft x 9ft 10in)
Endurance:	2224 km (1200nm)
Main Armament:	Four 120mm (4.7in) guns
Powerplant:	Twin screw geared turbines
Performance:	36 knots

Boudeuse

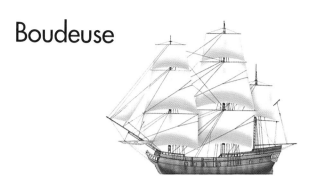

Launched in 1763, *Boudeuse* was a small frigate that proved fast and handy, carrying a large spread of canvas on light spars. Her hull was lightly sheathed and covered with flat-headed iron nails which rusted together to form a solid, yet easy to repair, layer. With the end of the Seven Years War (1756–63), Frenchman Louis de Bougainville established a colony on the Falkland Islands. When the Spanish forced the French to evacuate the islands, Bougainville set out across the Pacific in command of *Boudeuse* and eventually arrived at Tahiti, which he formally annexed in 1767. Bougainville in the Solomon Islands, scene of much bitter fighting in World War II, is named after him. The exploits of French explorers tended to be overshadowed by their British counterparts like Captain Cook, possibly because of the scientific nature of the British expeditions.

Country of origin:	France
Type:	Frigate
Launch date:	1763
Crew:	175
Displacement:	559 tonnes (550 tons)
Dimensions:	40m (131ft) long on the gun deck
Endurance:	Unlimited, depending on stores
Main Armament:	Twenty-six 18-pounder cannon
Powerplant:	Sail
Performance:	11 knots

Bourrasque

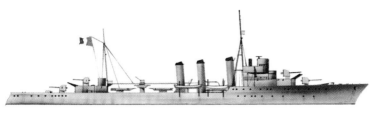

The 12 vessels of the Bourrasque class formed part of the 1922 programme by which France planned to upgrade her navy. *Bourrasque* was well armed and compared favourably with her contemporaries. However, any advantage that might have been gained from using a large-calibre gun was lost because the rate of fire was only four to five rounds per minute. All ships in the class underwent armament modifications, and some were stripped of the aft 127mm (6in) gun to improve stability. *Bourrasque* was lost while evacuating troops from Dunkirk on 30 May 1940, being shelled and mined off Nieuport. Two ships of this class, *Mistral* and *Ouragan*, were in British ports at the time of the armistice in June 1940, and were taken over. *Mistral* was manned by a Royal Navy crew until 1944 and *Ouragan* served with the Polish Navy for a time before being turned over to the Free French.

Country of origin:	France
Type:	Destroyer
Launch date:	5 August 1925
Crew:	104
Displacement:	1930 tonnes (1900 tons)
Dimensions:	105.7m x 10m x 4.2m (347ft x 31ft 9in x 14ft)
Endurance:	4630km (2500nm)
Main Armament:	Four 127mm (5in) guns
Powerplant:	Twin screw geared turbines
Performance:	26 knots

Boykiy

Boykiy was one of six Krupny-class destroyers built during the 1960s. They were originally completed as missile ships. Initial construction started in 1958 at Leningrad. Original armament was the SS-N-1 anti-ship missile, but when this became obsolete, the whole group was converted to the anti-submarine warfare role. Other ships in the class were the *Gnevnyi*, *Gordyi*, *Plamyonny* and *Zorkyi*. They were the first Soviet destroyers to have a helicopter platform fitted as standard, probably because a helicopter was necessary to provide mid-course corrections to the anti-ship missiles. They were also the last developments of the original *Kotlin* destroyer concept to be built, later designs making use of gas turbine propulsion or new high-pressure steam plant. Three ships of the class were converted to the SAM role.

Country of origin:	Russia
Type:	Destroyer
Launch date:	15 December 1960
Crew:	360
Displacement:	4826 tonnes (4750 tons)
Dimensions:	140m x 15m x 5m (458ft 9in x 45ft 9in x 16ft 6in)
Endurance:	11,112km (6000nm)
Main Armament:	Eight 57mm (2.25in) guns, plus missiles
Powerplant:	Twin screw geared steam turbines
Performance:	34 knots

Brandenburg

The four Type 123 Brandenburg-class frigates (the others are *Schleswig-Holstein*, *Bayern* and *Mecklenburg-Vorpommern*) were all commissioned between 1994 and 1996 and are based with the 6th Frigate Squadron of the German Navy at Vilhelmshaven. They were formerly known as the Deutschland class, and were ordered in 1989 to replace the deleted Hamburg class. They are extremely well armed and carry a formidable array of electronic equipment, including air search D-band and air/sea search F-band radars. They are fitted with the Atlas Elektronik/Paramax SATIR combat data system and their design, developed by Blohm und Voss, incorporates stealth technology. On-board space is allocated for a Task Group Commander and his battle staff. The ships of this class are optimised for combat in the relatively confined waters of the Baltic.

Country of origin:	Germany
Type:	Frigate
Launch date:	28 August 1992
Crew:	199 plus 19 aircrew
Displacement:	4775 tonnes (4700 tons)
Dimensions:	138.9m x 16.7m x 6.8m (455ft 8in x 54ft 9in x 22ft 3in)
Endurance:	6430km (3472nm)
Main armament:	One 76mm (3in) DP gun; four Exocet; 16 Sea Sparrow SAMs; four 324mm (12.75in) anti-submarine torpedo tubes
Powerplant:	Two shafts, two gas turbines, two diesels
Performance:	29 knots

Bremen

A Germanised modification of the gas turbine-powered Dutch Kortenaer design, the eight-ship Bremen class of Type 122 frigates replaced the German Navy's elderly Fletcher-class destroyers and Kïln-class frigates. The first order was placed in 1977, and the first ship was commissioned in May 1982. The ships are fitted with fin stabilisers; a complete NBC defence citadel system is also fitted. The eight ships in service are the *Bremen* (F207), *Niedersachsen* (F208), *Rheinland-Pfalz* (F209), *Emden* (F210), *Kïln* (F211), *Karlsruhe* (F212), *Augsburg* (F213) and *Lübeck* (F214). Like the Brandenburgs, the Bremen class were intended for operations in the Baltic, but some units have been deployed farther afield in recent years. All have received an updated EW fit since 1994, and current plans call for them to remain in first-line service well into the twenty-first century.

Country of origin:	Germany
Type:	Frigate
Launch date:	27 September 1979
Crew:	204
Displacement:	2977 tonnes (2930 tons)
Dimensions:	130.5m x 14.4m x 6m (428ft 1in x 47ft 3in x 19ft 7in)
Endurance:	12,970km (7000nm)
Main Armament:	Two quadruple Harpoon missile launchers; one octuple NATO Sea Sparrow SAM launcher; two RAM close-range SAM launchers; one 76mm (3in) gun; four 324mm (12.75in) torpedo tubes
Powerplant:	Two gas turbines, two diesels
Performance:	32 knots

Broadsword

The British Leander class of general-purpose frigate, which entered service in the 1960s, served the Royal Navy well for many years; 26 were built. The Leanders were to have been succeeded by 26 examples of the Type 22 Broadsword class, conceived as ASW ships for use in the Greenland-Iceland-UK gap against Soviet high-performance nuclear submarines, but in the event only 14 were produced. *Brilliant* and *Broadsword* distinguished themselves in action during the 1982 Falklands war. The other principal class of British frigate was the Type 21 Amazon class, of which eight were constructed. All the Batch 1 vessels were sold to Brazil: *Broadsword* on 30 June 1995, *Brilliant* and *Brazen* on 30 August 1996, and *Battleaxe* on 30 April 1997. The Batch 2 Broadswords, deployed with the 1st Frigate Squadron, are *Boxer*, *Beaver*, *Brave*, *London*, *Sheffield* and *Coventry*.

Country of origin:	Britain
Type:	Frigate
Launch date:	12 May 1976
Crew:	286
Displacement:	4470 tonnes (4400 tons)
Dimensions	131m x 14.8m x 4.2m (430ft 5in x 48ft 8in x 14ft)
Endurance:	7408km (4000nm)
Main Armament:	Four M38 Exocet launchers; two 30mm (1.6in) guns; two sextuple Sea Wolf SAM; Sting Ray torpedoes
Powerplant:	Twin screw gas turbine engines
Performance:	30 knots

Broadsword III

The Broadswords were built in three batches, of which Batch 3 was a general purpose variant. The four Batch 3 units are HMS *Cornwall*, *Cumberland*, *Campbeltown* and *Chatham*. All the Batch 3 vessels have enlarged flight decks for the operation of Sea King or EH101 Merlin helicopters, although a single Westland Lynx is usually embarked for peacetime operations. The Batch 3 ships are fitted with two Rolls-Royce Spey SM1A and two Rolls-Royce Tyne gas turbines; the more powerful Spey SM1C engines might be retrofitted in due course. The Seawolf GWS25 short-range SAM system is being progressively upgraded, as is the electronic warfare fit. The Batch 3 Broadswords are deployed with the 2nd Frigate Squadron. They are highly capable ships, and the appelation 'frigate' seems rather inappropriate when applied to vessels displacing some 5000 tonnes.

Country of origin:	Britain
Type:	Frigate
Launch date:	14 October 1985 (HMS *Cornwall*)
Crew:	273
Displacement:	4877 tonnes (4800 tons)
Dimensions:	148.1m x 14.8m x 6.4m (458ft 10in x 48ft 6in x 21ft)
Endurance:	7238km (3906nm)
Main armament:	Four 30mm (1.1in); two 20mm (0.7in) guns; Exocet SSMs; Seawolf SAMs; six 324mm (12.75in) Stingray torpedo tubes
Powerplant:	Two shafts, four gas turbines
Performance:	30 knots

Bullfinch

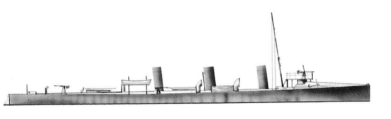

By the late nineteenth century, the combination of torpedo and torpedo boat represented a real threat to the Royal Navy's capital ships. The solution was to counter the torpedo boats with gun-armed 'catchers' that could be deployed from capital ships, and by the 1890s these had evolved into larger, independent vessels called 'torpedo boat destroyers' designed to accompany larger units. Between 1892 and 1893, the first six ships, now called simply 'destroyers', were ordered for service with the Royal Navy. By 1895, 36 destroyers, led by HMS *Gossamer* and HMS *Rattlesnake*, had been launched and were succeeded by an improved class, the first of which were HMS *Havoc* and HMS *Hornet*, which could make 30 knots and were armed with two torpedo tubes mounted on the centreline, one 12-pounder and five six-pounder guns. HMS *Bullfinch* was one of 68 built over these two classes.

Country of origin:	Britain
Type:	Destroyer
Launch date:	10 February 1898
Crew:	63
Displacement:	396 tonnes (390 tons)
Dimensions:	65m x 6m x 2.5m (214ft 6in x 20ft 6in x 7ft 10in)
Endurance:	2778km (1500nm)
Main Armament:	One 12-pounder; five six-pounders; two 457mm (18in) torpedo tubes
Powerplant:	Twin screw triple expansion engines
Performance:	30 knots

Byedovi

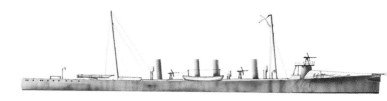

B<i>yedovi</i> was one of a group of 22 destroyers of this class laid down in Russian yards between 1900 and 1903 that followed the successful British-built <i>Sokol</i> of 1895 in general design. Many of the class saw service in the Russo-Japanese war of 1904–5, and gave good service. After the Battle of Tsushima in May 1905, <i>Byedovi</i> – one of the few Russian warships that was still undamaged - attempted to escape to Vladivostok with the wounded Russian commander, Admiral Rozhestvensky, on board. However, she was intercepted by Japanese destroyers and compelled to surrender. Impressed into service with the Imperial Japanese Navy, she was scrapped in 1922. Some of these vessels took part in the final evacuation of White Russian refugees from the Black Sea ports in 1920 and ferried them to North Africa, mostly to Bizerta. Their eventual fate is unknown.

Country of origin:	Russia
Type:	Destroyer
Launch date:	1902
Crew:	80
Displacement:	355 tonnes (349 tons)
Dimensions:	56.6m x 6m x 3m (185ft 6in x 19ft 6in x 9ft 8in)
Endurance:	2778km (1500nm)
Main Armament:	One 12-pounder and five three-pounder guns; three 380mm (15in) torpedo tubes
Powerplant:	Twin screw vertical triple expansion engines
Performance:	26.5 knots

Calatafimi

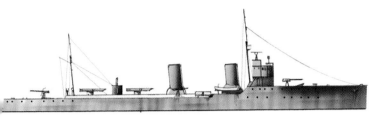

Originally ordered in 1915, *Calatafimi* and her three sisters were delayed due to a shortage of materials created by the demands of the army; *Calatafimi* herself was not launched until March 1923. In 1938 the vessels were reclassified as torpedo boats and their armament was altered, a single 102mm (4in) gun replacing the twin mount aft. After the Italian surrender in September 1943, *Calatafimi*, together with several other boats of her class, was impressed into service by the Germans for service in the Aegean. Renamed *TA19*, she took part in many escort operations with the 9th Torpedo Boat Flotilla before being torpedoed and sunk by the Greek submarine *Pipinos* on 9 August 1944. As the war in Europe approached its end this type of vessel was hounded to destruction not only by surface forces, but by rocket-armed aircraft like the Beaufighter and Hurricane.

Country of origin:	Italy
Type:	Destroyer
Launch date:	17 March 1923
Crew:	105
Displacement:	894 tonnes (880 tons)
Dimensions:	85m x 8m x 3m (278ft 9in x 26ft 3 in x 9ft 9in)
Endurance:	3333km (1800nm)
Main Armament:	Four 102mm (4in) guns; six 444mm (17.5in) torpedo tubes
Powerplant:	Two shaft geared turbines
Performance:	30 knots

Calliope

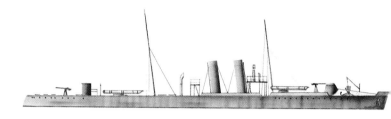

Launched in August 1906, *Calliope* was one of a group of eight torpedo boats based upon the design of Thorneycroft, who were among the world's leading builders of torpedo craft. Built by Pattison of Naples, the last of the class were launched in 1909 and were intended for service in the Adriatic. They were good, stoutly-built seagoing vessels, their hull plates thicker than those of the previous Perseo class. Two of the class were fitted with oil-burning boilers which slightly reduced the displacement and gave greater endurance. *Calliope*'s armament was later changed to two 76mm (3in) guns and one machine gun. All ships in the class gave good service during World War I. *Calliope* was stricken in 1924. *Calliope* was the second Italian torpedo boat to bear the name; the first was a member of the Euterpe class of 1883.

Country of origin:	Italy
Type:	Torpedo boat
Launch date:	27 August 1906
Crew:	65
Displacement:	220 tonnes (216 tons)
Dimensions:	53m x 5m x 2m (173ft 11in x 17ft 5in x 5ft 10in)
Endurance:	1482km (800nm)
Main armament:	Three 47mm (1.85in) guns; three 450mm (17.7in) torpedo tubes
Powerplant:	Twin screw vertical triple expansion engines
Performance:	26.5 knots

Carabiniere

The Italian frigates *Alpino* and *Carabiniere*, originally named *Circe* and *Climene*, were provided for under the 1959–60 programme. The original Circe-class project was modified in 1962, in respect of both machinery and armament. The new design was an improved version of the Centauro class, combined with the Bergamini class. They had similar basic characteristics, but a heavier displacement and increased engine power. Two other ships of the same type, to have been named *Perseo* and *Polluce*, were provided for under the 1960–61 programme, but were suspended for reasons of economy. The Alpino-class frigates were the first Italian warships to be powered by gas turbines, but they were capable of making a steady 22 knots on diesels alone. Part of their task was to provide an ASW screen for the US Sixth Fleet.

Country of origin:	Italy
Type:	Frigate
Launch date:	30 September 1967
Crew:	254
Displacement:	2743 tonnes (2700 tons)
Dimensions:	113m x 13m x 4m (371ft x 43ft 6in x 12ft 7in)
Endurance:	7408km (4000nm)
Main Armament:	Six 76mm guns; six 305mm (12in) torpedo tubes; one A/S mortar
Powerplant:	Twin screw, diesels, gas turbines
Performance:	28 knots (all engines)

Carlo Bergamini

The four frigates of this class – the others being the *Carlo Margottini*, *Luigi Rizzo* and *Virginio Fasan* – were all laid down in 1957 with the exception of the last-named, which was laid down in 1960. They were novel for their type in that they had diesel instead of steam propulsion. Later, the vessels were given an enhanced anti-submarine capability, being allocated an AB204 A/S helicopter each. The flight deck was enlarged, and this made it necessary to remove the single gun and mountings astern. The single-barrelled automatic depth charge mortars fitted to these frigates have a range of 915m (1000yds) and a rate of fire of 15 depth charges per minute. The Bergamini class were designed to be the smallest type of warship capable of operating an anti-submarine helicopter, but this was over-ambitious, and as originally built they were disappointing.

Country of origin:	Italy
Type:	Frigate
Launch date:	16 June 1960
Crew:	160
Displacement:	1676 tonnes (1650 tons)
Dimensions:	94m x 11m x 3m (308ft 3in x 37ft 3in x 10ft 6in)
Endurance:	7412km (4000nm)
Main Armament:	Three 76mm (3in) guns; six 305mm (12in) torpedo tubes; one A/S depth charge mortar
Powerplant:	Twin screw diesel
Performance:	26 knots

Cassard

Four destroyers of the Cassard class were originally laid down, but two were subsequently cancelled. The *Cassard* and her sister ship, *Jean Bart*, were laid down in September 1982 and March 1986 respectively at the Lorient Naval Dockyard, and commissioned in July 1988 and September 1991. The building programme was subjected to serious delays because of financial constraints and doubts about the effectiveness of the increasingly obsolescent Standard SM-1 surface-to-air missile system; there are plans to replace this with the Aster 30 system as the ships are refitted. The radar and countermeasures equipment carried by the two ships is of French design. The ships have a helicopter platform at the stern for use by a single Aerospatiale Panther, now replacing the Lynx which was carried earlier. Both ships were based at Toulon in 1999.

Country of origin:	France
Type:	Destroyer
Launch date:	6 February 1985
Crew:	225
Displacement:	4806 tonnes (4730 tons)
Dimensions:	139m x 14m x 6.5m (455ft 11in x 45ft 9in x 21ft 3in)
Endurance:	13,182km (7118nm)
Main armament:	One 100mm (3.9in) gun; Exocet; Mistral anti-sea-smimming missiles; standard SAMs; ASW torpedoes
Powerplant:	Two shafts, four diesel engines
Performance:	29.5 knots

Castle class

In terms of size, the Castle class of anti-submarine corvette was somewhat larger than the earlier Flower class, which it closely resembled. The Castles were elegant ships, and incorporated all the lessons learned from their forebears. They also incorporated the new Squid anti-submarine mortar, a weapon too heavy to be retrofitted into the Flower-class corvettes or River-class frigates. The Squid's big advantage was that it could lay a pattern of three heavy bombs around a submerged target up to 502m (550yd) ahead while the contact was still in the ship's sonar beam. The performance of the Castle-class vessels did not match that of the frigates, so they were not used as close convoy escorts; instead, they were formed into homogenous escort groups, which were later being deployed in large numbers towards the end of World War II.

Country of origin:	Britain
Type:	Corvette
Launch date:	June 1943 (first units)
Crew:	120
Displacement:	1070 tonnes (1060 tons)
Dimensions:	76.8m x 11.2m x 3.05m (252ft x 36ft 9in x 10ft)
Endurance:	6910km (3725nm)
Main armament:	One 102mm (4in) gun; 10 20mm (0.7in) AA; AS mortar and depth charges
Powerplant:	Single shaft, triple expansion steam engine
Performance:	16.5 knots

Centauro

Launched in April 1954, *Centauro* was one of a class of four vessels built to Italian plans and specifications and funded under the US off-shore programme of the 1950s which aimed to increase the military power of friendly nations. All units had automatic anti-submarine and medium anti-aircraft armament, plus US sonar equipment. The guns were mounted one above the other in twin gun houses and could fire 60 rounds per minute. All four ships underwent armament modification between 1966 and 1967, the changes including the mounting of three 76mm (3in) guns, replacing the two 2-barrelled 76mm (3in) and the four 40mm (1.5in) AA guns. The other vessels in the class were the *Canopo*, *Cigno* and *Castore*. In 1960 the four ships, originally classified as destroyers with 'D' pennant numbers, were reclassified as frigates and allocated 'F' pennant numbers.

Country of origin:	Italy
Type:	Destroyer
Launch date:	4 April 1954
Crew:	255
Displacement:	2255 tonnes (2220 tons)
Dimensions:	103.3m x 11.5m x 3.5m (339ft x 38ft x 11ft 6in)
Endurance:	4630 km (2500nm)
Main Armament:	Four 76mm (3in) guns
Powerplant:	Twin screw geared turbines
Performance:	26 knots

Chao Phraya

The four ships of the Chao Phraya class are basically Jianghu-class vessels, two of them Type IIIs. These vessels were built for the Thai Navy by the China State Shipbuilding Corporation under a contract signed in July 1988. Although plans were made to build two more in Thailand, they were subsequently shelved. The Thai Navy originally wanted only the hulls built in China, as it was planned to install equipment purchased in the USA, but as a condition for the deal, China insisted on fitting out the ships completely and on installing Chinese armament simultaneously. When the ships arrived in Thailand between 1991 and 1992, the shipbuilding standards were found to be so poor that they had to be docked for extensive repair, and also to improve damage control facilities. The poor workmanship in Chinese yards is due almost entirely to an over-emphasis on strict regimentation.

Country of origin:	Thailand
Type:	Frigate
Launch date:	24 June 1990
Crew:	168
Displacement:	1955 tonnes (1924 tons)
Dimensions:	103.2m x 11.3m x 10.2m (338ft 6in x 37ft 1in x 10ft 2in)
Endurance:	5626km (3038nm)
Main armament:	Two or four 100mm (3.9in) guns; eight 37mm (1.4in) guns; A/S mortars and depth charges
Powerplant:	Two shafts, four diesel engines
Performance:	30 knots

Charles

Launched in 1776, the *Charles* was one of the more unusual vessels built during the eighteenth century, being a large frigate equipped with a full set of sails plus oars, or sweeps, for use when the ship was becalmed. The oars were used from the lower deck and could drive the ship along at an approximate speed of 6 knots. *Charles* was used successfully in the battle against the Barbary pirates, who repeatedly attacked trade in the Mediterranean to deadly effect. The ship had two full decks running her entire length, and the deck below the sweep deck was used as a storage space. Crew quarters were forward; officers' aft. *Charles* handled well under sail, but this type of frigate galley generally was not a popular design. It was certainly not popular with the oarsmen, most of whom were criminals who had been sentenced to serve years as virtual galley slaves.

Country of origin:	France
Type:	Frigate galley
Launch date:	1776
Crew:	350
Displacement:	1016 tons (1000 tons)
Dimensions:	45.7m x 11.5m x 4.2m (150ft x 38ft x 14ft)
Endurance:	Unlimited, depending on provisions
Main Armament:	Forty guns
Powerplant:	Sail and oars
Performance:	10 knots

Chidori

Chidori was one of the Tomozuru class of four vessels laid down between 1931 and 1933. With their armament of three 127mm (5in) guns and two 533mm (21in) torpedo tubes, they were virtually small destroyers, but they turned out to be dangerously unstable because of excessive topweight. *Tomozuru* capsized in heavy weather while running trials in March 1934, but was brought into port and righted. All ships in the class were rebuilt to correct the defect, and had a lighter armament mounted, plus the additions of 61 tonnes (60 tons) of permanent ballast to increase displacement. Once modified, the Tomozurus were amongst the most efficient and dangerous of Japanese anti-submarine vessels. *Chidori* was sunk by the US submarine *Tilefish* (Lt-Cdr Kaithley) on 22 December 1944. The *Hatsukari* alone survived the war, being surrendered at Hong Kong.

Country of origin:	Japan
Type:	Torpedo boat
Launch date:	1 April 1933
Crew:	100
Displacement:	749 tonnes (737 tons)
Dimensions:	82m x 7.4m x 2.5m (269ft x 24ft 3in x 8ft 2in)
Endurance:	2779km (1500nm)
Main armament:	Three 127mm (5in) guns; two 533mm (21in) torpedo tubes
Powerplant:	Twin screw turbines
Performance:	28 knots

Chikugo

Chikugo was built by the Mitsui Zozen Company, Tamano, as part of the 1967 new construction programme and was launched on 13 January 1970. Designed and built with structural features to reduce noise and vibration, the Chikugo class ships – 11 of which were laid down in 1968 – are used primarily for coastal ASW missions around the Japanese home islands. To facilitate their use in this role, they are equipped to carry and operate the SQS35(J) variable-depth sonar from an open well which is located offset to starboard at the stern. They are also the smallest warships in the world designed to carry the ASROC ASW missile launcher system; the midships launcher is trained to the bearing and then elevated to fire a two-round salvo of the solid-fuel RUR-5A rockets with their Mk46 parachute-retarded torpedo payloads out to a maximum range of 9.2km (5.7 miles).

Country of origin:	Japan
Type:	Frigate
Launch date:	13 January 1970
Crew:	165
Displacement:	1493 tonnes (1470 tons)
Dimensions:	93m x 11m x 4m (305ft 5in x 35ft 5in x 11ft 6in)
Endurance:	6482km (3500nm)
Main Armament:	Two 76mm (3in) guns
Powerplant:	Twin screw diesels
Performance:	25 knots

Cigno

Launched in 1956, the *Cigno* and her three sister ships (see entry for *Centauro*) were built for the Italian Navy to Italian designs, but were financed by the US offshore programme. All had US sonar equipment and carried automatic anti-submarine and medium anti-aircraft armament. The Italian-made 76mm (3in) guns were mounted in twin turrets and could fire 60 rounds per minute. In the 1960s, the gun turrets were replaced by three single 76mm (3in) mounts. The main ASW weapon was the new Italian Menon mortar. The ships were in fact designed as escort destroyers rather than frigates, and their hull was a scaled-down version of the Impetuoso-class design. The ships were decommissioned in rotation as each vessel was replaced by one of the Maestrale class. All four vessels in the class had retired from service by the late 1980s.

Country of origin:	Italy
Type:	Frigate
Launch date:	20 March 1955
Crew:	255
Displacement:	2455 tonnes (2220 tons)
Dimensions:	103.3m x 11.5m x 4m (339ft x 38ft x 11ft 6 in)
Endurance:	4630km (2500nm)
Main Armament:	Four 76mm (3in) guns
Powerplant:	Twin screw geared turbines
Performance:	28 knots

Cleveland

In 1938, the worsening situation on the world stage caused great alarm in Britain, and efforts were made to increase the strength of the Royal Navy. However, when World War II broke out, Britain was still short of destroyers to escort her vital Atlantic convoys. By 1940 the Royal Navy decided to put in hand a programme of small destroyers that could be quickly and easily constructed. *Cleveland* was one of the first group of Hunt-class destroyers subsequently built. Originally they were designed to carry six 102mm (4in) guns, but this armament proved too top-heavy, and the number of guns was reduced to four. Although ballast and stabilisers were added to reduce roll in a seaway, movement was jerky. Launched in April 1940, *Cleveland* survived the war, only to be wrecked in June 1957, en route to the shipbreakers.

Country of origin:	Britain
Type:	Destroyer
Launch date:	1 November 1941
Crew:	146
Displacement:	922 tonnes (907 tons)
Dimensions:	85.3m x 8.8m x 3.8m (280ft x 29ft x 12ft 6in)
Endurance:	3704km (2000nm)
Main Armament:	Four 102mm (4in) guns
Powerplant:	Twin screw geared turbines
Performance:	26 knots

Comet

HMS *Comet*, launched in June 1944, was one of 31 C-class destroyers built in the last two years of World War II. They all followed the same basic pattern, with two guns firing ahead and two aft. There was a single sloping funnel behind the bridge. Additional anti-aircraft guns were added as the vessels entered service, and one of the class, HMS *Contest*, was the first British destroyer with an all-welded hull. All vessels in the class survived the war. Four went to Norway in 1946, and four were handed over to Pakistan in the 1950s. Two more saw service with the Royal Canadian Navy. HMS *Comet* was scrapped at Troon, Scotland, in November 1962. Together with the Battle class, the C class were among the last true destroyers built for the Royal Navy, for with the disappearance of the line of battle there was no further need for conventional destroyers.

Country of origin:	Britain
Type:	Destroyer
Launch date:	22 June 1944
Crew:	186
Displacement:	1737 tonnes (1710 tons)
Dimensions:	111m x 11m x 4m (362ft 9in x 35ft 8in x 14ft 5in)
Endurance:	4074km (2200nm)
Main Armament:	Four 114mm (4.5in) guns
Powerplant:	Twin screw turbines
Performance:	36.7 knots

Comte de Grasse

Built as replacements for the many Gearing-class destroyers, the Spruance class, to which *Comte de Grasse* belongs, are arguably the most capable anti-submarine warfare vessels ever built. Constructed by the modular assembly technique – whereby large sections of the hull are constructed in various parts of the shipyard and then welded together on the slipway – these were the first large US warships to employ all gas turbine propulsion. The successful hull design of the Spruance-class destroyers was used, with modifications, on two other classes of US warship, and has reduced rolling and pitching tendencies, so providing a better weapons platform. All vessels in the Spruance class have undergone major weapons changes over the years. Targets at long range are engaged by on-board ASW helicopters.

Country of origin:	USA
Type:	Destroyer
Launch date:	26 March 1976
Crew:	296
Displacement:	7925 tonnes (7800 tons)
Dimensions:	171.7m x 16.8m x 8.8m (563ft 3in x 55ft 2in x 29ft)
Endurance:	20,383km (11,000nm)
Main armament:	Two 127mm (5in) DP guns; Tomahawk and Harpoon SSM; Sea Sparrow SAM; Phalanx CIWS; ASROC
Powerplant:	Two shafts, four gas turbines
Performance:	32.5 knots

Confienza

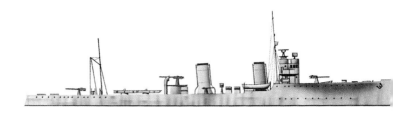

L aunched in December 1920, *Confienza* was one of a class of four vessels that were an improved version of the *Audace*, launched in 1913. In 1938 all vessels in *Confienza*'s class were reclassified as torpedo boats, but plans to revise the armament were never followed through. The smaller weapons carried included two 76mm (3in) anti-aircraft guns plus two machine guns and four 450mm (17.7in) torpedo tubes. Three of the group were war losses. These were the *Palestro*, sunk by HM submarine *Osiris*, *San Martino*, taken over by the Germans and sunk in an air raid, and *Solferino*, also taken over and sunk by British destroyers. On 18 December 1940, *Confienza* sank the British submarine *Triton* (Lt Cdr Watkins) in the Strait of Otranto. She herself was sunk in a collision with the naval auxiliary vessel *Capitano Cecchi* off Brindisi.

Country of origin:	Italy
Type:	Destroyer
Launch date:	18 December 1920
Crew:	190
Displacement:	1093 tonnes (1076 tons)
Dimensions:	82m x 8m x 3m (268ft 8in x 26ft 3in x 9ft 2in)
Endurance:	2778km (1500nm)
Main Armament:	Four 102mm (4in) guns
Powerplant:	Twin screw vertical triple expansion engines
Performance:	28 knots

Constitution

The *Constitution*, launched in 1797, was designed by Joshua Humphreys and built at Boston. Commissioned in 1798, she served in the war against France, and in 1799 captured two privateers. She was then taken out of service, but with the outbreak of a new conflict against the Barbary pirates in 1803, she was recommissioned. She saw action in the brief and pointless war that erupted between England and the United States over trade restrictions between Europe and North America. In 1812 she narrowly avoided capture by the British, and then underwent extensive repairs between 1812 and 1815. She was rebuilt in 1833, between 1871 and 1877, in 1906, and again between 1927 and 1930. Numerous plans to scrap the ship were thwarted by popular protest, and *Constitution* is now permanently based at Boston. She is the oldest commissioned warship still afloat.

Country of origin:	USA
Type:	Frigate
Launch date:	October 1797
Crew:	375
Displacement:	2236 tonnes (2200 tons)
Dimensions:	53m x 13m x 4m (175ft x 43ft 6in x 14ft 3in)
Endurance:	Unlimited, depending on provisions
Main Armament:	Twenty-eight 24-pounders; 10 12-pounders
Powerplan:	Sail
Performance:	13 knots

Conyngham

Launched in September 1935, the USS *Conyngham* was one of the Mahan class of American destroyers, closely related to the preceding Farragut class. Of the 18 ships in the class, six were lost in World War II. *Cassin* and *Downes* were virtually destroyed at Pearl Harbor but were later rebuilt; the USS *Tucker* survived the attack on Pearl Harbor but was lost in August 1942; the *Cushing* was sunk by Japanese gunfire and torpedoes off Guadalcanal on 13 November 1942; the *Preston* was sunk off Guadalcanal by a Japanese battle group on 14 November 1942; the *Perkins* went down in the Southwest Pacific on 29 November 1943; the *Mahan* was lost on 7 December 1944; and the *Reid* was lost on 11 December 1944. Another vessel, the *Lamson*, was expended at the Bikin atomic bomb tests in 1946, and the *Conyngham* herself was sunk as a target vessel on 2 July 1948.

Country of origin:	USA
Type:	Destroyer
Launch date:	14 September 1935
Crew:	250
Displacement:	1417 tonnes (1395 tons)
Dimensions:	104m x 10.4m x 2.69m (341.25ft x 34.16ft x 8.83ft)
Endurance:	6482km (3500nm)
Main Armament:	Five single 127mm DP guns; two quadruple 533mm (21in) torpedo tubes
Powerplant:	Two sets of geared steam turbines
Performance:	36.5 knots

Coronel Bolognesi

The *Coronel Bolognesi* was previously one of the Friesland class of Dutch destroyer escorts (DDE) built for the Royal Netherlands Navy. They formed the backbone of the Dutch anti-submarine groups until the late 1970s, when they were replaced by the newer Standaard-class frigate. Between 1980 and 1982, the ships were transferred to the Peruvian Navy, which had plans to arm them with Exocet missiles. The ships have side armour as well as deck protection. In Dutch service, plans were made to fit them with eight 533mm (21in) torpedo tubes, but this project was abandoned after only one ship had been so equipped (the tubes were subsequently removed). The primary anti-submarine weapon of these vessels is the Limbo-type rocket projector. Their 4.7in guns are fully automatic, with a rate of fire of 50 rounds per minute.

Country of origin:	Peru
Type:	Destroyer
Launch date:	8 August 1955
Crew:	284
Displacement:	3150 tonnes (3100 tons)
Dimensions:	116m x 12m x 5m (380ft 7in x 38ft 5in x 17ft)
Endurance:	4632km (2500nm)
Main Armament:	Four 120mm (4.7in) guns
Powerplant:	Twin screw turbines
Performance:	36 knots

Corrientes

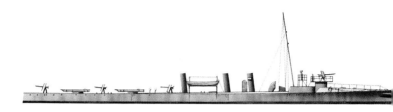

A permanent Argentine Navy was first established in 1872, when a number of vessels, including two armoured monitors, were ordered. Two small battleships were also commissioned at a later date. The contract speed for these vessels was 26 knots for three hours but they had difficulty achieving this. A border dispute with Chile in the 1890s led to a naval race, and four armoured cruisers were ordered from Italy, although two of these were cancelled when a treaty brought an end to the tension that had existed between the two countries. The two cruisers were sold to Japan. At the same time, Argentina – conscious of the threat presented to its small fleet by enemy torpedo boats – ordered four destroyers from the British company Yarrow shipbuilders on the River Clyde. *Corrientes* was one of them, and she served in the Argentinian Navy until she was taken off the active list in 1925.

Country of origin:	Argentina
Type:	Destroyer
Launch date:	1896
Crew:	98
Displacement:	284 tonnes (280 tons)
Dimensions:	58m x 6m x 2.2m (190ft x 19ft 6in x 7ft 4 in)
Endurance:	1482km (800nm)
Main armament:	One 14-pounder; three six-pounders; three 457mm (18in) torpedo tubes
Powerplant:	Twin screw triple expansion engines
Performance:	22 knots

Crescent

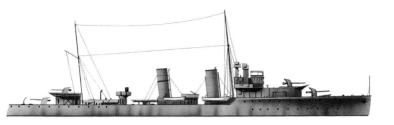

HMS *Crescent* formed part of the 1922 British naval rearmament programme, which was to be drastically curtailed due to the onset of the great worldwide economic Depression of the early 1930s. Crescent was one of the C and D classes of destroyer, which were slightly enlarged versions of the B class, having increased fuel capacity and a 76mm (3in) anti-aircraft gun in addition to the main armament of 120mm (4.7in) guns. The machinery developed 36,000hp for a designed speed of 35.5 knots. *Crescent* was launched in September 1931 and transferred to the Royal Canadian Navy in 1937, where she was renamed *Fraser*. She was lost in a collision with the British cruiser *Calcutta* off the Gironde on 26 June 1940 while taking part in Operation Aerial, in which British ships evacuated 191,870 troops from the Biscay ports.

Country of origin:	Britain
Type:	Destroyer
Launch date:	29 September 1931
Crew:	190
Displacement:	1927 tonnes (1897 tons)
Dimensions:	97m x 10m x 2.6m (317ft 9in x 33ft x 8ft 6in)
Endurance:	3704km (2000nm)
Main Armament:	Four 120mm (4.7in) guns
Powerplant:	Twin screw turbines
Performance:	36 knots

Curlew

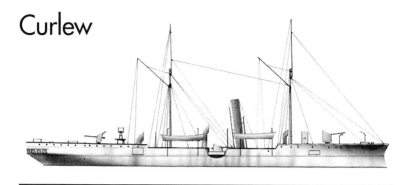

Classified as first-class gun vessels, *Curlew* and her sister *Landrail* were the last of the old-style gunboats that had filled the Royal Navy lists over the years. *Curlew* was a steel-hulled vessel with fine lines and a relatively shallow draught. Unfortunately, *Curlew* and her sister proved unsuitable as gunboats and were too slow to be cruisers. *Curlew* served in British waters until she was sold in 1906. The boats would have had much longer careers than they enjoyed had it not been for their inadequacies, since their armament was really quite formidable. Typically, their 152mm (6in) gun fired a 100lb shot and their three 127mm (5in) weapons a 60lb shot. *Curlew*'s sister ship, *Landrail*, was deployed first of all to the Cape station and spent almost all her operational life overseas. She was sunk as a target vessel in October 1906.

Country of origin:	Britain
Type:	Gunboat
Launch date:	23 October 1885
Crew:	75
Displacement:	965 tonnes (950 tons)
Dimensions:	59.5m x 8.5m x 3.2m (195ft x 28ft x 10ft 6in)
Endurance:	1760km (950nm)
Main Armament:	One 152mm (6in) and three 127mm (5in) guns.
Powerplant:	Twin screw horizontal direct-acting compound engines
Performance:	14.5 knots

Curtatone

Steel-hulled, three-masted and barque-rigged, *Curtatone* – launched in August 1888 – was a typical small gunboat of the period, built to police overseas possessions and supply trained crew for larger warships. The three boilers developed just over 1000hp, though during cruises reliance was usually placed on sail power alone. Boats like the *Curtatone* featured prominently in the navies of all the colonial powers of the day; they carried a crew of 30 or 40, and were commanded by a lieutenant. It was an ideal first command for an ambitious young officer in a navy where chances of promotion had hitherto often depended on the death of someone more senior. It is true to say that at the end of the gunboat era, senior naval officers tended to be much more youthful, and probably more efficient, than their predecessors.

Country of origin:	Italy
Type:	Gunboat
Launch date:	14 August 1888
Crew:	45
Displacement:	1292 tonnes (1272 tons)
Dimensions:	54m x 10m x 4.5m (177ft 2in x 32ft 10in x 14ft 10in)
Endurance:	Approx 1668km (900nm) on engine power
Main Armament:	Four 119mm (4.7in) guns
Powerplant:	Single screw compound engine
Performance:	14 knots

Cushing

The *Cushing* was the US Navy's first true purpose-designed torpedo boat, and wa laid down in April 1888. She was built by the Herreshof company, and unlike *Stiletto*, her wooden-hulled predecessor, she was built of steel. *Cushing* had a long, slim hull with a curved deck and an anachronistic ram bow. She was used initially on experimental torpedo development work at the Newport Naval Torpedo Station. In 1897, once the technology was regarded as being well proven, she was used as a despatch boat off the coast of Cuba, and saw active service during the war with Spain in 1898. In a single action in August of that year, she intercepted and captured four small Spanish transports. After the war she was returned to Newport, where she became a target hulk. She was sunk as a target vessel in September 1920, the fate of many of her kind.

Country of origin:	USA
Type:	Torpedo boat
Launch date:	23 January 1890
Crew:	22
Displacement:	118 tonnes (116 tons)
Dimensions:	42.6m x 4.6m x 1.5m (140ft x 15ft 1in x 4ft 10in)
Endurance:	926km (500nm)
Main armament:	Three 457mm (18in) torpedo tubes; three 6-pounder guns
Powerplant:	Twin screw vertical quadruple expansion engines
Performance:	23 knots

Cushing

The USS *Cushing* is one of the large Spruance warships; there are 31 units in all, built by Ingalls Shipbuilding Division of Litton Industries, Pascagoula, Mississipi, as replacements for the many Gearing-class destroyers, and they are arguably the most capable anti-submarine warfare vessels ever built. On trials *Spruance* made about 32 knots. Constructed by the modular assembly technique, whereby large sections of the hull are built in various parts of the shipyard and then welded together on the slipway, these were the first large US warships to employ all gas turbine propulsion. The successful hull design of the Spruance-class destroyers was used, with modifications, on two other classes of US warship, and has reduced rolling and pitching tendencies, so providing a better weapons platform. All vessels in the Spruance class have undergone major weapons changes and upgrades.

Country of origin:	USA
Type:	Destroyer
Launch date:	17 June 1978
Crew:	296
Displacement:	8168 tonnes (8040 tons)
Dimensions:	171.7m x 16.8m x 5.8m (563ft 4in x 55ft 2in x 19ft)
Endurance:	20,372km (11,000nm)
Main armament:	Two 127mm (5in) guns; Tomahawk and Harpoon missiles
Powerplant:	Twin screws, gas turbines
Performance:	32.5 knots

Dahlgren

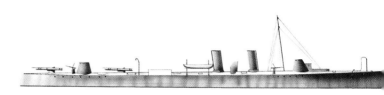

Dahlgren and her sister boat *Craven* were authorised in 1896, laid down in March 1897, and completed in 1899. They had closely spaced funnels, a single light pole mast, and two single torpedo tubes mounted aft. The efficiency of torpedo boats such as these was made possible by the drastic reduction in the size of powerplants that took place in the latter years of the nineteenth century. This was due to the development of new types of boiler and compound multi-cylinder engines operating at previously impossible temperatures and pressures. Such engines found application in warships and merchant vessels alike, bringing the necessary fuel economy to the latter and unheard-of speed to the former. During this period America became the world's major industrial power, a fact reflected in the strength of her navy.

Country of origin:	USA
Type:	Torpedo boat
Launch date:	29 May 1899
Crew:	29
Displacement:	148 tonnes (146 tons)
Dimensions:	46m x 5m x 1.5m (151ft 4in x 16ft 5in x 4ft 8in)
Endurance:	Not known
Main armament:	Four one-pounder guns; two 457mm (18in) torpedo tubes
Powerplant:	Twin screw vertical triple expansion engines
Performance:	31 knots

Danaide

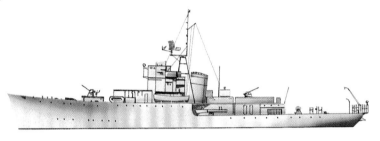

From 1942 onwards, the Italian Navy laid down a class of some 60 small escort vessels – the Gabbiano class. The last was not completed until 1948. Pressures of war caused the early ships in the class to be built extremely quickly. *Danaide* was one of the first, and was completed only four months after launching. She was originally fitted out for minesweeping, and operated extensively in the Mediterranean during World War II. Like her sister ships, she was modified extensively throughout her operational life. Many of the class survived the war, and 17 were still in Italian service in the mid-1960s. Some of the earlier vessels were seized by the Germans and pressed into service as submarine chasers; most were sunk by Allied air attack. One of the class, *Ape* (Bee) was converted to carry frogmen and commandos in the special duties role; others became target tugs.

Country of origin:	Italy
Type:	Corvette
Launch date:	21 October 1942
Crew:	101
Displacement:	812 tonnes (800 tons)
Dimensions:	64m x 8.5m x 2.5m (209ft 7in x 27ft 6in x 8ft 1in)
Endurance:	2778km (1500nm)
Main armament:	Four 40mm (1.6in) anti-aircraft guns
Powerplant:	Twin screw diesel engines
Performance:	17.5 knots

Dardo

Built under the 1960 programme, and laid down at Taranto in 1964, *Dardo* was one of four motor gunboats in the Freccia class, the others being *Saetta* and *Strale*. The design specification called for a fast vessel that was capable of being rapidly converted into an armed gunboat for use as a fast minelayer (with an anti-aircraft gun and eight mines) or as a torpedo boat (with one 40mm (1.5in) gun and 21 533mm (21in) torpedoes). The necessary conversions could be completed in under 24 hours as and when required. The boats were fitted with S-band navigation and tactical radar using a slotting waveguide antenna. All vessels in the class proved to be good seaboats and were well suited to the needs of the Italian Navy. The Italians developed several classes of motor gunboat in the 1960s and 1970s, all designed with specific tasks in mind.

Country of origin:	Italy
Type:	Motor gunboat
Launch date:	laid down 10 May 1964; not completed
Crew:	50
Displacement:	218 tonnes (215 tons)
Dimensions:	45.7m x 7.2m x 1.7m (150ft x 23ft 9in x 5ft 6in)
Endurance:	2037km (1100nm)
Main armament:	One 40mm (1.6in) gun; four 533mm (21in) torpedo tubes
Powerplant:	Twin screw diesels and gas turbines
Performance:	40+ knots

Daring

During the early 1890s, the British Admiralty requested designs for small destroyers that would be faster than the rapidly growing fleet of French torpedo boats. The French had needed most of the century to recover from the total destruction of their fleet during the Napoleonic wars and, in that interlude, they concentrated on the design of small, fast craft capable of attacking enemy capital ships. Thorneycroft and Yarrow subsequently came up with the design for *Daring*, based on their successful sea-going torpedo boats. The hull at the stern had a flat floor at the waterline, so enabling the screws to be lifted to allow for navigation in relatively shallow waters. *Daring* was scrapped in 1912. Her sister boat, *Decoy*, was lost in a collision in 1904. Both vessels were built by Thorneycroft, and were stronger than contemporary vessels built by Yarrow.

Country of origin:	Britain
Type:	Destroyer
Launch date:	25 November 1893
Crew:	98
Displacement:	264 tonnes (260 tons)
Dimensions:	56.6m x 5.7m (185ft 6in x 19ft.)
Endurance:	Not known
Main armament:	One 12-pounder; three six-pounders; three torpedo tubes
Powerplant:	Twin screw three-stage compound engines
Performance:	22 knots

Daring

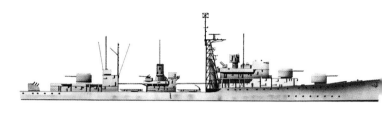

Launched in 1949, *Daring* and her seven sisters were expanded and improved versions of the earlier Battle-class and Weapon-class vessels, and were able to perform a variety of tasks, including anti-submarine and reconnaissance duties. They were the largest destroyers built for the Royal Navy and had an all-welded hull construction. The 120mm (4.5in) guns were radar-controlled and automatic. The lattice foremast was built around the fore funnel, giving *Daring* an unusual and distinctive appearance. During the early years of the Cold War, the vessels of the Daring class formed an important part of NATO's hunter-killer naval forces in the Atlantic. They were the first British destroyers specifically designed to perform multi-role funtions, and set the trend for future developments that would lead to today's highly effective craft.

Country of origin:	Britain
Type:	Destroyer
Launch date:	10 August 1949
Crew:	290
Displacement:	3636 tonnes (3579 tons)
Dimensions:	114m x 13m x 4m (375ft x 43ft x 13ft)
Endurance:	12,964km (7000nm)
Main armament:	Six 120mm (4.5in) guns
Powerplant:	Twin screw geared turbines
Performance:	31.5 knots

Davidson

The Garcia class of anti-submarine ships to which the USS *Davidson* belongs were built between 1962 and 1968 as successors to the Bronstein class of destroyer escorts. Ten were launched and were originally classed as ocean escorts, but their designation and role was soon changed to that of frigate. Gyro-driven stabilisers enable *Davidson* to operate effectively in heavy seas, and her anti-submarine capabilities have been significantly improved over those of earlier designs. As well as the two single gun mounts, she carries a large box launcher which holds eight ASROC anti-submarine missiles. She was also equipped with twin torpedo tubes in the stern, but these were later removed. Her combat effectiveness is enhanced by an SH-2 Seasprite helicopter which is housed in a hangar towards the stern.

Country of origin:	USA
Type:	Destroyer escort
Launch date:	2 October 1964
Crew:	241
Displacement:	3454 tonnes (3400 tons)
Dimensions:	126m x 13.5m x 7.3m (414ft 8in x 44ft 3in x 24ft)
Endurance:	7585km (4096nm)
Main armament:	Two 127mm (5in) DP guns
Powerplant:	Single screw, turbines
Performance:	27 knots

DE Type

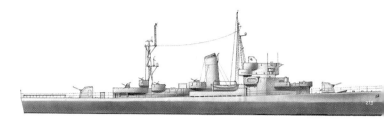

The first destroyer escorts (DEs) built in the United States were ordered under lend-lease for Britain early in 1941. The original order for 50 was expanded to 250 early in 1942, but only 55 were actually transferred. The remainder of these vessels were retained by the US Navy, which had not planned to build any. Of the 1005 destroyer escorts ordered by 1943, only 563 were completed. The DEs of this type were built after the fashion of American fleet destroyers, having a long flush deck with a prominent sheer line in place of the more commodious long forecastle decks preferred by the British. Far more emphasis was placed on gun armament. As anti-submarine warships, the DEs were extremely effective, although they arrived too late to prevent much of the carnage caused by the U-boats in the Battle of the Atlantic.

Country of origin:	USA
Type:	Destroyer Escort
Launch date:	9 January 1943 (Buckley class, first unit)
Crew:	220
Displacement:	1748 tonnes (1720 tons)
Dimensions:	93.27m x 11.27m x 2.89m (306ft x 37ft x 9ft 6in)
Endurance:	15,742km (8500nm)
Main armament:	Three 76mm (3in) guns; six 40mm (1.5in) and four 20mm (0.7in) AA; three 533mm (21in) torpedo tubes; depth charges
Powerplant:	Two shafts, two steam turbines, two propulsion motors
Performance:	24 knots

Decatur

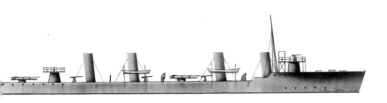

The Bainbridge class of five units was the largest destroyer class laid down before 1899. All previous destroyers had been 'one-off' vessels of between 238 and 283 tonnes (235 and 279 tons). The vessels of this class were authorized in 1898 and for most of their lives were based at Cavite in the Philippine Islands. In 1917, *Chauncey* was rammed and sunk by the steamer *Rose*, but all the remaining vessels in the class survived World War I and were sold in 1920. In general, American destroyers tended to be larger than their British counterparts, and more rakish: in fact, more like light cruisers in appearance. Some US destroyer flotillas operated from Irish bases in World War I. In fact, America's first act of war on 13 April 1917 was to deploy six destroyers to European waters to take part in the Atlantic Patrol alongside their Royal Navy counterparts.

Country of origin:	USA
Type:	Destroyer
Launch date:	26 September 1900
Crew:	110
Displacement:	426 tonnes (420 tons)
Dimensions:	77m x 7m x 2m (252ft 7in x 23ft 6in x 6ft 6in)
Endurance:	2778km (1500nm)
Main armament:	Two 76mm (3in) guns; five six-pounders; two 457mm (18in) torpedo tubes
Powerplant:	Twin screw verticle triple expansion
Performance:	29 knots

Delta

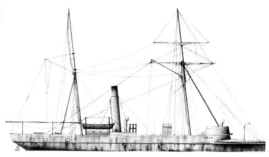

George Rendell designed a number of successful gunboats from between 1868 to 1879, starting with the British 183-tonne (180-ton) vessel, *Staunch*. Their common feature was the use of a single, very large gun mounted on a small, low profile hull with shallow draught. *Delta* was one of four units ordered by China in 1875 and completed in 1877. The other boats were named *Alpha*, *Beta* and *Gamma* They were effectively floating gun platforms rather than warships, but were useful for coastal defence. *Delta* was armed with a single 36-tonne (35-ton) gun, which could only be traversed a few degrees from dead ahead. To aim the gun, the boat had to be pointed directly at the target, and she was fitted with twin screws to enable her to manoeuvre quickly. All four of the Chinese Rendell gunboats were captured by the Japanese in 1895 and were broken up between 1906 and 1907.

Country of origin:	China
Type:	Gunboat
Launch date:	1876
Crew:	50
Displacement:	426 tonnes (420 tons)
Dimensions:	36.5m x 9m x 2.5m (119ft 9in x 39ft 6in x 8ft 4in)
Endurance:	Not known
Main armament:	One 317mm (12.5in) gun
Powerplant:	Twin screw horizontal compound engines
Performance:	9.6 knots

Des Geneys

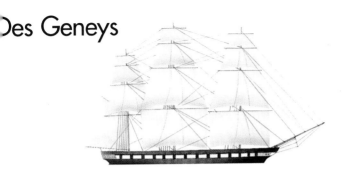

aunched in December 1828, *Des Geneys* was originally named *Haute Combe* and was part of the Sardinian Fleet until 1839. She formed part of the early alian Navy. She was a typical frigate of the period, with a single gun deck running er full length. In 1854 she became a transport and her armament was reduced to our cannon. *Des Geneys* was removed from service in 1865. The Italian Navy – ounded as it was in 1860 following the unification of the country – was forced to ely entirely on such warships as *Des Geneys* until it acquired its first armoured ronclad) frigates . These frigates were all built in foreign yards, including two of hem in the United States. In 1866 the Italian Navy consisted of 12 ironclads, 29 crew fighting ships, 49 steam warships and 13 sailing ships, about half of which vere based in the Adriatic.

Country of origin:	Italy
Type:	Frigate
Launch date:	1828
Crew:	350
Displacement:	1532 tonnes (1508 tons)
Dimensions:	47m x 12.6m x 5.7m (154ft 6in x 41ft 4in x 18ft 8in)
Endurance:	Unlimited, depending on provisions
Main armament:	Thirty-six cannon
Powerplant:	Sail
Performance:	12 knots

D'Estienne d'Orves

Designed for coastal ASW, the D'Estienne d'Orves class could also be used for scouting missions, training and 'showing the flag' overseas, for which role one officer and 17 men of the Naval Infantry (Marines) could also be accommodated. Since entering service in the mid-1970s, the design has been sold to the Argentine Navy, whose three ships the *Drummond*, *Guerrico* and *Granville* saw service in the 1982 Falklands war. In this campaign, the *Guerrico* was damaged by shore fire from small arms and 'Carl Gustav' anti-tank rocket launchers operated by a contingent of Royal Marines defending South Georgia. She was hit by 1275 rounds of rifle and machine-gun fire and three rockets, one exploding on her side, a second on her Exocet launcher, and a third on her gun turret. She had to be dry-docked for three days in order for repairs to be carried out.

Country of origin:	France
Type:	Frigate
Launch date:	1 June 1973
Crew:	105
Displacement:	1351 tonnes (1330 tons)
Dimensions:	80m x 10m x 3m (262ft 6in x 33ft 10in x 9ft 10in)
Endurance:	7408km (4000nm)
Main armament:	One 100mm (3.9in) DP gun; two single MM40 Exocet surface-to-surface missile launchers with two missiles (replacing earlier MM38 Exocet missiles)
Powerplant:	Twin screw diesel engines.
Performance:	24 knots

Devonshire

Devonshire and *Hampshire*, designed to embody improvements in the destroyer field, were projected between 1955 and 1956, and it was later found possible to arm these 'super-destroyers' with guided weapons instead of anti-aircraft guns, and to carry modern anti-submarine detection equipment. *Kent* and *London*, provided under the 1956–57 estimates, had the mainmast stepped further aft. The next four ships – *Fife*, *Glamorgan*, *Antrim* and *Norfolk* – all had the updated Seaslug MkII SAM system, later retrofitted in the first four. All the ships were fitted with stabilisers. The County class, together with the Tribals were the first ships to have Combined Steam and Gas turbine (COSAG) machinery. Their lengthy endurance enabled them to operate independently, in the same way as cruisers. The class was superseded by the Type 42 destroyer.

Country of origin:	Britain
Type:	Destroyer
Launch date:	10 June 1960
Crew:	471
Displacement:	6299 tonnes (6200 tons)
Dimensions:	158.6m x 16.4m x 6m (520ft 6in x 54ft x 20ft)
Endurance:	12,964km (7000nm)
Main armament:	Four 114mm (4.5in) guns; twin launcher for long-range Seaslug SAM
Powerplant:	Two sets geared steam turbines, four gas turbines
Performance:	32.5 knots

Deyatelnyi

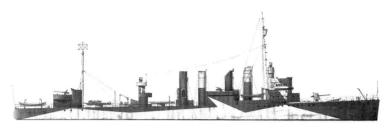

The *Deyatelnyi* was originally an American Clemson-class destroyer of 1919 vintage, the USS *Herndon*. Transferred to the Royal Navy early in World War II, she was renamed HMS *Churchill* and served on convoy escort duty in the North Atlantic until 1944, when she was handed over to the Soviet Navy and renamed *Deyatelnyi*. After some months on escort duty in the Arctic, she was escorting coastal convoy KB1 in the White Sea with the flotilla leader *Baku* and seven other destroyers, with three Pe-2 bombers providing air escort, when the convoy was attacked by German submarines. The *U997* (Lt Lehmann) sank the *Deyatelnyi* (Lt-Cdr Kravchenko) with a T-5 acoustic homing torpedo. Russian destroyers, in fact, rarely ventured outside coastal waters in World War II, leaving the burden of escort duty mostly to their Allies.

Country of origin:	USA (Transferred to UK and USSR)
Type:	Destroyer
Launch date:	31 May 1919
Crew:	146
Displacement:	1209 tonnes (1190 tons)
Dimensions:	95.78m x 9.37m x 2.82m (314ft 4in x 30ft 9in x 9ft 3in)
Endurance:	2778km (1500nm)
Main armament:	Four single 102mm (4in) and one 76mm (2.9in) AA guns; four triple 533mm (21in) torpedo tubes
Powerplant:	Two sets of geared steam turbines
Performance:	35 knots

Dido

The 26-strong Leander class became the backbone of the Royal Navy's frigate force during the 1960s and early 1970s. Vessels of this class followed the basic pattern of the Rothesay/Whitby class, but were more versatile and had improved fighting capabilities. *Dido*, launched in December 1961, was equipped with a powerful early-warning radar, a bow-mounted sonar, and variable-depth sonar. In addition to her gun and missile armament, she carried a triple-barrelled anti-submarine mortar. She also carried a Wasp light helicopter (later replaced by a Lynx) which could be equipped with anti-submarine homing torpedoes. Some ships in this class had their guns replaced by the Exocet sea-skimming missile, while others, *Dido* included, had their guns replaced by the Ikara anti-submarine missile system. Several nations bought Leanders, or built them under licence.

Country of origin:	Britain
Type:	Frigate
Launch date:	22 December 1961
Crew:	263
Displacement:	2844 tonnes (2800 tons)
Dimensions:	113.3m x 12.4m x 5.4m (372ft x 41ft x 18ft)
Endurance:	8334km (4500nm)
Main armament:	Two 114mm (4.5in) guns; one quadruple launcher for Seacat SAMs
Powerplant:	Twin screw turbines
Performance:	30 knots

Dolphin

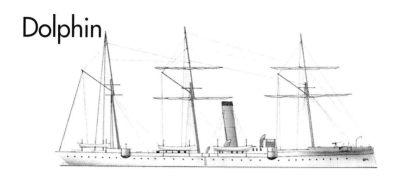

Dolphin was the first warship iof America's so-called 'New Navy', which came into being in parallel with an upsurge of overseas commercial interests. Launched in April 1884, *Dolphin* was the first all-steel warship in the US Navy. She originally had a light barque rig, but was re-rigged as a three-masted schooner before a third rig of only two masts was settled upon. She served mostly in the West Indies, but nearly became involved in hostilities with Chilean naval forces after the death of two American seamen during a revolt in Chile, which, during this period, was in a state of almost continual warfare. In a conflict with Peru, the Chilean navy was almost completely annihilated, and during the civil war which broke out in 1891, several naval actions were fought between rebel forces and government vessels. The *Dolphin* was sold in 1922.

Country of origin:	USA
Type:	Gunboat
Launch date:	12 April 1884
Crew:	75
Displacement:	1509 tonnes (1486 tons)
Dimensions:	78m x 9.7m x 4.6m (256ft 6in x 32ft x 15ft 3in)
Endurance:	1852km (1000nm)
Main armament:	One 152mm (6in) gun
Powerplant:	Single screw vertical compound engines
Performance:	14 knots

Donetz

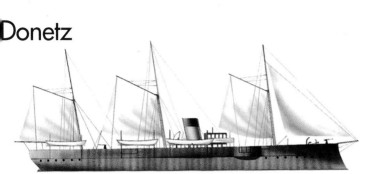

Launched in November 1887, *Donetz* was one of six ships of the Kubanetz class, all of which were built for operations in the Black Sea. They were considered to have been poorly designed and, in the case of the vessels built at Nikolaiev, to have suffered from poor workmanship. On 29 October 1914, *Donetz* was torpedoed in Odessa harbour by the Turkish destroyer *Gairet*. Although she was subsequently salvaged and repaired and put back into service, she was finally sunk in May 1919. The class leader, *Kubanetz*, saw service as an oiler during World War II as the *Krasni Kuban*, and was lost in unknown circumstances during the conflict. Another of the class, *Teretz* (renamed *Znamya Sozialisma*) was used as a school ship after the Russian Revolution. Most of the ships were rearmed with different gun calibres, and surviving vessels of the class had their fore and mizzen masts removed.

Country of origin:	Russia
Type:	Gunboat
Launch date:	November 1887
Crew:	180
Displacement:	1219 tonnes (1200 tons)
Dimensions:	64m x 10.6m x 3m (210ft x 35ft x 10ft)
Endurance:	1666km (900nm)
Main armament:	One 152mm (6in) and two 203mm (8in) guns
Powerplant:	Twin screw horizontal compound engines
Performance:	14 knots

Doudart de Lagrée

Nine vessels of the Commandant Riviere class were built under the French Navy's 1956–57 estimates by the Lorient Naval Dockyard. They were good general-purpose anti-submarine vessels of small displacement, and were intended for patrol work or escort duties. Their speed was not particularly high, but they packed a reasonable amount of equipment into a light hull. One vessel was fitted with an experimental combined gas turbine/diesel installation, which gave a dramatic increase in maximum range. *Doudart de Lagrée* had a wartime crew complement of 214, and could also carry some 80 commandos. In later life, one of her 100mm (3.9in) gun turrets was replaced by four Exocet missile launchers. The other vessels in the class were *Amiral Charner, Balny, Commandant Bory, Commandant Bourdais, Ensigne de Vaisseau Henry, Protet* and *Victor Schoelcher*.

Country of origin:	France
Type:	Frigate
Launch date:	15 April 1961
Crew:	214
Displacement:	2235 tonnes (2200 tons)
Dimensions:	102m x 11.5m x 3.8m (334ft x 37ft 9in x 12ft 6in)
Endurance:	7408km (4000nm)
Main armament:	Three 100mm (3.9in) guns; twin AA weapons
Powerplant:	Twin screw diesels
Performance:	25 knots

Downes

At the time of their building, the 46 Knox-class ocean escorts, of which *Downes* was one, comprised the largest group of destroyer-escort type warships built to the same design in the west since World War II. The ships were almost identical to the earlier Garcia and Brooke classes, but slightly larger. Original planning provided for the vessels to have the Sea Mauler, a short-range anti-aircraft missile adapted from a missile being developed by the US Army, but the Mauler/Sea Mauler programme was abandoned because of technical difficulties. Mauler/Sea Mauler was a slim high-acceleration missile carried in a box of 12 and operated by a two-man crew; it could be used to spearhead amphibious assaults and engage low-flying aircraft. The ships had a very large superstructure and a distinctive cylindrical structure combining masts and engine exhaust stacks.

Country of origin:	USA
Type:	Frigate
Launch date:	13 December 1969
Crew:	220
Displacement:	4165 tonnes (4100 tons)
Dimensions:	126.6m x 14m x 7.5m (415ft 4in x 46ft 9in x 24ft 7in)
Endurance:	8338km (4500nm)
Main armament:	One 127mm (5in) gun; one eight-tube Sea Sparrow missile launcher; Phalanx CIWS
Powerplant:	Single screw, turbines
Performance:	27 knots

Doyle

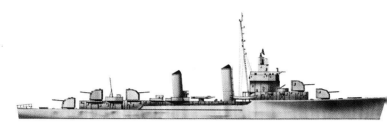

Developed from the Sims class, the large Benson-Livermore class to which *Doyle* belonged was the last destroyer class to be designed and built for the US Navy before the Americans entered World War II. Production was speeded up by the elimination of unnecessary curves in the superstructure, and many of the class were completed with straight-fronted bridge structures. Many ships in the class were transferred to friendly foreign navies after World War II, and continued to give good service for many years. The USS *Doyle*, launched in March 1942, spent her war service on convoy escort and ASW duty in the central Atlantic, and supported the Allied landings in Normandy and the south of France in June and August of 1944. Along with 23 of her sister ships, Doyle was converted to the role of high-speed minesweeper in 1945.

Country of origin:	USA
Type:	Destroyer
Launch date:	17 March 1942
Crew:	250
Displacement:	2621 tonnes (2580 tons)
Dimensions:	106m x 11m x 5.4m (348ft 6in x 36ft x 18ft)
Endurance:	5556km (3000nm)
Main armament:	Four 127mm (5in) guns; five 533mm (21in) torpedo tubes
Powerplant:	Twin screw, turbines
Performance:	37 knots

Doyle

The vessels of the Oliver Hazard Perry class of guided-missile frigate, to which USS *Doyle* belongs, were tailored to cost, and as a result many limitations became apparent in service. (The British had the same problem with their Type 42 destroyers). For example, the USS *Stark* suffered intense fire damage after being hit by two Exocet missiles in the Persian Gulf on 17 May 1987. Since then, there have been many improvements in damage control procedures and equipment to cope with residual missile-propellant-induced fires. On 14 April 1988, the *Samuel B. Roberts* was mined in the Gulf. Fourteen ships of this class were active in the 1991 war with Iraq. In all, 39 units were built for the US Navy; Australia bought four of the class and has since built two more. Spain has six of the class and Taiwan is building seven, while others have been either leased or sold to Bahrain and Egypt.

Country of origin:	USA
Type:	Frigate
Launch date:	22 May 1985
Crew:	200
Displacement:	3696 tonnes (3638 tons)
Dimensions:	135.6m x 13.7m x 7.5m (444ft 10in x 45ft x 24ft 7in)
Endurance:	7408km (4000nm)
Main armament:	One 76mm (3in); four Harpoon SSM; Standard SAM system
Powerplant:	Single screw, gas turbines
Performance:	29 knots

Dragone

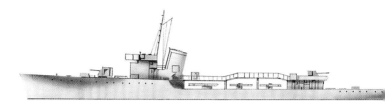

Dragone and her sisters were enlarged versions of the previous Spica class, but were slower, in spite of an increase in machinery power. *Dragone* was taken over by the Germans after Italy's surrender and numbered *TA30*. In May 1944, she joined other destroyers of her type in minelaying operations in the Ligurian Sea which lies between the northern tip of Corsica and Genoa, and was of strategic importance at this time. The destroyers were challenged by American PT boats, most notably in a clash on 30 May, when both sides sustained light damage. On the night of 15–16 June, *TA26* (formerly *Ardito*) and *TA30* were carrying out a mining operation when they were attacked by the American boats *PT558*, *PT552* and *PT559*. Both the *TA26* and the *TA30* were sunk in the engagement. It is sometimes stated that *Dragone* was sunk by Royal Navy light forces, which was not the case.

Country of origin:	Italy
Type:	Destroyer
Launch date:	14 August 1943
Crew:	175
Displacement:	1117 tonnes (1100 tons)
Dimensions:	83.5m x 8.6m x 3.1m (274ft x 28ft 3in x 10ft 4in)
Endurance:	1851km (1000nm)
Main armament:	Two 102mm (4in) guns; six 450mm (17.7in) torpedo tubes; plus smaller weapons
Powerplant:	Twin screw, turbines
Performance:	31.5 knots

Dragonfly

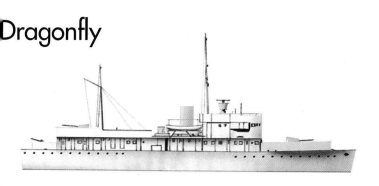

Launched in December 1938, *Dragonfly* was similar to the *Scorpion* of 1937, but slightly smaller. Five vessels were originally planned for this class of river gunboat, but one (*Bee*) was ultimately cancelled, while *Locust* and *Mosquito* were not completed until 1940. The engines developed 3800hp and carried 91.5 tonnes (90 tons). The vessels were intended primarily for river patrols in the Far East. Small and compact, with a shallow draught, they were able to navigate up most of the shallow rivers in the Malay peninsula, policing areas often unsettled by warring local chieftains. On 14 February 1942, *Dragonfly* and her sister ship HMS *Grasshopper* were bombed and sunk by Japanese aircraft south of Singapore. Another of the class, *Mosquito*, had been sunk two years previously during the evacuation of Dunkirk on 1 June 1940.

Country of origin:	Britain
Type:	River gunboat
Launch date:	December 1938
Crew:	74
Displacement:	726 tonnes (715 tons)
Dimensions:	60m x 10m x 1.8m (196ft 6in x 33ft 8in x 6ft 2in)
Endurance:	1852km (1000nm)
Main armament:	Two 102mm (4in) guns
Powerplant:	Two-shaft geared turbines
Performance:	17 knots

Duguay-Trouin

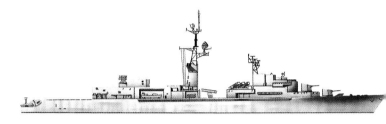

Duguay-Trouin was one of three vessels in a class that were designed to follow on from the earlier Aconite class destroyer. The single-screw propulsion of the earlier class had proved unsuccessful, leading to a doubling-up of the machinery in Duguay-Trouin. This resulted in an increase in speed of four knots. Helicopter facilities were included, plus essential backup, making the *Duguay-Trouin* and her sister vessels the first French warships of destroyer size to operate anti-submarine helicopters. The missile launcher is mounted forward of the funnel, which also carries the mast, with extensive magazines below. *Duguay-Trouin* was launched in June 1973. She was named after Admiral René Duguay-Trouin (1673-1736), who distinguished himself particularly in the wars of Louis XIV, was revered by his sailors, and died in virtual poverty.

Country of origin:	France
Type:	Destroyer
Launch date:	1 June 1973
Crew:	250
Displacement:	5892 tonnes (5800 tons)
Dimensions:	152.5m x 15.3m x 6.5m (500ft 4in x 50ft 2in x 21ft 4in)
Endurance:	9630km (5200nm)
Main armament:	Two 100mm (3.9in) guns; one eight-cell Crotale missile launcher
Powerplant:	Twin screw, turbines
Performance:	32 knots

Duncan

HMS *Duncan* was one of 14 C and D class destroyers laid down in 1931 and 1932 respectively. They were slightly enlarged versions of the B class. Whereas the C-class boats served in the Western Approaches and North Atlantic, the D class were all transferred to the Mediterranean from China when war broke out. *Duncan* was fitted out as a destroyer leader and spent two years on the Gibraltar station as apart of Force H, escorting Mediterranean convoys, and taking part in the Allied landings at Diego Suarez, Madagascar, before being transferred to the Western Approaches. In May 1943, while on convoy escort duty, she helped to sink the *U381* and damaged the *U707*. She was scrapped at Barrow in November 1945. No fewer than nine of the other ships in her class were lost during the war, including three of the five that were transferred to the Royal Canadian Navy.

Country of origin:	Britain
Type:	Destroyer
Launch date:	7 July 1932
Crew:	145
Displacement:	1973 tonnes (1942 tons)
Dimensions:	100m x 10m x 4m (329ft x 32ft 10in x 12ft 10in)
Endurance:	2778km (1500nm)
Main armament:	Four 120mm (4.7in) guns
Powerplant:	Twin screw, turbines
Performance:	35.5 knots

Duncan

The second destroyer to bear the name (the earlier one was lost on 12 October 1942 off Guadalcanal), the USS *Duncan* was part of an extensive World War II building programme of ocean-going destroyers, all of which were equipped with a powerful armament and strengthened by a good radius of action. Thirty-six of the original group, known as the Gearing class, were converted in 1949 and fitted with enemy aircraft early-warning systems. Of the class of nearly 100 units, several were still in service as late as 1980. *Duncan* herself, launched in October 1944, arrived in the Pacific just in time to participate in Japan's surrender, functioning as a radar picket ship with the destroyer USS *Rogers* as part of Rear-Admiral Ballentine's Task Group 38.2. She served for many years post-war, being finally stricken from the Navy list in 1973.

Country of origin:	USA
Type:	Destroyer
Launch date:	27 October 1944
Crew:	350
Displacement:	3606 tonnes (3550 tons)
Dimensions:	120m x 12.5m x 5.8m (390ft 6in x 41ft x 19ft)
Endurance:	5556km (3000nm)
Main armament:	Six 127mm (5in) guns; six torpedo tubes
Powerplant:	Twin screw, turbines
Performance:	35 knots

Dunois

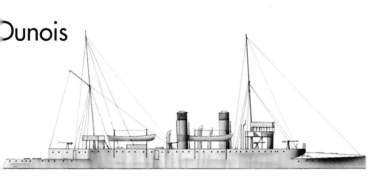

aunched in October 1897, *Dunois* was a twin-funnelled vessel with two pole masts, a straight stem and a turtle-backed foredeck. No torpedoes were fitted in this group, and the main armament was situated on the upper deck near the funnels. In service, neither *Dunois* nor her sister ship made their designed speed of 21.7 knots, but they were able to make 20 knots for lengthy periods. Although the French Navy classed the ships as contre-torpilleurs (destroyers) they were much too slow to be so rated. *Dunois* was deactivated in 1920. The French still had nine river gunboats in service at the outbreak of World War II, two of them assigned to duty in China and the others in French Indo-China. Most were laid down just after World War I and completed in the early 1920s. All were scuttled in the face of the Japanese advance, or sunk by enemy action.

Country of origin:	France
Type:	Gunboat
Launch date:	October 1897
Crew:	75
Displacement:	903 tonnes (889 tons)
Dimensions:	78m x 8.4m x 3.8m (256ft x 27ft 10in x 12ft 8in)
Endurance:	2037km (1100nm)
Main armament:	Six nine-pounder guns
Powerplant:	Twin screw vertical triple expansion engines
Performance:	20 knots

Dupleix

Launched in October 1975, the *Dupleix* was one of eight ships built at Brest Naval Dockyard for service as anti-submarine vessels. The class, also known as the C70 ASW class, was actually divided into two sub-groups, the first fitted out for anti-submarine warfare and the other for air defence. A major innovation was the use of gas turbine engines. These can develop 52,000hp for a speed of 30 knots, compared with the diesels, which develop 10,400hp for 18 knots. The use of gas turbines, however, produced severe limitations on the available space amidships due to the requirement for the extensive intake and uptake trunking. This forced a choice between the Malafon anti-submarine missile and AS helicopters; the latter were chosen, and all ships in the class carry a double hangar aft. In time of war, an extra battery of four Exocet anti-ship missiles can be fitted.

Country of origin:	France
Type:	Destroyer
Launch date:	2 December 1978
Crew:	250
Displacement:	4236 tonnes (4170 tons)
Dimensions:	139m x 14m x 5.7m (456ft x 46ft x 18ft 8in)
Endurance:	8334km (4500nm)
Main armament:	One 100mm (3.9in) gun; two fixed torpedo launchers
Powerplant:	Twin screw gas turbines, plus diesels
Performance:	30 knots

Duquesne

Originally classed as light cruisers, the *Duquesne* and her sister ship *Suffren* were the first French destroyers designed specifically to carry surface-to-air missiles, in this case the Masurca, mounted on a twin-round launcher. They were intended to provide both anti-aircraft and anti-submarine protection for the new generation of French aircraft carriers. *Duquesne* is also fitted with four Exocet missile launchers. *Suffren* became operational in July 1968, and *Duquesne* followed in January 1969. The structure of the ships provided the best possible resistance to atomic blast, and carefully studied habitability was a feature of the design. The *Duquesne* was named after the celebrated sixteenth-century French Admiral Abraham Duquesne (1610–1688), who achieved some notable sea victories in the Mediterranean.

Country of origin:	France
Type:	Destroyer
Launch date:	12 February 1966
Crew:	446
Displacement:	6187 tonnes (6090 tons)
Dimensions:	157.6m x 15.2m x 7.2m (517ft x 50ft x 23ft 9in)
Endurance:	9260km (5000nm)
Main armament:	Two 100mm (3.9in) guns; one Malafon anti-submarine missile launcher; four torpedo launchers
Powerplant:	Twin screw turbines
Performance:	34 knots

Durandal

Launched in February 1899, *Durandal* was France's first destroyer, and the lead ship of a four-strong class ordered in 1896 as prototypes for a new type of anti-torpedo-boat vessel. The ships were built by Normand, who already had wide experience in building torpedo craft. Two Normand water tube boilers supplied the engines, which developed 4800hp. Coal supply was about 38 tons. *Durandal* had a flying deck which ran nearly her entire length, with funnels and gun mounts passing up through it. As originally completed, she had two masts. All vessels in the class could make 26 knots in bad weather and were generally good sea boats. *Durandal* was named after the sword of the legendary French medieval hero, Roland. According to the legend, Roland died while covering the retreat of Charlemagne's army in the Pass of Ronceveaux.

Country of origin:	France
Type:	Destroyer
Launch date:	11 February 1899
Crew:	98
Displacement:	300 tonnes (296 tons)
Dimensions:	57.5m x 6.3m x 3.1m (188ft 8in x 20ft 8in x 10ft 5in)
Endurance:	1852km (1000nm)
Main armament:	One 65mm (2.6in) and six 47mm (1.85in) guns; two 380mm (15in) torpedo tubes
Powerplant:	Twin screw triple expansion engines
Performance:	26 knots

Edinburgh

With the cancellation of a planned new generation of aircraft carriers in the mid-1960s, a Naval Staff Requirement was issued for a small fleet escort capable of providing area defence. This resulted in the Type 42 class design, which suffered considerably during gestation from constraints that were placed on the dimensions as a result of the British Treasury pressure to minimise costs. As built, the ships lacked any close-range air defence system, had reduced endurance on full power output from their gas turbines, and suffered from a short forecastle which resulted in a very wet forward section. The main armament included the Sea Dart SAM system, which proved to be a very effective area defence in the Falklands and the Gulf. The ships were built in three batches, HMS *Edinburgh* being issued as part of Batch 3.

Country of origin:	Britain
Type:	Destroyer
Launch date:	14 April 1983
Crew:	300-312
Displacement:	4851 tonnes (4775 tons)
Dimensions:	141.1m x 14.6m x 5.8m (463ft x 48ft x 19ft)
Endurance:	5185km (2800nm)
Main armament:	One 114mm (4.5in) gun; helicopter-launched Mk44 torpedoes; two triple mounts for Mk46 AS torpedoes; one Sea Dart SAM launcher
Powerplant:	Twin screw, gas turbines
Performance:	30 knots

Elan

At the outbreak of World War II, the French fleet was poorly served for escorts in the accepted sense of the word, those available being designed primarily for colonial service. For effective anti-submarine work, therefore, the Free French Navy relied on frigates, corvettes and DEs transferred from the Royal Navy or the US Navy. The exception was the 15-strong Elan-class vessels, completed between 1939 and 1940 and fitted out as minesweepers. Those that escaped capture by Axis forces after the fall of France were pressed into service in the ASW role; despite their relatively low speed compared with that of the Royal Navy's Flower class, they had an excellent endurance. The class leader, *Elan*, captured the German cargo ship *Rostock* on 10 February 1940 and later took part in the short Syrian campaign. Afterwards, she was interned in Turkey until December 1944.

Country of origin:	France
Type:	Corvette
Launch date:	27 July 1938
Crew:	Not known
Displacement:	752 tonnes (740 tons)
Dimensions:	78m x 8.5m x 2.4m (255ft 11in x 27ft 11in x 7ft 11in)
Endurance:	16,645km (8988nm)
Main armament:	Two 100mm (3.9in) guns
Powerplant:	Two shafts, two diesel engines
Performance:	20 knots

Electra

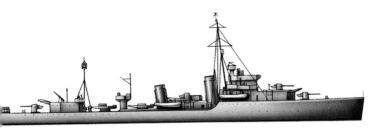

aunched on February 1934, HMS *Electra* was one of nine E-class destroyers. She saw initial action off Norway in April 1940, and a year later, as part of the escort to the battleship *Prince of Wales*, she participated in the hunt for the German battleship *Bismarck*. In October 1941, together with the destroyer *Express*, she accompanied the *Prince of Wales* to Singapore, and was present when the battleship and the battlecruiser *Repulse* were sunk off Malaya by Japanese air attack on 10 December 1941. On 27 February 1942, she formed part of a mixed force of British, Dutch, and American warships that sailed to intercept Japanese invasion forces in the Java Sea. In a confused short-range action with eight enemy destroyers and the cruiser *Naka*, the *Electra* attacked through a smokescreen and was seen no more.

Country of origin:	Britain
Type:	Destroyer
Launch date:	15 February 1934
Crew:	145
Displacement:	1397 tonnes (1375 tons)
Dimensions:	100.2m x 10.3m x 2.6m (329ft x 33ft 9in x 8ft 6in)
Endurance:	3889km (2100nm)
Main armament:	Four 120mm (4.7in) guns; eight 533mm (21in) torpedo tubes
Powerplant:	Two-shaft geared turbines
Performance:	35.5 knots

Emanuele Pessagno

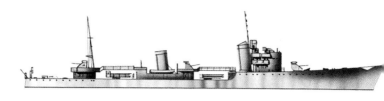

The *Emanuele Pessagno* was ordered in 1926 and laid down between 1927 and 1928. She and the other 11 vessels that made up her class all saw extensive service in World War II. Although smaller than their French rivals of the Guepard and Jaguar classes, the Italian vessels carried the same powerful armament and ha a three-knot speed advantage over them. During trials, one of *Emanuele Pessagno* sisters was reported to have achieved 45 knots. When first completed, the vessels were classified as scouts, but by 1938 they were listed as destroyers. Only one vessel survived the war; eight were sunk in combat, two were scuttled, and one wa mined. In May 1942, the *Emanuele Pessagno*, while escorting Italian supply convoys to Benghazi, was torpedoed and sunk by the British submarine HMS *Turbulent* (Cdr Linton).

Country of origin:	Italy
Type:	Destroyer
Launch date:	12 August 1929
Crew:	225
Displacement:	2621 tonnes (2580 tons)
Dimensions:	107.3m x 10.8m x 3.4m (352ft x 33ft 6in x 11ft 2in)
Endurance:	3426km (1850nm)
Main armament:	Six 120mm (4.7in) guns; six 533mm (21in) torpedo tubes
Powerplant:	Twin screw, turbines
Performance:	38 knots

Erato

aunched in 1883, *Erato* was one of a class of light units built by Thorneycroft.
She was designed for inshore service. Upon completion, *Erato* and her sisters
were classified as fourth-class torpedo boats. They were discarded between 1896
and 1899, two being transferred to the Customs Service in 1898. In the last two
decades of the nineteenth century, the Italians were preoccupied with establishing
a naval force capable of challenging the Austro-Hungarian Navy for command of the
Adriatic. As a result, small attack craft such as *Erato* were in great demand as the
ideal vessels for infiltrating the many anchorages and inlets on the coast of
Dalmatia, where much of the Austro-Hungarian fleet was based. The other boats in
the class were *Euterpe, Talia, Melpomene, Tersicore, Polimnia, Urania* and
Calliope. The two transferred to the Customs Service were *Talia* and *Tersicore*.

Country of origin:	Italy
Type:	Torpedo boat
Launch date:	1883
Crew:	9–15
Displacment	3.7 tonnes (13.5 tons)
Dimensions:	19.2m x 2.2m x 1.1m (63ft x 7ft 6in x 3ft 9in)
Endurance:	Not known
Main armament:	One 25mm (1in) revolver; two 355mm (14in) torpedo tubes
Powerplant:	Single screw vertical triple expansion engine
Performance:	c.19 knots

Erie

The USS *Erie* (PG50), launched in 1936, was built to an unusual design in which the needs for peacetime patrols and wartime missions were successfully combined in a vessel that also provided adequate accommodation for its crew and Marine contingent. It was also economical to run. *Erie's* unique hull design enable her relatively low 5941hp to drive her along at 20 knots, and her long bow helped keep the vessel dry. A scouting aircraft was carried, but it was not possible to fit a catapult and so the machine was lowered into the water and retrieved by crane. *Erie* and her sister *Charleston* were the first US ships to carry the new 152mm (6in 47-calibre weapon with its combined shell and charge. On 12 November 1942 *Erie* weas torpedoed off Curacao by the *U163* (Cdr Engelmann); she was consequently beached and burnt out.

Country of origin:	USA
Type:	Gunboat
Launch date:	1936
Crew:	236
Displacement:	2376 tonnes (2339 tons)
Dimensions:	100m x 12.5m x 3.4m (328ft 6in x 41ft 3in x 11ft 4in)
Endurance:	5556km (3000nm)
Main armament:	Four 152mm (6in) guns
Powerplant:	Two-shaft geared turbines
Performance:	20 knots

rmanno Carlotto

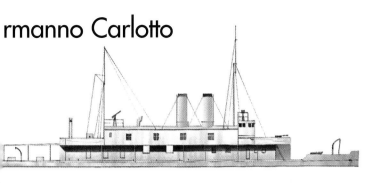

aunched in 1918, *Ermanno Carlotto* was a shallow-draught river gunboat built by the Shanghai Dock and Engineering Company. Two Yarrow boilers provided am for the 1100hp engines, and the twin screws operated in tunnels to achieve ximum benefit from the shallow draught. She was assigned to the Italian Far East onial Station and was based at Shanghai. On 9 September 1943, following the ian armistice with the Allied powers, *Ermanno Carlotto* was scuttled in anghai to prevent her falling into Japanese hands. The Japanese, however, oated her and named her *Narumi*. Enlisted into the Imperial Navy on 15 October 43, she was used in Chinese waters before being surrendered in 1945. She was ded over to China, who renamed her *Kian Kun*, and was captured by the inese Communists in 1949.

Country of origin:	Italy
Type:	Gunboat
Launch date:	19 June 1918
Crew:	75
Displacement:	221 tonnes (218 tons)
Dimensions:	48.8m x 7.5m x 0.9m (160ft x 24ft 7in x 3ft)
Endurance:	Not known
Main armament:	Two 76mm (3in) guns
Powerplant:	Twin screw vertical triple expansion engines
Performance:	13 knots

Erne

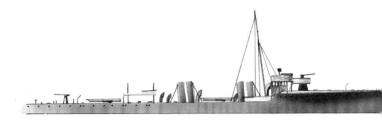

Part of the 1901–1904 naval building programme included a large group of destroyers known as the E or River class. *Erne* was the first ship of the 34-strong class to be launched, in January 1903. Experience with earlier types of destroyer had shown that concentrating on high trial speed was a snare and a delusion. The combination of seaworthiness with the ability to maintain a less spectacular speed when it became rough was of far more value. The larger size, sturdiness and raised forecastle of these ships made them much more seaworthy than their predecessors. These vessels thus marked the real break between the torpedo boat and the true destroyer, and set the trend for future British destroyer development. *Erne* was one of eight British destroyers wrecked during World War I; the Royal Navy's total destroyer loss, from all causes, was 64, of which one-third were the victims of mines.

Country of origin:	Britain
Type:	Destroyer
Launch date	14 January 1903
Crew:	110
Displacement:	630 tonnes (620 tons)
Dimensions:	71m x 7.1m x 2.9m (233ft 6in x 23ft 6in x 9ft 9in)
Endurance:	2038km (1100nm)
Main armament:	One 12-pounder; two 457mm (18in) torpedo tubes
Powerplant:	Twin screw, triple expansion engines
Performance:	25.6 knots

Esmereldas

Although strictly speaking rated as missile corvettes rather than small light frigates, the units of the Esmeraldas class approximate more closely to small light frigates because of their multipurpose capabilities. Ordered in 1978 from the Italian firm CNR del Tirreno, the design is based on that of the Assad class built for Libya, but with more powerful diesel engines, a helicopter landing platform amidships (but no hangar) , and a SAM launcher aft of the bridge. All six units of the class – *Esmeraldas*, *Manabi*, *Los Rios*, *El Oro*, *Galapagos* and *Laja* – are in service with the Ecuadorean Navy as the country's primary anti-ship surface strike force. *El Oro* was out of commission for two years from 1985 after a bad fire. Only self-defence ASW torpedo tubes are fitted, together with a hull-mounted sonar set for sub-surface warfare operations.

Country:	Ecuador
Type:	Corvette
Launch date:	1 October 1980
Crew:	51
Displacement:	696 tonnes (685 tons)
Dimensions:	62.3m x 9.3m x 2.5m (204ft 5in x 30ft 6in x 8ft 2in)
Endurance:	7037km (3800nm)
Main armament:	One 76mm gun; Exocet SSMs; Aspide SAMs
Powerplant:	Four shafts, four diesel engines
Performance:	37 knots

Espero

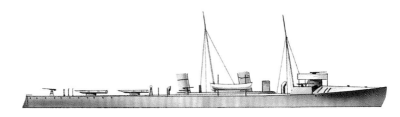

E_spero_ was one of the six vessels of the Nembo class built for the Italian Navy by Pattison of Naples. From 1908 to 1912 all were reboilered (fuel oil) and from 1909 their armament was altered. Minelaying gear (10-16 mines) was added in 1915-18. Three of the class were sunk in action during World War I. In 1921 the three remaining vessels were reclassified as torpedo boats, and two years after that _Espero_ was discarded. The confines of the Adriatic Sea, where engagments between Italian destroyers and their Austro-Hungarian counterparts were fought, lent themselves very well to actions by naval light forces, which were able to penetrate the waterways and the deep, sheltered passages that lay between the maze of islands off the coasts of Dalmatia and Albania. Italian destroyers also operated in the Dardanelles in support of the Allied naval forces deployed there.

Country of origin:	Italy
Type:	Destroyer
Launch date:	9 July 1904
Crew:	210
Displacement:	386 tonnes (380 tons)
Dimensions:	64m x 5.9m x 2.2m (210ft x 19ft 6in x 7ft 6in)
Endurance:	2778km (1500nm)
Main armament:	Five 57mm (2.24in) guns; four 355mm (14in) torpedo tubes
Powerplant:	Triple expansion engines
Performance:	26 knots

Espero

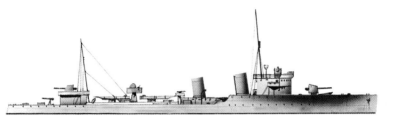

All eight units in the Espero class were laid down in 1925 and were slightly larger and more powerful versions of the previous Sauro class. The crew, which numbered 142 in peacetime, could be increased to 179 in time of war. All the vessels in the class underwent minor changes to their armament early in World War II. The entire class was lost during the war, with six of the group being sunk in 1940. On 28 June 1940, the Italian destroyers *Espero*, *Ostro* and *Zeffiro* were ferrying supplies from Taranto to Tobruk when they were sighted by a reconnaissance aircraft, which summoned the British 7th Cruiser Squadron to intercept. The *Espero* (Flotilla Cdr Baroni) attacked the British force to cover the withdrawal of the others, and was sunk by the Australian cruiser *Sydney*. This was one of the most gallant Italian Naval actions of World War II.

Country of origin:	Italy
Type:	Destroyer
Launch date:	31 August 1927
Crew:	142
Displacement:	1696 tonnes (1670 tons)
Dimensions:	93.2m x 9.2m x 2.9m (305ft 9in x 30ft 2in x 9ft 10in)
Endurance:	3890km (2100nm)
Main armament:	Four 120mm (4.7in) guns
Powerplant:	Twin screw, turbines
Performance:	36 knots

Essex

Essex was a large sailing frigate paid for by popular subscription. Although she and four other frigates, also paid for by popular subscription, were completed too late to see much action in the war with France, they proved valuable additions to the newly formed US Navy. As built, *Essex* was a very fast frigate, but numerous changes made to her by different commanders greatly reduced her speed. She first saw action early in 1800, and became the first US warship to round the Cape of Good Hope. In 1812 a brief war broke out between Britain and the United States over trade restrictions, resulting in several naval actions. Early in 1814, *Essex* was captured by two British frigates after an action lasting nearly three hours. From 1833 onwards, *Essex* served as a prison ship at Kingston, Jamaica, until she was sold at auction in 1837.

Country of origin:	USA
Type:	Frigate
Launch date:	1799
Crew:	350
Displacement:	863 tonnes (850 tons)
Dimensions:	43m x 11m (141ft 9in x 36ft 6in)
Endurance:	Unlimited, depending on provisions
Main armament:	Twenty-six 12-pounders and 10 six-pounders
Powerplant:	Sail
Performance:	12 knots

Étendard

Both France and Britain had large colonial empires in the second half of the nineteenth century which required policing to maintain order. Consequently, both nations produced large numbers of gunboats: cheap and simple vessels able to operate for long periods away from sophisticated bases and logistic support, but powerful enough to deal with most small incidents in farflung colonies. *Étendard* (Standard) was one of an eight-strong class of gunboats built in Bordeaux. Her hull was of wooden construction, and came complete with a full brigantine rig of sail and twin screw coal-fired engines. Her bunkers could only carry a maximum of 56 tonnes (55 tons) of coal, and so she was expected to rely on sail power for most of the time. *Étendard* was one of the longest serving boats in the group, and was only removed from the effective list in 1882.

Country of origin:	France
Type:	Gunboat
Launch date:	1868
Crew	69
Displacement:	508 tonnes (500 tons)
Dimensions:	43.4m x 7.3m x 2.7m (142ft 6in x 24ft 3in x 8ft 10in)
Endurance:	2592km (1400nm)
Main armament:	One 120mm (4.7in)gun; one 140mm (5.5in) gun
Powerplant:	Twin screw vertical compound engines
Performance:	9 knots

Euro

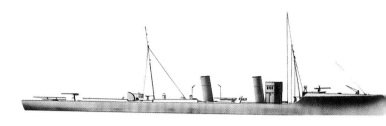

Launched in August 1900, *Euro* was one of six vessels in the first major destroyer class to be built for the Italian Navy. They were fast, strongly built ships, with a range of 551km (297 nautical miles) at 26 knots, increasing to 3792km (2048nm) at 12 knots. During World War I, five ships in the class were converted to the role of minelayer. Minelaying was a major activity of the Italian Navy in the Adriatic, where the Austro-Hungarian fleet had the benefit of many small inlets and harbours from which it could operate. The other boats in the class were *Lampo* (class leader), *Freccia, Dardo, Strale* and *Ostro*. Between 1922 and 1923, *Euro* served as a target ship. When *Strale* was discarded in January 1924 *Euro* was allocated her name so that *Euro* could be allocated to a new boat then under construction; *Euro/Strale* was discarded in November that year.

Country of origin:	Italy
Type:	Destroyer
Launch date:	27 August 1900
Crew:	150
Displacement:	353 tonnes (348 tons)
Dimensions:	62m x 6.5m x 2.6m (203ft 5in x 21ft 4in x 8ft 6in)
Endurance:	3800km (2048nm)
Main armament:	One 76mm (3in) gun; two 355mm (14in) torpedo tubes
Powerplant:	Twin screw triple expansion engines
Performance:	26 knots

Euro

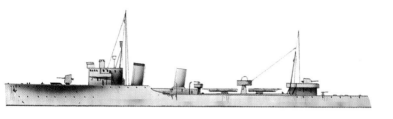

Euro was part of a class of six vessels which were slightly larger versions of the previous Sauro class. All were laid down in 1925, the last unit being launched in 1928. All the vessels of this class adopted the names of their immediate predecessors. Designed to reach a speed of 36 knots with 40,000hp, *Euro* actually achieved 38.9 knots during a four-hour full-power trial. In service, however, her best sea speed was about 30 knots. After Italy's entry into World War II, she was employed on minelaying and convoy escort operations, and in November 1941 she was damaged while escorting a convoy that was attacked by the cruisers of the British Force K from Malta. All seven merchantmen were sunk, together with the destroyer *Libeccio*, which sank while under tow by the *Euro*. On 1 October 1943, following Italy's surrender, the *Euro* was sunk by German aircraft in Leros harbour.

Country of origin:	Italy
Type:	Destroyer
Launch date:	7 July 1927
Crew:	142
Displacement:	1696 tonnes (1670 tons)
Dimensions:	93.2m x 9.2m x 3m (305ft 9in x 30ft 2in x 9ft 10in)
Endurance:	3890km (2100nm)
Main armament:	Four 120mm (4.7in) guns; six 533mm (21in) torpedo tubes
Powerplant:	Twin screw turbines
Performance:	36 knots

Euro

Following the success of the Lupo-class frigate, Italy decided to build an enlarged version, the Maestrale class, incorporating a hangar for two helicopters. The first six vessels were ordered in 1976 and the last pair in 1980. *Euro* entered service in 1984. The aft flight deck is 27m (88ft 6in) long and 12m (39ft 4in) wide, and there is a stern well for a new variable depth towed sonar array which is streamed out on a 600m (1968ft) long cable; this was later increased to 900m (2953ft). From 1994, hull and sonars were modified to give better shallow water performance and a mine detection capability. The eight vessels of the Lupo class are scheduled for replacement from the year 2000, although it is likely that they will be updated and retained in service. The ships of this class have seen much service in the Adriatic with the NATO peacekeeping force operational in the area since 1991.

Country of origin:	Italy
Type:	Destroyer
Launch date:	25 March 1983
Crew:	232
Displacement:	3088 tonnes (3040 tons)
Dimensions:	122.7m x 12.9m x 8.4m (402ft 6in x 42ft 4in x 27ft 6in)
Endurance:	7408km (4000nm)
Main armament:	One 127mm (5in) gun plus missiles
Powerplant:	Twin screw diesels and gas turbines
Performance:	29 knots (diesels), 32 knots (turbines)

Euterpe

A sister ship of the *Erato*, *Euterpe* was one of eight small craft designed and built by Thorneycroft and intended for coastal defence. During the time of her construction, torpedo boats were posing a serious threat to battle fleets, especially at night. The Imperial Russian Navy had already proved the concept of the torpedo boat in the 1870s, during Russia's conflict with Turkey during which several attacks were made on Turkish warships, both offshore and in harbour, with varying degrees of success. *Euterpe*'s torpedo tubes were carried in the bow and were loaded from a ramp behind the turtle-backed foredeck. Launched in 1883, *Euterpe* was numbered Torpedo Boat 37 in 1886, and was discarded around 1897. Sister ships *Talia* and *Tersicore* were transferred to Customs service in 1898. Thorneycroft also built a second group of eight torpedo boats in this class in 1883.

Country of origin:	Italy
Type:	Torpedo boat
Launch date:	1883
Crew:	9–15
Displacement:	13.5 tonnes (13.3 tons)
Dimensions:	19.2m x 2.2m x 1.1m (63ft x 7ft 6in x 3ft 9in)
Endurance:	Not known
Main armament:	One 25mm (1in) machine gun; two 355mm (14in) torpedo tubes
Powerplant:	Single screw vertical triple expansion engines
Performance:	c.19 knots

Exeter

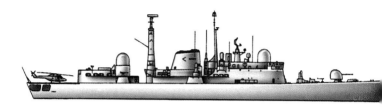

HMS *Exeter*, launched in April 1978 and commissioned in September 1980, is one of four Batch 2 Type 42 destroyers, the others being *Southampton*, *Nottingham* and *Liverpool*. The Type 42s were originally designed to provide are defence for a task force with their British Aerospace Sea Dart surface-to-air missil these have a range of 40km (21.5nm) under radar or semi-active radar guidance a have a height envelope of 100-18,300m (328-60,042ft). The weapons also have a limited anti-ship capability. Generally, each Type 42 is armed with 22 Sea Dart rounds. The ships' Lynx helicopter carries the Sea Skua air-to-surface missile for u against lightly defended surface-ship targets, such as fast attack craft, and has bee operationally proved in the Falklands and Gulf conflicts, being especially effectiv against small, fast targets such as missile boats.

Country of origin:	Britain
Type:	Destroyer
Launch date:	25 April 1978
Crew:	253
Displacement:	4166 tonnes (4100 tons)
Dimensions:	125m x 14.3m x 5.8m (412ft x 47ft x 19ft)
Endurance:	6430km (3472nm)
Main armament:	One 114mm (4.5in) gun; Sea Dart SAM; 20mm (0.7in) and Phalanx AA.
Powerplant:	Twin shafts, four gas turbines
Performance:	29 knots

xmoor

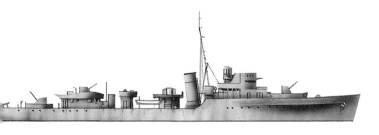

In 1941 the Type II Hunt-class destroyer HMS *Burton* was renamed *Exmoor*, following the loss of the Hunt Type I ship of that name. The choice of the original name was perhaps unfortunate, in view of the then current slang expression 'gone for a Burton', which meant that someone or something had met an untimely end. Exmoor served in the North Atlantic and in the Mediterranean with the Gibraltar-based Force H and was part of the naval support force in Operation Husky, the Allied landings on Sicily in July 1943, and the Salerno landing in September. On 10 March 1944 she participated in the destruction of the U450 off Anzio. In 1953 Exmoor was transferred to the Royal Danish Navy as the Valdemar Sejr, together with the other Hunt-class ships *Blackmore* (*Esbern Snare*) and Calpe (*Rolf Krake*). She was stricken in 1962.

Country of origin:	Britain
Type:	Destroyer
Launch date:	12 March 1941
Crew:	168
Displacement:	1067 tonnes (1050 tons)
Dimensions:	85.3m x 9.6m x 3.7m (280ft x 31ft 6in x 12ft 5in)
Endurance:	3333km (1800nm)
Main armament:	Six 102mm (4in) guns
Powerplant:	Twin screw turbines
Performance:	26 knots

Exmouth

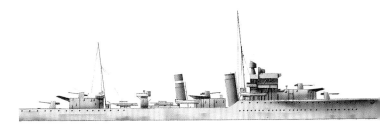

E*xmouth* was one of the E-class destroyers that were improved versions of the C and D-class vessels. The E class had increased fuel capacity and higher speed, plus extra stowage. Two of *Exmouth*'s sisters, *Esk* and *Express*, were fitted out as minelayers, but *Exmouth* was an enlarged version of the flotilla destroyer, with one more 120mm (4.7in) gun and a higher speed. In spite of poor weather conditions, trials run in September 1934 produced good results. At 20 knots, just over two tons of fuel oil were used per hour. In November 1939, *Exmouth* was one of the destroyers that provided an escort for the battlecruiser HMS *Hood*, searching for the German battlecruisers *Scharnhorst* and *Gneisenau* in the North Atlantic. In January 1940, *Exmouth* was sunk with all hands in the Moray Firth by the *U22* (Lt-Cdr Jenisch).

Country of origin:	Britain
Type:	Destroyer (Flotilla Leader)
Launch date:	7 February 1934
Crew:	175
Displacement:	1397 tonnes (1375 tons)
Dimensions:	104.5m x 10.2m x 3.8m (342ft 10in x 33ft 9in x 12ft 6in)
Endurance:	3889km (2100nm)
Main armament:	Five 120mm (4.7in) guns
Powerplant:	Twin screw turbines
Performance:	35.5 knots

Falco

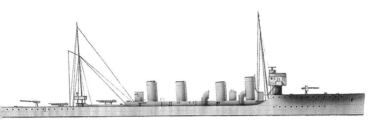

In 1913 Romania ordered four large, powerful destroyers from Pattison of Naples for service in the Black Sea where they needed to have an endurance of ten hours at full speed. *Falco* was laid down as *Viscol* but was taken over by the Italian Navy in 1916, when she was renamed and reclassified as a scout. She was completed in 1920. In 1937 she entered Spanish service for the Nationalists and was renamed *Ceuta*. The Italians were a principal supplier of arms and equipment to General Franco's forces during the Spanish Civil War, the other supplier being Nazi Germany, and much of the equipment supplied was retained after the conflict was over. The former *Falco* was discarded in 1948, when Spain received a batch of ex-American destroyers. Prior to this, the Spanish Navy was very much the same as it had been in 1939, development having stagnated during the war.

Country of origin:	Italy
Type:	Flotilla Leader
Launch date:	16 August 1919
Crew:	150
Displacement:	1788 tonnes (1760 tons)
Dimensions:	94.7m x 9.5m x 3.6m (310ft 8in x 31ft 2in x 11ft 10in)
Endurance:	1667km (900nm)
Main armament:	Three 152mm (6in) guns
Powerplant:	Twin screw turbines
Performance:	35.2 knots

le Fantasque

The le Fantasque class was the penultimate class in a series that set new destroyer standards, yet which had little real influence on construction abroad because it stemmed largely from naval rivalry between the French and the Italians. The six ships of the class were magnificent-looking vessels with an imposing freeboard and an extra 3m (9.84ft) in overall length that allowed for a fifth gun and three triple sets of torpedo tubes. After France's collapse, *le Fantasque* and *le Terrible* deployed to Dakar, and after a refit at Boston, USA. Subsequently, these ships and *le Malin* served with distinction in the Mediterranean, forming part of the naval force that landed in southern France in August 1944 and carried out many raiding sorties in the Aegean. At the end of the war, *le Fantasque* was deployed to the Far East to support French forces reoccupying Indo-China.

Country of origin:	France
Type:	Destroyer
Launch date	15 March 1934
Crew:	210
Displacement:	3404 tonnes (3350 tons)
Dimensions:	132.4m x 12.35m x 5.0m (434ft 4in x 40ft 6in x 16ft 4in)
Endurance:	7408km (4000nm)
Main armament:	Five single 138.6mm (5.46in) and two twin 37mm (1.4in) AA guns; three triple 553mm (21in) torpedo tubes.
Powerplant:	Two sets of geared steam turbines
Performance:	37 knots

Farragut

The USS *Farragut*, launched in July 1898, was the US Navy's first destroyer, although when originally authorised she was described as a torpedo boat. She was laid down in July 1897 at the Union Iron Works, and was completed in March 1899. Her engines developed 5878hp, and steam was supplied by three Thorneycroft boilers. Coal supply was 96 tonnes (95 tons). In August 1918, *Farragut* was renamed Coast Torpedo Boat No 5. She was sold in 1919. The *Farragut* entered service during an exciting period in US naval development. Victories in the Philippines had established the USA as a sea power, and with the acquisition of new territory in the Caribbean and the Far East, the prestige of the US Navy began to climb rapidly. Its development was helped by the fact that the USA was now the leading industrial nation.

Country of origin:	USA
Type:	Destroyer
Launch date:	16 July 1898
Crew:	66
Displacement:	283 tonnes (279 tons)
Dimensions:	65m x 6.3m x 1.8m (214ft x 20ft 8in x 6ft)
Endurance:	1852km (1000nm)
Main armament:	Six six-pounder guns; two 457mm (18in) torpedo tubes
Powerplant:	Twin screw vertical triple expansion engines
Performance:	33.7 knots

Fasana

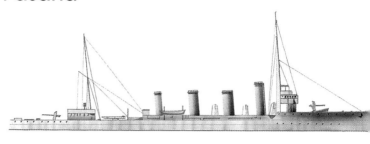

Fasana was formerly the Austrian *Tatra*, one of a class of seven vessels that wer
the best and most powerful destroyers in the Austro-Hungarian Navy. In the
years prior to World War I, the Archduke Franz Ferdinand (the heir to the Austrian
throne whose assassination at Sarajevo was to precipitate the war) had made
strenuous efforts to build up his country's fleet with modern warships, and the
Tatra, launched in November 1912, was part of the building programme. As war
reparations, she was transferred to the Italian Navy in August 1920 and renamed
Fasana, though she was neither refitted nor commissioned into the Italian Navy
because of her poor condition. Once in Italian service the armament of the other
vessels was changed, their 533mm (21in) torpedo tubes being reduced to the
standard 450mm (17.7in).

Country of origin:	Austria (transferred to Italy)
Type:	Destroyer
Launch date:	5 November 1912
Crew:	120
Displacement:	1052 tonnes (1036 tons)
Dimensions:	83.5m x 7.8m x 3m (274ft x 25ft 7in x 9ft 10in)
Endurance:	2778km (1500nm)
Main armament:	Two 100mm (3.9in) guns
Powerplant:	Twin screw turbines
Performance:	32.6 knots

Fatahillah class

The Fatahillah class of Dutch-designed and -built ASW frigates was ordered in August 1975 as the first major new-build warship type for the Indonesian Navy since the acceptance of Soviet ships in the 1950s and 1960s. The class numbers only three, one of which, the *Nala*, has a flight deck to accommodate a light helicopter. The vessels of the Fatahillah class carry an anti-ship missile armament comprising two pairs of container-launchers for the MM39 Exocet. It is this armament which enables the ships to operate as effective supports for the considerable force of missile- and gun-armed attack units which the Indonesian Navy employs among the myriad islands which go to make up the republic. The Indonesians also use three ex-Royal Navy Tribal-class frigates. Indonesia began to expand its navy following the confrontation with Malaysia in the early 1960s.

Country of origin:	Netherlands/Indonesia
Type:	Frigate
Launch date:	22 December 1977
Crew:	89
Displacement:	1473 tonnes (1450 tons)
Dimensions:	84m x 11m x 3.3m (275ft 7in x 36ft 4in x 10ft 11in)
Endurance:	3333km (1800nm)
Main armament:	One 120mm (4.7in) DP gun; one 40mm (1.5in) and two 20mm (0.7in) AA guns; two triple 324mm (12.76in) torpedo tubes; ASW rockets and anti-ship missiles
Powerplant:	Two shafts, one gas turbine, two diesels
Performance:	30 knots

Faulknor

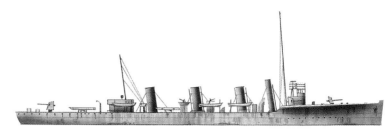

Designed by J.S. White in 1912, *Faulknor* was one of four large, powerful destroyers ordered for the Chilean Navy which was British-trained and the best in Latin America. Previously named *Almirante Simpson*, the ship was taken over by the Royal Navy in August 1914, whereupon the fore funnel was raised and a more powerful radio outfit installed. Unlike other British destroyers of the day, which had a single gun firing forward, *Faulknor* and her sisters were heavily armed with three or four guns firing forward. In 1915 *Faulknor* joined other light forces in hunting U-boats in the Irish Sea, and in November 1916, she operated intensively against enemy submarine traffic off the Norwegian coast. After World War I, *Faulknor* was refitted and returned to Chile, where she served until she was removed from the effective list in 1933.

Country of origin:	Britain
Type:	Destroyer (Flotilla Leader)
Launch date:	26 February 1944
Crew:	190
Displacement:	2024 tonnes (1993 tons)
Dimensions:	100m x 10m x 6.4m (330ft 10in x 32ft 6in x 21ft 1in)
Endurance:	3704km (2000nm)
Main armament:	Six 102mm (4in) guns; four 533mm (21in) torpedo tubes
Powerplant:	Triple screw turbines
Performance:	29 knots

La Fayette

The first three of five La Fayette-class frigates were ordered in July 1988, but construction was delayed because of funding problems. *La Fayette* was commissioned in March 1996, and *Surcouf* and *Courbet* in February and March 1997 respectively. *Aconit* had a commission date of December 1999 and *Guepratte* of January 2002. The La Fayette class-frigates are intended for out-of-area operations on overseas stations, and the first three are assigned to the Indian Ocean. Super Frelon helicopters may be operated from the flight deck, and the vessels can launch inflatable boats from a hatch in the stern which hinges upwards. The ships incorporate many stealth features, and extensive use is made of radar absorbent paint. Protruding equipment such as capstans and bollards are either hidden or fitted as flush as possible.

Country of origin:	France
Type:	Frigate
Launch date:	13 June 1992
Crew:	139
Displacement:	3658 tonnes (3600 tons)
Dimensions:	124.2m x 15.4m x 5.9m (407ft 6in x 50ft 6in x 19ft 5in)
Endurance:	14,467km (7812nm)
Main armament:	One 100mm (3.9in) DP gun; Exocet SSM; Crotale SAM
Powerplant:	Two shafts, four diesel engines
Performance:	25 knots

Ferret

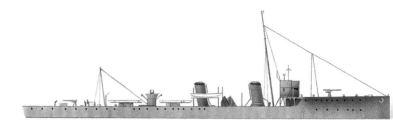

Ferret was the lead ship in a group of destroyers that were originally intended to be repeats of the previous Acorn class. She was laid down in September 1910 and was completed in October 1911. Twenty other ships of the class were also begun in 1910, but six others were put out to private firms to see if they could improve upon the Acorn design. On trials, *Ferret* maintained slightly over 30 knots for eight hours, a credit to her builder, J.S. White. However, although the fore funnel was set well back from the bridge, the exhaust fumes still caused problems for those on the bridge. This was rectified later when the funnel was raised. Destroyers of this type performed good service with the coastal flotillas in World War I, patrolling into the Heligoland Bight and securing the Channel area. *Ferret* was scrapped in 1921.

Country of origin:	Britain
Type:	Destroyer
Launch date:	12 April 1911
Crew:	98
Displacement:	762 tonnes (750 tons)
Dimensions:	75m x 7.8m x 2.6m (246ft x 25ft 8in x 8ft 9in)
Endurance:	2037km (1100nm)
Main armament:	Two 102mm (4in) guns
Powerplant:	Twin screw turbines
Performance:	33 knots

Fervent

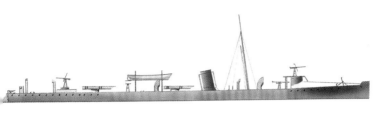

Fervent was part of the building programme of 1894–95 which was designed to combat the strength of the French Navy. The ship followed the design of earlier destroyers, but was fitted with old-style locomotive boilers and had only one funnel. At this time, new ideas and inventions in shipbuilding were emerging so quickly that a new vessel could be obsolete before it was launched. Much of this problem was created by Britain's own naval policy, which was described as a 'two-power standard' and which kept the Royal Navy equal in numbers to any two foreign navies. In simple terms, warships were being built at too fast a rate to incorporate the latest technological advances. *Fervent* and her sister ship, *Zephyr*, failed entirely to meet their contract speed, and their builder eventually went out of business. She was scrapped in 1920.

Country of origin:	Britain
Type:	Destroyer
Launch date:	20 March 1895
Crew:	80
Displacement:	280 tonnes (275 tons)
Dimensions:	61m x 5.7m x 2.4m (200ft 4in x 19ft 1in x 8ft)
Endurance:	1760km (950nm)
Main armament:	Three six-pounders; one 12-pounder
Powerplant:	Twin screw triple expansion engines
Performance:	22 knots

Fionda

Italian war estimates provided for the building of 42 boats in *Fionda*'s class. Only 15 were laid down, the lead ship *Ariete* being the only one actually delivered to the Italian Navy. *Fionda* was laid down in 1942, but she was captured by the Germans while still on the slips and designated *TA46*. On 20 February 1945 she was damaged in an Allied air attack. She was repaired and assigned to Yugoslavia as the *Velebit*, but she was never completed. Two of her sister ships, however, did serve with the Yugoslav Navy; these were the *Ariete*, which was renamed *Durmitor*, and the *Balestra*, renamed the *Ucka*. The latter vessel, designated *TA47* by the Germans, was also damaged by air attack in February 1945, and was completed by Yugoslavia in 1949. The *Ucka* and *Durmitor* were removed from the active list in 1963 and 1968 respectively.

Country of origin:	Italy
Type:	Destroyer
Launch date:	31 January 1943
Crew:	175
Displacement:	1138 tonnes (1120 tons)
Dimensions:	82.2m x 8.6m x 2.8m (270ft x 28ft 3in x 9ft 2in)
Endurance:	1852km (1000nm)
Main armament:	Two 100mm (3.9in) guns
Powerplant:	Twin screw turbines
Performance:	31.5 knots

Flamingo

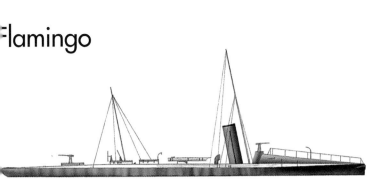

Flamingo was one of a group of 20 small torpedo boats built for the Austrian Navy in the late 1880s and 1890s. They were based on the earlier and successful *Schichau* design, and incorporated a number of improvements. *Flamingo* herself was laid down in 1888 and completed in the following year. All the boats of this design underwent major reconstruction between 1900 and 1910. During this refit, *Flamingo* had her boiler replaced by two Yarrow units, and eventually re-entered service bearing pennant number 26. She was mined and sunk off Pola on 23 August 1914. Eighteen remaining boats were converted to the minesweeping role in 1917, and 16 of these were transferred to Italy in 1920. Most were scrapped soon after, but four operated as customs patrol boats until 1925. The Austro-Hungarian fleet had dozens of similar craft at this time.

Country of origin:	Austria
Type:	Torpedo boat
Launch date:	1889
Crew:	15
Displacement:	91.4 tonnes (90 tons)
Dimensions:	39.9m x 4.8m x 1.9m (130ft 11in x 15ft 9in x 6ft 3in)
Endurance:	2276km (1229nm)
Main armament:	Two 350mm (13.8in) torpedo tubes
Powerplant:	Single screw triple expansion engine
Performance:	19 knots

Fletcher

Though the extensive Benson class achieved the aim of putting the US destroyer-building industry on to a war footing, the design had limitations for a Pacific war, both in terms of endurance and its curtailed weapons fit. Even before the end of the programme, therefore, the first of an improved class were coming off the slipways. The first two of this Fletcher class went down the ways in February 1942 and the last four of 175 ships on the same day in September 1944 at Puget Sound Navy Yard. Although the vessels in the Fletcher class were generally rushed out to the Pacific on completion, those built on the Atlantic seaboard saw some service in that ocean. The USS *Fletcher* herself served on convoy protection duty in the western Atlantic before being deployed to the Pacific in time for the naval actions off Guadalcanal. She was reclassified as a destroyer escort (DDE) in 1949.

Country of origin:	USA
Type:	Destroyer
Launch date:	3 May 1942
Crew:	295
Displacement:	2083 tonnes (2050 tons)
Dimensions:	114.76m x 12.04m x 5.41m (376ft 6in) x 39ft 6in x 17ft 9in)
Endurance:	7412km (4000nm)
Main armament:	Five single 127mm (5in) D; three twin 40mm (1.5in) AA and four single 20mm(0.7in) AA guns; two quintuple 533mm (21in) torpedo tubes
Powerplant:	Two sets of geared steam turbines, two shafts
Performance:	37 knots

Floréal

Floréal is the leader of a class of six ships, all commissioned between 1992 and 1994. Officially described as 'Ocean Capable Patrol Vessels', they are designed operate in the offshore zone in low-intensity operations. The frigates, all of which were built at the Chantiers de l'Atlantique, St Nazaire, were constructed to merchant passenger ship standards, with air conditioning and stabilisers, which enables them to operate a helicopter up to Sea State 5. The ships proved to have a better range than expected during their sea trials, and have an endurance of 50 days. *Floréal* is stationed in the South Indian Ocean and the others at various points in the Far East where the French have interests, such as the sensitive nuclear st site at Mururoa. The ships are named after the months of the French evolutionary Calendar.

Country of origin:	France
Type:	Frigate
Launch date:	6 October 1990
Crew:	86
Displacement:	2997 tonnes (2950 tons)
Dimensions:	93.5m x 14m x 4.3m (306ft 10in x 45ft 11in x 14ft 1in)
Endurance:	16,075km (8680nm)
Main armament:	One 100mm (3.9in) gun; Exocet SSMs; Matra Simbad SAMs
Powerplant:	Two shafts, four diesel engines
Performance:	20 knots

Flower class

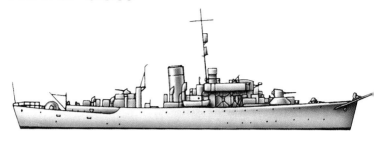

Possibly because of their homely names or their rather unwarlike appearance, the units of the Flower class (45 built in the UK and 113 in Canada for launch between 1940 and 1942) came to be regarded by the British as the archetypal escort ship. Though they made their reputation in the early days of the Battle of the Atlantic, they were not really suited to the job, this type having been developed primarily as a coastal escort fitted for minesweeping. Paradoxically, however, the design was based on that of a commercial whale-catcher, a hull form meant to withstand the worst of weathers. They were superb seaboats, but being so short, were horribly lively and wet in the deep ocean, so that crews quickly became exhausted. Thirty-one were lost in World War II, and the Flower class was immortalised by the fictitious *Compass Rose* in the book and film *The Cruel Sea*.

Country of origin:	Britain
Type:	Corvette
Launch date:	14 January 1940 (HMS *Gladiolus*, first unit)
Crew:	85
Displacement:	179 tonnes (1160 tons)
Dimensions:	62.5m x 10.1m x 3.5m (205ft 1in x 33ft 1in x 11ft 6in)
Endurance:	6389km (3450nm)
Main armament:	One 102mm (6in) gun; one two-pounder or one quadruple 12.7mm (0.5in) AA mounting; depth charges
Powerplant:	Single shaft, triple expansion steam engine
Performance:	16 knots

Folaga

aunched in November 1942, *Folaga* was one of a class of 60 vessels designed
early in World War II as cheap anti-submarine escorts for service in the
editerranean. They could be quickly built, some being completed in less than
ven months, and had a range of 4822km (2604nm). To allow for silent running
ring anti-submarine operations, two electric motors were fitted, although
durance in this mode was only 25.5km (13.8nm). *Folaga*'s wartime career was
ite unremarkable. She escaped the fate of many of her sister vessels, which were
ized by the Germans after Italy's armistice with the Allies, pressed into service as
bmarine hunters, and later sunk in action or scuttled. Some of the latter were
ised by the Italians and recommissioned in the post-war years. *Folaga* survived
e war and was stricken in 1965.

Country of origin:	Italy
Type:	Corvette
Launch date:	14 November 1942
Crew:	150
Displacement:	740 tonnes (728 tons)
Dimensions:	64m x 8.7m x 2.5m (210ft x 28ft 7in x 8ft 4in)
Endurance:	4822km (2604nm)
Main armament:	One 100mm (3.9in) gun
Powerplant:	Twin screw diesel engines
Performance:	19 knots

Folgore

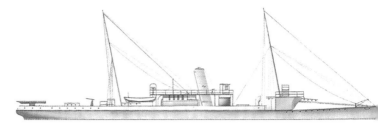

Launched in 1886, *Folgore* was designed by Benedetto Brin and built at Castellammare Naval Dockyard. She was completed in 1887 and originally listed as a torpedo despatch vessel. She and her sister, *Saetta*, were among the first of this type of fast torpedo-armed vessel to be built for the Italian Navy. They were steel-hulled with engines by Hawthorn Leslie and Co. On 5 July 1889, *Folgore* was damaged in a collision off Capri with the cruiser *Bausan*; she was placed in reserve and eventually sold in 1900. *Saetta* was used in oil-fuel experiments, later becoming a torpedo training ship and a target ship until being discarded in 1908. Italy's torpedo boat construction programme in the 1880s was in response to the fact that Austria-Hungary, part of whose territory lay on the other side of the Adriatic, was also building this type of craft in considerable numbers.

Country:	Italy
Type:	Torpedo despatch vessel
Launch date:	29 September 1886
Crew:	57–70
Displacement:	370 tonnes (364 tons)
Dimensions:	56.7m x 6.3m x 2.2m (186ft x 20ft 8in x 7ft)
Endurance:	Not known
Main armament:	Two 57mm (2.25in) guns; three 356mm (14in) torpedo tubes
Powerplant:	Twin screw double expansion engines
Performance:	17 knots

Folgore

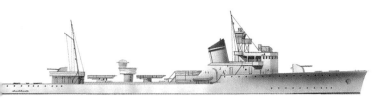

Folgore was one of a class of four fast destroyers which were developed from the earlier Freccia class. The new ships had a narrower beam than before, which reduced hull drag and ensured a high sustained speed. The penalty for this was less internal storage space, which reduced the amount of weapons, equipment and fuel they could carry. All four ships had their armament upgraded at various times, and were eventually modified to carry 52 mines. They were popular as minelaying vessels, as their high speed enabled them to transit to and from the mining area quicker than most other ships, leaving them less vulnerable to detection and interception. The whole class saw extensive active service during World War II. Three were sunk in action, including *Folgore*, which was destroyed by British cruisers in December 1942.

Country of origin:	Italy
Type:	Destroyer
Launch date:	26 April 1931
Crew:	175
Displacement:	2123 tonnes (2090 tons)
Dimensions:	96m x 9.2m x 3.3m (315ft x 30ft 2in x 10ft 10in)
Endurance:	6840km (3693nm)
Main armament:	Four 119mm (4.7in) guns; six 533mm (21in) torpedo tubes
Powerplant:	Twin screw turbines
Performance:	38.8 knots

Forban

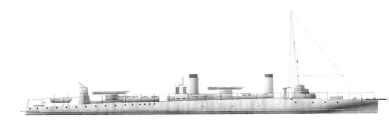

Launched in July 1895, *Forban* was a major milestone in the development of torpedo boats, being the first vessel to exceed 30 knots. Ordered in 1893, she was designed and built by Normand. She followed on from the three vessels in the Filibustier class, which possessed fine sea-keeping qualities and were ideal for service in the Bay of Biscay and English Channel areas. Indeed, the threat posed by these vessels persuaded the British Admiralty to build the first true destroyers in reply. *Forban* was a superb sea boat, with more powerful engines than the vessels of the Filibustier class. In 1907 her torpedo tubes were replaced by 457mm (18in) ones. She was sold in 1920. *Forban* was followed into service by *Mangini*, which was one of the most successful torpedo boats of the period. She could reach a top speed of 24 knots, and once averaged 18 knots for 24 hours.

Country of origin:	France
Type:	Torpedo boat
Launch date:	25 July 1895
Crew:	57
Displacement:	152 tonnes (150 tons)
Dimensions:	44m x 4.6m x 1.3m (144ft 4in x 15ft 3in x 4ft 5in)
Endurance:	1852km (1000nm)
Main armament:	Two 355mm (14in) torpedo tubes
Powerplant:	Twin screw triple expansion engines
Performance:	30+ knots

Foudre

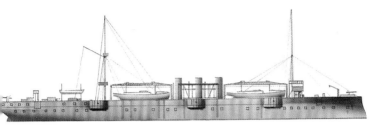

Foudre was built as a special depot ship for 10 small 18m (60ft) torpedo boats, each fitted with one 380mm (15in) torpedo tube. These boats were carried on cradles positioned in groups on either side of the central superstructure. *Foudre* had three funnels, close together, and was fitted with overhead gear for handling her torpedo boats, nine of which were built. *Foudre* underwent many conversions including to repair ship, minelayer, aircraft depot ship and seaplane carrier. She served in the latter role during World War I. Before that, she had demonstrated the feasibility of aircraft operation during the 1913 manoeuvres, hoisting out one seaplane and launching the other from a ramp. She carried armour ranging from a maximum of 16mm (0.6in) on the slopes to 58mm (2.3in) on the flat. She was scrapped in 1921.

Country of origin:	France
Type:	Torpedo depot ship
Launch date:	October 1895
Crew:	410
Displacement:	6186 tonnes (6089 tons)
Dimensions:	118.7m x 17.2m x 7.2m (389ft 5in x 56ft 5in x 23ft 7in)
Endurance:	Not known
Main armament:	Eight 100mm (3.9in) guns; four nine-pounder guns
Powerplant:	Twin screw triple expansion engines
Performance:	19 knots

Framée

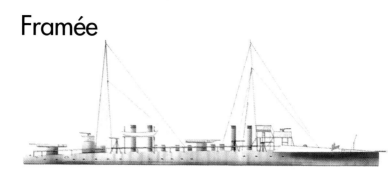

The threat posed by small torpedo boats was the catalyst for the development of a new class of warship: the destroyer. These were supposed to be powerful enough to overcome such boats, but light and fast enough to catch them. They used the new pattern of watertube boiler to feed fast-running engines. Full design speed was rarely achieved. A more critical problem was that of weight distribution. By packing the necessary weapons and equipment into a narrow hull, the designers produced a ship which was top-heavy and rolled excessively. Later modifications were removal of the main mast and aft control area, but the problem remained. The class to which *Framée* belonged was never repeated, although lessons learned were incorporated in later designs. Launched in October 1899, *Framée* was accidentally rammed and sunk off Cape St Vincent on 11 August 1900 by the battleship *Brennus*

Country of origin:	France
Type:	Destroyer
Launch date:	21 October 1899
Crew:	66
Displacement:	354 tonnes (348 tons)
Dimensions:	58.1m x 6.3m x 3m (190ft 7in x 20ft 8in x 9ft 10in)
Endurance:	1482km (800nm)
Main armament:	One 65mm (2.56in) gun
Powerplant:	Twin screw triple expansion engines
Performance:	26 knots

Francesco Mimbelli

The Italian guided-missile destroyers *Luigo Durand de la Penne* and *Francesco Mimbelli* were originally named *Animoso* and *Ardimentoso*. Their names were changed in 1992 to honour former Italian naval heroes. On 10 June 1942 Cdr Francesco Mimbelli lost his life while commanding Italian MTB units in action against Soviet shipping attempting to supply the fortress of Sevastopol. It was Lt Cdr de la Penne who led the small force of Italian frogmen when they successfully placed explosive charges under the British battleships *Valiant* and *Queen Elizabeth* at Alexandria harbour in December 1941. Both vessels are fitted with Kevlar armour plating. Their three super-rapid fire 76mm (3in) guns are used as a combined medium-range anti-surface weapon and as a close-in defence system against missiles. Weapons of this kind were first developed during the Pacific war.

Country of origin:	Italy
Type:	Destroyer
Launch date:	13 April 1991
Crew:	377
Displacement:	5486 tonnes (5400 tons)
Dimensions:	148.5m x 16.1m x 8.6m (487ft 5in x 52ft 10in x 28ft 2in)
Endurance:	11,252km (6076nm)
Main armament:	One 127mm (5in) and three 76mm (3in) guns; antiship missiles and ASW rockets; six 324mm (12.75in) torpedo tubes
Powerplant:	Two shafts, two gas turbines and two diesels
Performance:	31 knots

Francesco Nullo

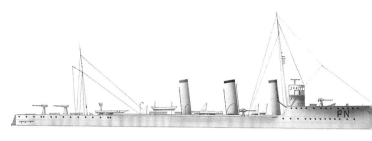

Francesco Nullo was one of a class of eight destroyers laid down between 1913 and 1914. She was the first Italian destroyer to have a single-calibre gun armament. Built by Pattison of Naples, she was completed in 1915 and this design set the pattern for the next major destroyer groups. The armament of these ships underwent several changes and, during World War I, they were all fitted out as minelayers. They were reclassified as torpedo boats in 1929 and *Francesco Nullo* herself was renamed *Fratelli Cairoli* so that the original name could be passed on to a modern destroyer. She was finally sunk by an enemy mine in December 1940. The other ships in the class serving in World War II were the *Giuseppe Cesare Abba*, *Giuseppe Dezza* (formerly *Pilade*), *Giuseppe Missori*, *Antonio Mosto*, *Rosolino Pilo* and *Simone Schiaffino*.

Country of origin:	Italy
Type:	Destroyer
Launch date:	24 July 1915
Crew:	145
Displacement:	914 tonnes (900 tons)
Dimensions:	73m x 7.3m x 2.7m (239ft 6in x 24ft x 9ft)
Endurance:	2222km (1200nm)
Main armament:	Five 76mm (3in) guns
Powerplant:	Twin screws, turbines
Performance:	28 knots

reccia

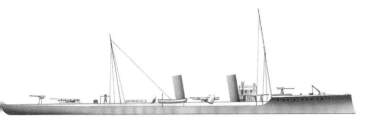

aid down in 1899 and completed in 1902, *Freccia* was designed and constructed
by the German builders Schichau. She and her five sisters formed the first major
up of destroyers built for the Italian Navy. She was lost on 12 October 1911, in
Italo-Turkish war, when she went aground at the entrance to Tripoli harbour.
e Italian Navy played a key part in this bitter little conflict, bombarding Turkish
ongpoints at Benghazi and other coastal locations. The naval bombardment of
poli, in fact, was the first action of the war, and for some time the Italian Navy
re the brunt of the fighting because the Italian Army was not ready. After
mbarding the forts of Tripoli in late September 1911, Italian warships
embarked 1700 sailors, who occupied the town and pushed the Turkish troops
ck towards the interior.

Country of origin:	Italy
Type:	Destroyer
Launch date:	23 November 1899
Crew:	102
Displacement:	354 tonnes (4348 tons)
Dimensions:	62.1m x 6.5m x 2.6m (203ft 7in x 21 ft 4in x 8ft 6in)
Endurance:	2778km (1500nm)
Main armament:	One 76mm (3in) gun
Powerplant:	Twin screw, triple expansion engines
Performance:	31 knots

Freccia

$\mathbf{F}$*reccia* was one of a class of four units, which were a complete break with the previous classes of two- and three-funnelled destroyers of the Italian Navy, and set the pattern for destroyer design in Italy for several years. Two sets of triple 533mm (21in) torpedo tubes were carried between the single, raked funnel and the main mast. During World War II, *Freccia* served with the 7th Destroyer Flotilla, her first major battle being the 'Action off Calabria' in July 1940. She subsequently saw action against the British Mediterranean convoys, in between escorting axis convoys to North Africa. One of the most hectic actions in which she fought took place in June 1942, when all available Italian warships were thrown against two vital Malta convoys. On 9 August 1943, she was sunk during an air raid while lying off Genoa.

Country of origin:	Italy
Type:	Destroyer
Launch date:	3 August 1930
Crew:	175
Displacement:	2134 tonnes (2100 tons)
Dimensions:	96m x 9.75m x 2.3m (315ft x 32ft x 10ft 4in)
Endurance:	3592km (1940nm)
Main armament:	Four 119mm (4.7in) guns
Powerplant:	Twin screw, turbines
Performance:	36 knots

Frunze

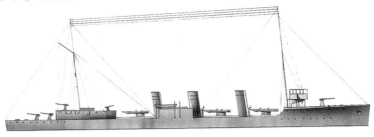

Originally named *Bystry*, the *Frunze* belonged to a class whose design was heavily influenced by the successful *Novik* design. The original specification called for a destroyer which would be capable of 35 knots and which would be armed with two 102mm (4in)- and four 457mm (18in) torpedo tubes. This in fact was altered before the ships were ordered, and additional armament of a single gun and six torpedo tubes was fitted. Out of the nine ships in the class, three, including the *Bystry*, were scuttled by loyalist crews during the Russian Revolution. *Bystry* was later raised by the Soviet Government and renamed *Frunze*. Two 47mm guns were added as anti-aircraft armament. On 21 September 1941, while on active service with the Black Sea Fleet, *Frunze* was finally sunk off the Tendra peninsula by Ju87 Stuka divebombers of StG77, together with the gunboat *Krasnaya Armeniya*.

Country of origin:	Russia
Type:	Destroyer
Launch date:	7 June 1914
Crew:	160
Displacement:	1321 tonnes (1300 tons)
Dimensions:	93m x 9.3m x 2.8m (305ft x 30ft 6in x 9ft 2in)
Endurance:	3333km (1800nm)
Main armament:	Three 102mm (4in) guns; one 75mm (3in) gun
Powerplant:	Twin shaft geared turbines
Performance:	34 knots

Fubuki

At the time of their construction between 1927 and 1931, the Fubuki-class ships were among the trend-setters of the destroyer world. Previously, Japanese destroyers had been influenced by British and German designs but now, Japanese designers went their own way to produce a destroyer so advanced that it was still formidable at the end of World War II. In 1943, the X turret was removed from surviving Fubuki-class destroyers in favour of more light AA guns. The original AA armament of two 13mm (0.5in) machine guns was changed to four 13mm (0.5in) and 14 25mm (0.9in) weapons. The class served widely in all theatres of war. Only the *Ushio* survived the conflict. Badly damaged in Manila Bay on 14 November 1944, she was towed to Yokosuka, and surrendered there at the war's end. *Fubuki* herself was sunk by US warships off Guadalcanal on 11 October 1942.

Country of origin:	Japan
Type:	Destroyer
Launch date:	15 November 1927
Crew:	197
Displacement:	2123 tonnes (2090 tons)
Dimensions:	118.35m x 10.36m x 3.2m (388ft 3in x 34ft x 10ft 6in)
Endurance:	8684km (4689nm)
Main armament:	Three twin 127mm (5in) guns; three triple 610mm (24in) torpedo tubes
Powerplant:	Two sets of geared steam turbines
Performance:	37 knots

Fu Lung

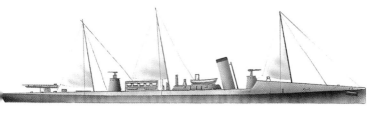

In the 1890s, the Chinese were making frantic efforts to modernize their fleet, which was then a collection of four autonomous navies based at Canton, Foochow, Shanghai and in the Yellow Sea. The *Fu Lung* was a steel-hulled, first-class ocean-going torpedo boat, with two torpedo tubes mounted side by side in the bows, for which two reloads were carried. She was one of two torpedo boats with the barbette ships *Ting Yuen* and *Kwang Ting* in the Chinese Inshore Squadron at the battle of the Yalu in 1894, and the presence of such vessels contributed to the Japanese decision not to carry on the naval action into the night. Nevertheless, the 1894–95 war with Japan saw the loss of China's only capital ships, when the Yellow Sea Fleet was destroyed. *Fu Lung* was captured by the Japanese on 8 February 1895 at the fall of Wei-Hai-Wei and renamed *Fukuryu*. She was broken up in 1908.

Country of origin:	China
Type:	Torpedo boat
Launch date:	1885
Crew:	25
Displacement:	130 tonnes (128 tons)
Dimensions:	44m x 5m x 2.3m (144ft 4in x 16ft 5in x 7ft 6in)
Endurance:	Not known
Main armament:	Two 356mm (14in) torpedo tubes
Powerplant:	Single screw, triple expansion engine
Performance:	19 knots

Fulmine

In July 1897, at the Odero yard at Sestri Ponente, Italy laid down the first destroyer to join the Italian Navy. Designed by Engineering Inspector General Martinez, it followed the standard destroyer design of the period, with a long, sleek hull and a turtleback forecastle. The design speed was 26.5 knots, but initially only 24 knots was achieved. In fact, by 1908 *Fulmine* had been credited with as many as 28 knots. Much experience was gained with this vessel and Italy went on to produce the fastest destroyers in the world. Despite this, however, she purchased her next batch from Germany. The *Fulmine* underwent some significant changes during her career. The number of torpedo tubes was reduced from three to two and her gun armament was changed to one 76mm (3in) and three 57mm (2.25in) guns. *Fulmine* was essentially an experimental ship, and was stricken in 1921.

Country of origin:	Italy
Type:	Destroyer
Launch date:	4 December 1898
Crew:	120
Displacement:	347 tonnes (342 tons)
Dimensions:	62m x 6.5m x 2.25m (204ft x 21ft x 7ft 6in)
Endurance:	2224km (1200nm)
Main armament:	Five 57mm (2.25in) guns; three 356mm (14in) torpedo tubes
Powerplant:	Twin screw triple expansion engines
Performance:	26 knots

Fulmine

The *Fulmine* was one of a class of eight vessels divided into two sub-groups, one ordered in 1928 and the other, to which she belonged, ordered a year later. They were among the few single-funnel destroyers built prior to World War II and all were good sea boats with a splendid turn of speed. As originally designed, the boats had two funnels and a straight bow, but during construction this was changed to one wider funnel and an overhang on the bow to improve sea-keeping. Six vessels of this class were lost in action during World War II, including the *Fulmine* herself: she was sunk during a skirmish with Royal Navy warships. At the time she was one of six destroyers escorting a large Italian supply convoy bound for North Africa; as well as *Fulmine*, the two British cruisers and two destroyers sank all seven merchant ships.

Country of origin:	Italy
Type:	Destroyer
Launch date:	2 August 1931
Crew:	174
Displacement:	2124 tonnes (2090 tons)
Dimensions:	94.5m x 9.25m x 3.35m (309ft 6in x 30ft 6in x 11ft)
Range:	3952km (2134nm)
Main armament:	Four 12mm (4.7in) guns
Powerplant:	Twin screw turbines
Performance:	38 knots

Fulton

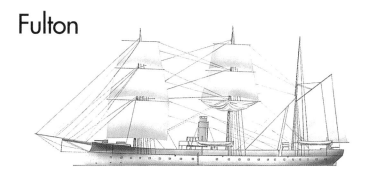

Laid down in 1882, *Fulton* was a wooden-hulled sloop with iron beams, rigged as a barque. She had a short, high forecastle, a pronounced ram bow, overhanging stern, and single, tall funnel. One of her 140mm (5.5in) guns was mounted on the forecastle and two amidships on the centreline, with the 100mm (3.9in) aft on a raised platform. She was not completed until 1888, the delay being caused by problems over the supply of engines. This occurred at a time when naval development was making rapid, dramatic strides and a long construction time could lead to vessels becoming dated before completion. *Fulton* was scrapped in 1900, but sister vessels *Inconstant* and *Papin* served in Ecuador's navy from 1901 to 1920. At about this time Ecuador also had a 19.8m (65ft) Yarrow-built torpedo boat in service; she was called the *Tungurahua*.

Country of origin:	France
Type:	Gunboat
Launch date:	January 1887
Crew:	116
Displacement:	838 tonnes (825 tons)
Dimensions:	60.8m x 8.7m x 3.9m (199ft 5in x 28ft 5in x 12ft 8in)
Endurance:	Not known
Main armament:	Three 140mm (5.5in) guns; one 100mm (3.9in) gun
Powerplant:	Single screw horizontal compound engine
Performance:	13 knots

Furor

Built at Clydebank, Scotland, *Furor* was the first destroyer to go into service with the Spanish Navy, and formed part of Admiral Ceveras's squadron which was sent to Cuba in 1898. The USA, following the destruction of their battleship USS *Maine* in Havana harbour on 21 February 1898, had decided on armed intervention in Cuba where the Spanish were attempting to crush a rebellion. There was little fierce resistance against the American intervention force, and when Admiral Ceveras attempted to escape from Santiago, whose garrison had held out for some time, he was resoundingly defeated by the American warships waiting to ambush him offshore. Three of his ships, including the *Furor*, were run ashore in flames, and another, with the Americans in hot pursuit, got as far as the Rio Turquino, where she was beached.

Country of origin:	Spain
Type:	Destroyer
Launch date:	1896
Crew:	98
Displacement:	376 tonnes (370 tons)
Dimensions:	67m x 6.7m x 1.7m (219ft 10in x 22ft x 5ft 7in)
Endurance	1667km (900nm)
Main armament:	Two 14-pounder guns; two 356mm (14in) torpedo tubes
Powerplant:	Twin screw triple expansion engines
Performance:	28 knots

Fuyutsuki

The *Fuyutsuki* was ordered in 1939 as part of the large Akitsuki class of ocean-going destroyers, originally planned as fast anti-aircraft escorts to work with the Japanese carrier task forces. However, the design was modified to incorporate one quadruple torpedo mount. At the end of the war, *Fuyutsuki* was surrendered at Moji in a badly damaged condition, and her sister ship *Suzutsuki* was surrendered at Sasebo in a similar state. Of the other four surviving ships, all of which surrendered at Kure, *Hanatsuki* was handed over to the Americans for use as a target ship; *Natsutsuki* was given to the British in June 1947 and subsequently scrapped; *Harutsuki* was handed over to the Russians and served for a time in the Soviet Navy; and *Yoitsuki* was impressed by Nationalist China and renamed *Fen Yang*.

Country of origin:	Japan
Type:	Destroyer
Launch date:	20 January 1944
Crew:	175
Displacement:	3759 tonnes (3700 tons)
Dimensions:	134.2m x 11.6m x 4.2m (440ft 3in x 38ft x 13ft 9in)
Endurance:	7408km (4000nm)
Main armament:	Eight 96mm (3.8in) guns; four 607mm (23.9in) torpedo tubes in one quadruple mount
Powerplant:	Twin screw turbines
Performance:	33 knots

G5

G5 was one of a class of about 295 vessels, first conceived in the early 1930s. As the series progressed, their displacement grew, until finally it reached 17 tons (16.7 tonnes). Some units claimed to have reached 60 knots. Many were fitted with Isotta Fraschini engines, which proved very reliable, but those fitted with Russian-built versions had a poorer record. Torpedoes were launched from tubes aft of the conning tower, and as they struck the water, the boat had to make a sharp turn to veer out of their way. At the time of the German invasion in June 1941, there were a total of 44 boats in this class in commission with the Baltic Fleet, 77 with the Black Sea, and 135 with the Pacific Fleet. During the German invasion, 73 were lost and 41 were discarded or decommissioned. A few were transferred to North Korea after the war.

Country of origin:	Russia
Type:	Torpedo gunboat
Launch date:	1934
Crew:	6–7
Displacement:	14 tonnes (13.7 tons
Dimensions:	19.1m x 3.3m x 0.76m (62ft 6in x 11ft x 2ft 6in)
Endurance:	Not known
Main armament:	Two 533mm (21in) torpedo tubes; two 12.7mm (0.5in) guns
Powerplant:	Twin screw petrol engines
Performance:	45 knots

G40

Although successful, *G40* and her three sister ships, launched between 1914 and 1915, were regarded as too big to act in concert with a tight battleline, and many later groups were scaled-down versions. The high, long forecastle made for good seaworthiness. A large bridge structure was positioned at the aft end of the forecastle, and almost level with this were two single torpedo tubes, one on each side. The rest of the torpedo tubes were placed in pairs in the centreline. All ships saw active wartime service. Of the four ships in this class, *G37* was mined and sunk in the North Sea on 4 November 1917; the others were all scuttled by their own crews at Scapa Flow on 21 June 1919, and were later raised and scrapped. The Germans consistently failed to exploit their destroyer force to the full in World War I, except during the final months.

Country of origin:	Germany
Type:	Destroyer
Launch date:	27 February 1915
Crew:	87
Displacement:	1068 tonnes (1051 tons)
Dimensions:	79.5m x 8.36m x 3.74m (261ft x 27ft 6in x 12ft 1in)
Endurance:	3335km (1800nm)
Main armament:	Three 85mm (3.3in) guns; six 508mm (20in) torpedo tubes
Powerplant:	Twin screw turbines
Performance:	34.5 knots

G101

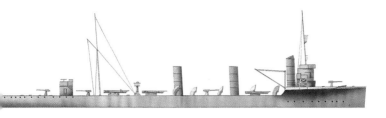

One of a quartet laid down for Argentina at the yard of Germaniawerft, Kiel, in 1914 and completed in 1915 (but subsequently taken over by the German Navy), *G101* was originally named *Santiago,* the other three *San Luis, Santa Fe* and *Tecuman.* Had these vessels entered service with the Argentinian Navy, they would have been among the most powerful destroyers in South American waters. The turbines of *G101* and her sisters developed 29,500hp. All four were interned after the war and scuttled by their crews at Scapa Flow on 21 June 1919. *G101* was raised and scrapped at Charleston, USA, in 1926; *G102* was salved and sent to the USA, where she was sunk as a bombing target by US aircraft off Cape Henry; *G103* was raised and foundered in a storm north of Scotland while en route to the breakers in November 1925, and *G104* was also scrapped at Charleston.

Country of origin:	Germany
Type:	Destroyer
Launch date:	12 August 1914
Crew:	104
Displacement:	1873 tonnes (1843 tons)
Dimensions:	98m x 9.4m x 3.9m (321ft 6in x 30ft 9in x 12ft 9in)
Endurance:	(3704km) 2000nm
Main armament:	Four 85mm (3.3in) guns; six 508mm (20in) torpedo tubes
Powerplant:	Twin screw turbines
Performance:	36.5 knots

G132

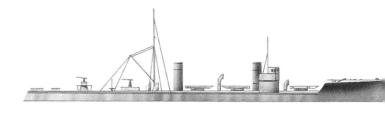

An improved version of the basic German destroyer design, *T132* and her four sisters (originally designated *G132–G136*, but re-lettered in 1916) were built ▶ Germaniawerft, Kiel, in 1906. A follow-on boat, *G137* (*T137*) had a greater displacement and and was used in experiments with Parsons turbine engines. Six were fitted: one high pressure, two low pressure, one cruising and two reverse. *G137* was two knots faster than *T132* but burnt more fuel. At the time, Germany was building up a large force of destroyers designed to act with the Battle Fleet by breaking through the enemy battleline and attacking it with torpedoes. This tactic would leave attacks on enemy destroyers as a secondary function for the German vessels, and was thereby in accordance with the aggressive doctrine of Admiral von Tirpitz, which failed somewhat in its actual implementation during WWI.

Country of origin:	Germany
Type:	Destroyer
Launch date:	12 May 1906
Crew:	102
Displacement:	553 tonnes (544 tons)
Dimensions:	65.7m x 7m x 2.6m (215ft 6in x 23ft 1in x 8ft 6in)
Endurance:	1575km (850nm)
Main armament:	Four 51mm (2in) guns; three 450mm (17.7in) torpedo tubes
Powerplant:	Twin screw triple expansion engines
Performance:	28 knots

Gabbiano

The lead ship of a very large class of Italian corvettes laid down between 1942 and 1943, *Gabbiano* was heavily involved in escorting Axis convoys that were taking desperately needed supplies and reinforcements from Italy to Tunisia. They were also involved in evacuating the wounded on the return trip. The convoys were heavily attacked by Allied aircraft and British submarines, which sank several merchantmen with severe loss of life. However, on 16 April, *Gabbiano* (Cdr Ceccacci) attacked and sank HM submarine *Regent*, and then, on 24 April, she also attacked HM submarine *Sahib* near the Lipari Islands. As a result, the British boat was forced to the surface and sunk by a German Junkers 88 dive-bomber. *Gabbiano* and a dozen of her sister ships served in the Italian Navy until the mid-1970s.

Country of origin:	Italy
Type:	Corvette
Launch date:	23 June 1942
Crew:	109
Displacement:	740 tonnes (728 tons)
Dimensions:	64.3m x 9m x 2.5m (211ft x 28ft 7in x 8ft 4in)
Endurance:	5556km (3000nm)
Main armament:	One 102mm (4in) gun; depth charges
Powerplant:	Twin screw diesel engines
Performance:	18 knots

Gadfly

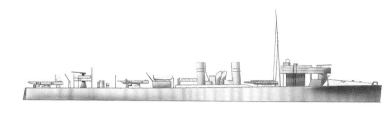

Gadfly was one of a large class of 36 coastal-defence destroyers, built as a cheap alternative to the Tribal-class destroyers, which were primarily intended for service with the fleet. The design followed that of the large first-class torpedo boats of the period, and was an economical way of creating a large fleet of destroyers for coastal defence and coastal roles. *Gadfly* was numbered TB6 soon after completion, and scrapped in 1920. During World War I, boats of this type were used to patrol the flanks of the Dover Barrage, which was intended to prevent the passage of U-boats through the Straits of Dover into the Western Approaches. The Dover passage could save a small U-boat based in Flanders nearly eight days on its 14-day cruise, and a larger boat from the German Bight six days out of 25. By 1917, the U-boat campaign was causing Britain serious problems.

Country of origin:	Britain
Type:	Destroyer
Launch date:	24 June 1906
Crew:	120
Displacement:	406 tonnes (400 tons)
Dimensions:	54.9m x 5.3m x 1.8m (180ft x 17ft 4 in x 5ft 11in)
Endurance:	4076km (2200nm)
Main armament:	Two 12-pounder guns; three 457mm (18in) torpedo tubes
Powerplant:	Triple screw turbines
Performance:	26 knots

Galatea

One of the Leander class designed in the late 1950s, planned as improved versions of the Type 12 Rothesay class, and intended to be built in five batches spread over 10 years, *Galatea* was part of the first group of seven vessels. In all, 24 were to be constructed, with the later ships increasing in size and carrying a greater amount of equipment, including Exocet and updated electronics. The hull had a long, unbroken form, with a raised forecastle. The hangar for one or two ASW helicopters was situated aft. The Ikara ASW missile system in *Galatea* was housed forward on the extended superstructure in front of the bridge. The class was updated in batches during the 1970s and 1980s, and progressively withdrawn from 1988 onwards. The success of the class was measured by the fact that it sold overseas, and was built under licence in some countries.

Country of origin:	Britain
Type:	Frigate
Launch date:	23 May 1963
Crew:	263
Displacement:	2906 tonnes (2860 tons)
Dimensions:	113.4m x 12.5m x 4.5m (372ft x 41ft x 14ft 9in)
Endurance:	8519km (4600nm)
Main armament:	One anti-submarine Ikara missile launcher
Powerplant:	Twin screws, turbines
Performance:	28 knots

Garibaldino

Originally intended as a follow-on group to the Nembo class, launched in 1901, *Garibaldino* incorporated improvements gained through operational experience. The six vessels in this class were all laid down in 1905 and completed between 1907 and 1910. *Garibaldino* was one of the group laid down in 1905. All in this 1905 group were coal burners, but a second group, known as the Soldato or Alpino class, were oil burners. *Garibaldino*'s engines developed 6000hp, and the ship had an endurance of 2894km (1536nm) at 12 knots, or 760km (410nm) at 23.5 knots. She was sunk on 16 July 1918, after colliding with the British destroyer HMS *Cygnet* off Villefranche in southern France. In effect, the Garibaldino class formed a kind of stepping-stone between the coal-burning pre-war destroyers and the oil-burning postwar ones.

Country of origin:	Italy
Type:	Destroyer
Launch date:	12 February 1910
Crew:	98
Displacement:	419 tonnes (412 tons)
Dimensions:	65m x 6.1m x 2.1m (213ft 3in x 20ft x 7ft)
Endurance:	1890km (1020nm)
Main armament:	Three 76mm (3in) guns; three 450mm (17.7in) torpedo tubes
Powerplant:	Twin screw triple expansion
Performance:	28 knots

Garland

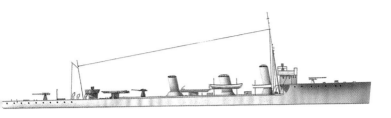

HMS *Garland* was one of a class of 20 destroyers which originated in the British naval construction programme of 1911–12. Designed to counter the considerable threat posed by the latest German destroyers, they were to be armed with two 102mm (4in) guns, plus four 12-pounders, but three 102mm (4in) guns were chosen instead, making them the most powerful destroyers of that period. Ships of this class were normally deployed in support of the Royal Navy's light cruiser forces, which were based at locations such as Harwich, from where they could readily intercept German excursions into the North Sea area. After Jutland, such excursions were rare. However, there were some spirited engagements between opposing destroyer forces in the Heligoland Bight, particularly in March and April 1918.

Country of origin:	Britain
Type:	Destroyer
Launch date:	23 April 1913
Crew:	147
Displacement:	1005 tonnes (989 tons)
Dimensions:	81.5m x 8.2m x 2.8m (267ft 6in x 27ft x 9ft 3in)
Endurance:	3335km (1800nm)
Main armament:	Three 102mm (4in) guns; two 533mm (21in) torpedo tubes
Powerplant:	Twin screw semi-geared turbines
Performance:	28 knots

Gatineau

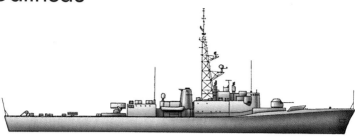

G *atineau*, completed in February 1959, was one of seven escort destroyers of the Restigouche class built for the Royal Canadian Navy, the others being *Chaudiere*, *Colombia*, *Kootenay*, *St Croix* and *Terra Nova*. The class was converted in order to carry variable-depth sonar, advanced electronics, and ASROC in the early 1970s, the latter supplementing the ASW mortars. The ships were developed from the original St Laurent class and were generally similar to other destroyer escorts completed at about the same time, namely the *Annapolis*, *Nipigon*, *Mackenzie*, *Saskatchewan*, *Qu'appelle* and *Yukon*. All ships of the Restigouche, Annapolis, and Mackenzie classes were capable of operating a Sea King ASW helicopter. Surviving ships of the Restigouche class were in reserve in the late 1990s.

Country of origin:	Canada
Type:	Destroyer
Launch date:	3 June 1957
Crew:	246
Displacement:	2946 tonnes (2900 tons)
Dimensions:	111.5m x 12.8m x 4.1m (366ft x 42ft x 13ft 6in)
Endurance:	12,970km (7003nm)
Main armament:	Two 76mm (3in) DP guns; Limbo 3-barrelled depth charge mortars
Powerplant:	Two shafts, geared turbines
Performance:	28 knots

Gatling

The USS *Gatling* was a Fletcher-class destroyer and, as such, was one of the largest classes built for the US Navy. Launched in June 1943, she went into action in the Pacific in late January 1944, when she formed part of a US naval task force attacking Japanese bases in the Marshall Islands. In June 1944, she was operating in support of US carriers attacking enemy bases in the Marianas, and in October of that same year she was conducting similar operations off Formosa along with 13 other destroyers of Task Group 38.3. From 30 December 1944 to 25 January 1945, her Task Group carried out many attacks on Japanese airfields in the Central and Southwest Pacific, and fought on to the Japanese surrender. A highly successful design, the Fletcher class formed the backbone of the Pacific Fleet. Many were sold after the war. *Gatling* was stricken from the Navy List in 1974.

Country of origin:	USA
Type:	Destroyer
Launch date:	20 June 1943
Crew:	300
Displacement:	2971 tonnes (2924 tons)
Dimensions:	114.7m x 12m x 4.2m (376ft 5in x 39ft 4in x 13ft 9in)
Endurance:	8334km (4500nm)
Main armament:	Five 127mm (5in) guns
Powerplant:	Twin screw turbines
Performance:	37 knots

Gearing

Yet more space and endurance requirements stretched the hull of the Sumner class of US destroyers – which had evolved from the Fletcher class – by 4.27m (14ft) to produce the Gearing class. This development into the Gearing class was to prove the ultimate stage in this family of closely related warships. Externally, these larger ships were distinguishable primarily through their more widely spaced funnels. Although the backbone of the Japanese surface fleet had been broken by 1945, the air threat remained considerable, and some of the Gearing class were fitted with a braced tripod bearing an air surveillance radar or an extra quadruple 40mm (1.5in) mounting. However, the 76.2mm (3in) automatic guns that could literally disintegrate a low-flying suicide aircraft did not generally become available until peacetime when they were fitted to most warships.

Country of origin:	USA
Type:	Destroyer
Launch date:	18 February 1945
Crew:	350
Displacement:	2971 tonnes (2924 tons)
Dimensions:	114.7m x 12.5m x 5.79m (376ft 5in x 41ft x 19ft)
Enmdurance:	8338km (4500nm)
Main armament:	Three twin 127mm (5in) DP and three quadruple 40mm (1.5in) AA guns; two quintuple 533mm (21in) torpedo tubes
Powerplant:	Two sets of geared steam turbines
Performance:	36.5 knots

Gemlik

The *Gemlik* started life as the *Emden*, a Kïln-class frigate of the West German Navy. She and her sisters were among the first modern warships built for the federal German Navy after World War II. She was laid down in 1958 and completed in October 1961. She is of a compact design, and is equipped with a wide range of anti-submarine weapons, sophisticated sensors, and electronic countermeasures. Her 100mm (3.9in) guns can fire a 13.5kg (30lb) projectile up to 15km (9 miles), at a maximum rate of 60–80 shells per minute. She has four launch tubes used for anti-submarine acoustic homing torpedoes, supplemented by four twin-barrelled anti-submarine mortars. She is also capable of carrying up to 80 anti-ship and anti-submarine mines. She was transferred from Germany to the Turkish Navy in September 1983.

Country of origin:	Germany (transferred to Turkey)
Type:	Frigate
Launch date:	21 March 1959
Crew:	210
Displacement:	2743 tonnes (2700 tons)
Dimensions:	109.9m x 11m x 5.1m (360ft 7in x 36ft x 16ft 9in)
Endurance:	5662km (3052nm)
Main armament:	Two 100mm (3.9in) guns; four 533mm (21in) torpedo tubes
Powerplant:	Twin screw gas turbines/diesel engines
Performance:	28 knots

General Pike

Although the American Navy was not large during the war of 1812, its warships were among the best in the world. The *General Pike* is a good example of such a vessel. She was a flush-decked frigate with all her guns carried on the one deck and she was larger than the contemporary British frigates that carried the same armament. She was built by Henry Eckford, a New York shipbuilder, and was laid down in 1813, but was set on fire by British forces in the brief war that erupted between Britain and America in 1812, when the British landed punitive expedition. The unfinished ship was saved and she was soon in action against the Royal Navy. Her principal task was to escort troop transports, but she was also part of the squadron that blockaded the British port of Kingston, Ontario. After the war, she was laid up. She was finally sold in 1825.

Country of origin:	USA
Type:	Frigate
Launch date:	June 1813
Crew:	275
Displacement:	889 tonnes (875 tons)
Dimensions:	44.2m x 11.3m (145ft x 37ft)
Endurance:	Unlimited, depending on provisions
Main armament:	Twenty-six 24-pounder guns
Powerplant:	Sail
Performance:	12 knots

Georges Leygues

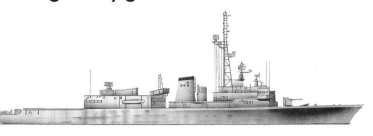

There are seven ships in the Georges Leygues class of guided-missile destroyer, all of which were commissioned between 1979 and 1990. Primary missile armament is the Exocet; anti-aircraft missile armament is the Thomson-CSF Crotale, which has a range of 13km (7 miles) and a speed of 2.4 Mach. Some of the vessels have undergone an air defence upgrade, the various weaponry and sensors (Matra Sadral sextuple SAM launchers; Breda-Mauser 30mm guns; and jammers) being controlled from a large command structure fitted above the bridge. Sea trials were conducted by the *Jean de Vienne* in 1996. Apart from the *Georges Leygues* and *Jean de Vienne*, the other vessels in this class are the *Dupleix, Montcalm, Primauguet, La Motte-Picquet* and *Latouche-Tréville*. The main role of the Georges Leygues class is surface-to-surface attack.

Country of origin:	France
Type:	Destroyer
Launch date:	17 December 1976
Crew:	218
Displacement:	4236 tonnes (4170 tons)
Dimensions:	139m x 14m x 5.7m (456ft x 46ft x 18ft 8in)
Endurance:	14,816km (8000nm)
Main armament:	One 100mm (3.9in) gun; Exocet missiles
Powerplant:	Twin screw, gas turbines and diesel engines
Performance:	30 knots

Gepard

The Gepard-class frigate is the successor to the Koni class. The first (and so far the only) ship, built at Zelenodolsk, was laid down in 1991 and completed at the end of 1994. However, due to the failure of the Russian Government to pay for it, its builders have been forced to make efforts to sell the class to overseas navies of countries such as Iran and India. *Gepard* is a logical development of existing light frigate classes with the addition of the Zvezda (SS-N-25) surface-to-surface missile system. A second ship of the class, featuring a helicopter platform, was scrapped, but an improved follow-on design with better armament is being projected. The builders claim that *Gepard* has stealth features, and the vessel is equipped with roll stabilisers and an air-conditioning system. The Russians had a second new frigate design, the Novik (Grom class) building at Kaliningrad in 1999.

Country of origin:	Russia
Type:	Frigate
Launch date:	July 1993
Crew:	110
Displacement:	1961 tonnes (1930 tons)
Dimensions:	102m x 13.6m x 4.4m (334ft 7in x 44ft 7in x 14ft 5in)
Endurance:	5626km (3038nm)
Main armament:	One 76mm (3in) gun; SS-N-25 sea-skimming missiles; SA-N-4 SAMs; four 533mm (21in) torpedo tubes
Powerplant:	Twin shafts, two gas turbines, two diesels
Performance:	26 knots

Gillis

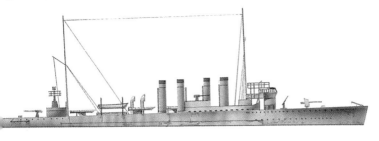

Launched on 29 May 1919, *Gillis* was one of a large class of vessels that were improved versions of the Wickes class of destroyer. Between 1938 and 1940 Gillis and 13 other old flush-deck destroyers were converted as seaplane tenders, having two of their boilers and their torpedo tubes removed. The USS *Williamson*, *George E. Badger*, *Clemson*, *Goldsborough*, *Hulbert*, *Belknap*, *Osmond Ingram*, *Greene* and *McFarland* reverted to destroyers in November 1943, but *Gillis* (AVD12) continued to serve as a seaplane tender together with the USS *Childs*, *William B. Preston*, *Ballard* and *Thornton*. Between 11 and 13 June 1942, Catalina aircraft, supported by the *Gillis*, attacked Japanese ships and installations on Kiska in the Aleutians in an intense 48-hour attack, exhausting the tender's bomb and fuel supplies, but failing to drive the enemy from the island. *Gillis* was scrapped in 1946.

Country of origin:	USA
Type:	Destroyer
Launch date:	29 April 1919
Crew:	150
Displacement:	1328 tonnes (1308 tons)
Dimensions:	95.8m x 9.4m x 3m (314ft 4in x 30ft 10in x 9ft 10in
Endurance:	4741km (2560nm)
Main armament:	Four 102mm (4in) guns; 12 533mm (21in) torpedo tubes
Powerplant:	Twin screw geared turbines
Performance:	25 knots

Giuseppe la Masa

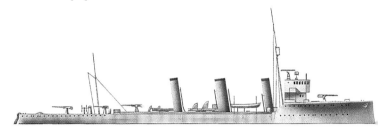

Launched in 1917, the *Giuseppe la Masa* was one of eight ships that formed the third series of the Indomito class destroyers. In 1929, she was reclassified as a torpedo boat. During World War II, her anti-aircraft armament was increased. Only one ship in the class, the *Giacinto Carini*, survived the war. Italy's fleet at the end of World War I depended to a great extent on its destroyers, which, with some 50 in service, were by far the most numerous of any of its warship categories. The vessels like the *Giuseppe la Masa* that were still in commision at the outbreak of World War II were used as harbour defence vessels, whereas the first-line destroyer forces were composed of fast, modern ships which were laid down during the inter-war 'treaty years'. *Giuseppe la Masa* was scuttled in September 1943 while in dock at Naples, where she was undergoing repairs, after Italy's armistice with the Allies.

Country of origin:	Italy
Type:	Destroyer
Launch date:	6 September 1917
Crew:	174
Displacement:	823 tonnes (810 tons)
Dimensions:	72.5m x 7.3m x 2.9m (238ft x 24ft x 9ft 6in)
Endurance:	3333km (1800nm)
Main armament:	Six 102mm (4in) guns; four 450mm (17.7in) torpedo tubes
Powerplant:	Twin screw, turbines
Performance:	34 knots

Gladiator

By the mid-1850s, the Royal Navy had 77 paddle-wheel warships, 41 of them serving on foreign stations. In 1860 HMS *Gladiator* was part of a combined British and US squadron sent to capture William Walker, the last of the famous American filibusters (sea captains who, while not strictly pirates, engaged in unlawful warfare against a foreign state), who had declared himself President of Nicaragua. He and his men were taken back to New Orleans on board *Gladiator*; Walker was tried and consequently executed. Filibusters were very much in the nature of privateers, although the latter were civilian vessels sailing under a 'letter of marque' which made them virtually legalised pirates provided they attacked only enemy ships. They often carried larger crews than normal to allow captured vessels to be sailed home as prizes.

Country of origin:	Britain
Type:	Corvette
Launch date:	1844
Crew:	75
Displacement:	1229 tonnes (1210 tons)
Dimensions:	67m x 8.5m x 3m (220ft x 28ft x 10ft)
Endurance:	Not known
Main armament:	Six 24-pounder guns
Powerplant:	Paddle wheels, oscillating engines, sail assisted
Performance:	9.5 knots

Glasgow

One of the first batch of Type 42 destroyers, HMS *Glasgow* was deployed to the South Atlantic in 1982 as part of the British task force assembled to retake the Falkland Islands. One of her sister ships, HMS *Sheffield*, was sunk by an Exocet missile launched by an Argentine Navy Super Etendard, while another, HMS *Coventry*, sustained three bomb hits on 25 May and sank within 45 minutes. Earlier, on 12 May, the *Glasgow* herself had narrowly missed serious damage – and perhaps even destruction – when a bomb passed through her hull amidships from side to side without exploding. The lack of any close-range air defence systems was a significant factor in each case, and was one of many shortcomings caused by economic restraints. On the credit side, the ships' Sea Dart missiles were credited with the destruction of five enemy aircraft.

Country of origin:	Britain
Type:	Destroyer
Launch date:	14 April 1976
Crew:	253
Displacement:	4165 tonnes (4100 tons)
Dimensions:	125m x 14.3m x 5.8m (410ft x 47ft x 19ft)
Endurance:	8334km (4500nm)
Main armament:	One 115mm (4.5in) gun; one twin Sea Dart launcher
Powerplant:	Twin screw, gas turbines
Performance:	30 knots

Godavari

Launched in May 1980, the *Godavari* is a modified version of the British Leander class. Two helicopters are housed in a large hangar aft, and the vessel carries a unique mixture of Russian, European, and Indian weapons. The Styx missiles with active radar or infrared homing capability have a range of 69km (43 miles) at 0.9 Mach with a 500kg (1100lb) warhead. Gecko has semi-active radar homing to 13km (8 miles) at 2.5 Mach with a 50kg (110lb) warhead. The Godavari class are longer and wider than the basic vessels of the Leander class. The other two vessels are the *Ganga* and *Gomati*. India has always maintained strong naval forces, based on carrier task groups, and used her naval power to good effect in the wars with Pakistan which took place in 1965 and 1971, when she used both naval gunfire and aircraft to attack shore targets.

Country of origin:	India
Type:	Frigate
Launch date:	15 May 1980
Crew:	330
Displacemenmt:	4064 tonnes (4000 tons)
Dimensions:	126.5m x 14.5m x 9m (415ft x 47ft 7in x 29ft 6in)
Endurance:	8334km (4500nm)
Main armament:	Two 57mm (2.25in) guns; four SS-N-2C Styx missiles; plus SA-N-4 Gecko missiles
Powerplant:	Twin screw, turbines
Performance:	27 knots

Gossamer

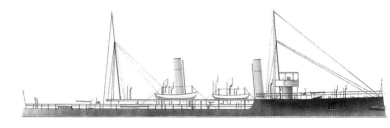

Gossamer and her 12 sisters were built to counter the threat posed by France's expanding torpedo boat fleet. To improve seakeeping qualities, the extended forecastle deck ran aft to the main mast, but initially the class suffered from hull weakness. One torpedo tube was carried in the bows; the others in paired mounts on either side amidships. The 120mm (4.7in) quick-firing guns eventually installed in this class had five times the rate of fire as the earlier breechloaders. Although properly titled the Sharpshooter class, the 13 boats were often called the Gossamer class. Four of the boats were allocated to colonial stations: two to the Royal Indian Marine, and two to the Australian station. Between 1908 and 1909, *Gossamer*, *Seagull*, *Skipjack* and *Spanker* were converted to the minesweeping role. *Gossamer* was sold in 1920.

Country of origin:	Britain
Type:	Torpedo gunboat
Launch date:	9 January 1890
Crew:	91
Displacement:	746 tonnes (735 tons)
Dimensions:	70m x 8.2m x 3.2m (230ft x 27ft x 10ft 6in)
Endurance:	Not known
Main armament:	Five 355mm (14in) torpedo tubes; two 120mm (4.7in) guns
Powerplant:	Twin screws, triple expansion engines
Performance:	19 knots

Göteborg

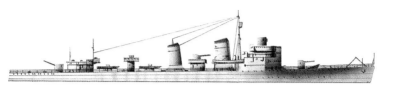

By 1934, it was clear that Sweden's destroyer force needed modernising. The ships already in service with the Swedish Navy were being outclassed by those coming off the slips in Germany and elsewhere. A new construction programme was begun and a class of six units began building, with the aim that they would be completed by 1941. The 120mm (4.7in) guns were housed in single mounts, one forward, one aft, and one on a raised platform amidships. Göteborg was sunk by an internal explosion in 1941, but was raised and continued in service until 1958. She was expended as a gunnery target on 14 August 1962. In effect, Sweden's navy is essentially a coastal force, and as such, its task is to defend the neutral country's long and rugged coastline against infiltration by hostile vessels. It was not until the Cold War era that the perceived threat to her security became serious.

Country of origin:	Sweden
Type:	Destroyer
Launch date:	14 October 1935
Crew:	220
Displacement:	1219 tonnes (1200 tons)
Dimensions:	94.6m x 9m x 3.8m (310ft 4in x 29ft 6in x 12ft 6in)
Endurance:	3333km (1800nm)
Main armament:	Three 120mm (4.7in) guns; six 533mm (21in) torpedo tubes
Powerplant:	Twin screws, turbines
Performance:	35 knots

Grafton

One of the Blackwood class of 12 post-World War II frigates, *Grafton* was built in pre-fabricated sections before final assembly on the launching ramp. The Blackwood-class vessels were very lightly gunned, having only two 40mm (1.6in) Bofors AA weapons. Their anti-submarine weaponry consisted of two Limbo three-barrelled depth charge launchers which could fire a pattern of large depth charges with great accuracy over a wide area. Three ships of this class – *Duncan*, *Palliser* and *Russell* – originally formed the 1st Division of the Fishery Protection Squadron, later incorporated in the Western Fleet. Some vessels incorporated four 533mm (21in) torpedo tubes, but these were removed. Between 1958 and 1959, all the Blackwoods had their hulls strengthened to withstand prolonged and severe conditions on fishery protection duty in Icelandic waters.

Country of origin:	Britain
Type:	Frigate
Launch date:	13 September 1954
Crew:	175
Displacement:	1480 tonnes (1456 tons)
Dimensions:	94.5m x 10m x 4.7m (310ft x 33ft x 15ft 6in)
Endurance:	7037km (3800nm)
Main armament:	Two 40mm (1.6in) guns
Powerplant:	Single screw, turbines
Performance:	27.8 knots

Grasshopper

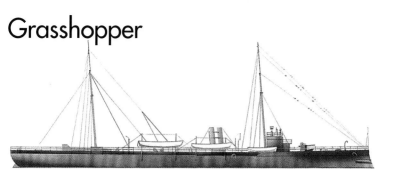

Grasshopper and her two sister vessels, *Sandfly* and *Spider*, formed the first true class of British torpedo gunboats. They were similar to the one-off *Rattlesnake*, but were somewhat larger and their performance was not as good. By the time they entered service there had been a steady increase in the range, speed reliability and explosive power of the torpedo, and the 355mm (14in) weapon, standard for some time, was being supplanted in the early 1890s by the 457mm (18in). *Grasshopper* was sold in 1905. The end of the nineteenth century saw the introduction of gyroscopic torpedo guidance and internal combustion in torpedoes, leading to still further improvements in range and accuracy. The combination of gun and torpedo was seen as the ideal mix of naval armament, and the torpedo gunboat was about to enjoy its brief but heady day.

Country:	Britain
Type:	Torpedo gunboat
Launch date:	30 August 1887
Crew:	66
Displacement:	558 tonnes (550 tons)
Dimensions:	60.9m x 7m x 3m (200ft x 23ft x 10ft 4in)
Endurance:	7585km (4096nm) at 10 knots
Main armament:	One 102mm (4in) gun; four 355mm (14in) torpedo tubes
Powerplant:	Twin screws, triple expansion engines
Performance:	17 knots

Grasshopper

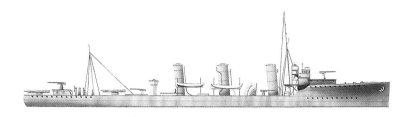

In 1907 the British Admiralty obtained plans of the latest German destroyers. Immediately, the Admiralty set a new construction programme in motion to counter these German designs. Initial plans for *Grasshopper* and her 15 sisters specified oil fuel, but this was soon changed to the more readily available coal fuel. The class carried a new torpedo, which was fitted with a heater to improve performance and which had a range of 10,972m (12,000yd) at 30 knots. *Grasshopper*, launched in November 1909, served with the Harwich Force on North Sea patrol duty during World War I, and was the second ship to bear the name. The first was a torpedo gunboat, launched in 1887, which carried a single 102mm (4in) gun and had four 355mm (14in) torpedo tubes. The second *Grasshopper* was withdrawn in 1921.

Country of origin:	Britain
Type:	Destroyer
Launch date:	23 November 1909
Crew:	150
Displacement:	937 tonnes (923 tons)
Dimensions:	82.6m x 27.5m x 9.7m (271ft x 27ft 10in x 9ft 6in)
Endurance:	2407km (1300nm)
Main armament:	One 102mm (4in) and three 12-pounder guns
Powerplant:	Triple screws, turbines
Performance:	27 knots

Gravina

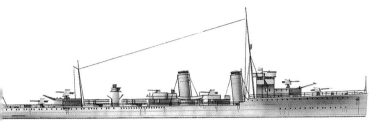

Gravina belonged to the largest class of destroyers built for the Spanish Navy. The class of 16 vessels was made up two groups, *Gravina* being part of the second group. The destroyers were virtual copies of the British Scott-class flotilla leaders. All vessels in *Gravina's* class were built at Cartagena and launched between 1926 and 1933. The ships of the second group all featured large gun shields. Engines developed 42,000hp, and oil fuel capacity was 548 tonnes (540 tons). Range at 14 knots was 8550km (5312 miles). One ship in *Gravina's* group, the *Ciscar*, was sunk in the Spanish Civil War in October 1957. All ships in this class were withdrawn from use in the late 1950s and early 1960s, *Gravina* herself being stricken from the Navy List in 1964. By this time, Spain had launched an ambitious naval expansion scheme.

Country of origin:	Spain
Type:	Destroyer
Launch date:	24 December 1931
Crew:	275
Displacement:	2209 tonnes (2175 tons)
Dimensions:	101.5m x 9.6m x 3.2m (333ft x 31ft 9in x 10ft 6in)
Endurance:	8534km (4608nm)
Main armament:	Five 120mm (4.7in) guns; six 533mm (21in) torpedo tubes
Powerplant:	Twin screws, turbines
Performance:	35 knots

Grisha class

Built as a small anti-submarine ship between 1968 and 1974, the Grisha-class vessels had a relatively short production run, ending after only 14 units had been built. They were followed by eight Grisha II border patrol ships, which were assigned to the Maritime Border Directorate of the KGB. These differed from the Grisha I class in having a second twin 57mm (2.2in) anti-aircraft mounting in place of the SAM launcher. The main Soviet Navy production model was the *Grisha III*, with a construction rate of about five per year in the early 1980s. Two vessels of the Grisha II class went to Lithuania in 1992, and four were transferred to the Ukraine in 1994. The latest variant is the Grisha V class, one of which was also delivered to the Ukraine in 1996. With their relatively shallow draught the Grishas are ideal craft for patrolling the shallow waters of river estuaries.

Country of origin:	Russia
Type:	Frigate
Launch date:	1968 (first unit)
Crew:	80
Displacement:	1219 tonnes (1200 tons)
Dimensions:	72m x 10m x 3.7m (236ft 2in x 32ft 10in x 12ft)
Endurance:	2779km (1500nm)
Main armament:	One twin 57mm (2.2in) and one 30mm (1.2in) AA gun; ASW rocket launchers; SAMs
Powerplant:	Twin shafts, one gas turbine, four diesels
Performance:	30 knots

Grom

The *Grom* (*Thunderbolt*) was the former Russian Skory-class destroyer *Smetlivy*. This was the largest class of Soviet destroyers to be built after World War II, and the ships, which were adapted from a pre-war design, incorporated many of the best design features of Germany's later destroyers. The other ex-Russian destroyer, the *Wicher* (*Hurricane*) was in fact the class prototype, the *Skory* herself. More than 70 Skory-class units were completed between 1950 and 1953. At a later date, the two Polish vessels were augmented by the transfer of a Kotlin-class destroyer. During the years of the Cold War, the Polish Navy, as a satellite of the USSR, would have had an important part to play in operations in the Baltic. By the early 1980s, its strength was centred on fast-attack craft and patrol boats, together with five submarines all supplied by the Soviet Union.

Country of origin:	USSR/Poland
Type:	Destroyer
Launch date:	17 November 1951
Crew:	280
Displacement:	3150 tonnes (3100 tons)
Dimensions:	120.5m x 11.8m x 4.6m (395ft 4in x 38ft 9in x 15ft)
Endurance:	7037km (3800nm)
Main armament:	Four 130mm (5.1in) guns; two 76mm (3in) AA guns
Powerplant:	Twin screws, turbines
Performance:	36 knots

Gromki

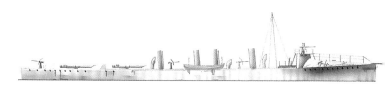

The *Gromki* belonged to the Boykiy class – one of the largest group of destroyers built for the Imperial Russian Navy – and formed part of the Second Pacific Squadron. During the Battle of Tsushima in 1905, she was attacked by a group of Japanese warships. After a two-hour running battle, she was crippled and dead in the water. She sank at midday on 28 May 1905, two-thirds of her crew having been killed or wounded. Another vessel of this class, the *Byedovi*, which was carrying the badly wounded Russian Admiral Rozhdestvensky, was also captured by Japanese ships after the Battle of Tsushima and was recommissioned into the Japanese Navy as the *Satsuki*. All of the destroyers in this class, including *Gromki*, were built at the Nevsky yards in St Petersburg, apart from five which were constructed by the Belgian Works yard at Nicolaiev.

Country of origin:	Russia
Type:	Destroyer
Launch date:	1904
Crew:	68
Displacement:	355 tonnes (350 tons
Dimensions:	64m x 6.4m x 2.5m (210ft x 21ft x 8ft 6in)
Endurance:	2222km (1200nm)
Main armament:	One 11-pounder, five three-pounder guns; three 350mm (15in) torpedo tubes
Powerplant:	Twin screws, vertical triple expansion engines
Performance:	26 knots

Gromki

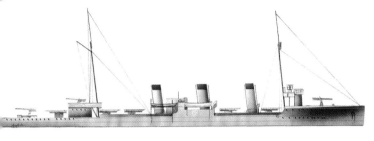

The *Gromki* of 1913 was one of the Bespokoiny class of nine destroyers that were reduced versions of the 1300-tonne (1280ton) *Novik*. They were part of a new naval construction programme whose primary aim was to increase the size of the Black Sea Fleet. Design studies had begun in 1907, and revised designs showed a 0.8-tonne (50-ton) increase in displacement to enable the vessels to carry more armament. Five twin torpedo tubes were carried on the centreline, with one 102mm (4in) gun forward and two aft. The engines developed 25,500hp, but not all vessels in the class reached the designed top speed, and other faults became apparent in service. All the ships served in World War I. Some vessels were built at Nikolaiev on the Black Sea, but *Gromki* was built at the Nevski yard. She was scuttled at Novorossisk on 18 June 1918.

Country of origin:	Russia
Type:	Destroyer
Launch date:	18 December 1913
Crew:	160
Displacement:	1483 tonnes (1460 tons)
Dimensions:	98m x 9.3m x 3.2m (321ft 6in x 30ft 6in x 10ft 5in))
Endurance:	3333km (1800nm)
Main armament:	Three 102mm (4in) guns; 10 457mm (18in) torpedo tubes
Powerplant:	Two-shaft geared turbines
Performance:	34 knots

Grondeur

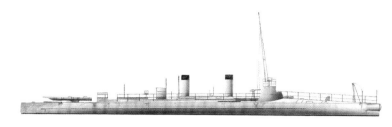

Launched in December 1892, *Grondeur* was a development of the *Coureur*, launched in 1888 to test the new Thorneycroft Watertube Boiler. This type of boiler gave the vessel a very high power output compared to weight. *Grondeur* was slightly larger and more strongly constructed than *Coureur*, and living accommodation for the crew was greatly improved. The torpedo tubes were positioned forward and aft. She was sold in 1926. France's torpedo boats suffered heavily during World War I, particularly in the Dardanelles. Little attention was paid to the development of this type of craft between the wars, and altough a building programme of MTBs was launched in the late 1930s, only a handful saw action before France's collapse. A few of the latter found their way into the Royal Navy in World War II and were manned by British, French and Polish crews.

Country of origin:	France
Type:	Torpedo boat
Launch date:	13 December 1892
Crew:	75
Displacement:	133 tonnes (131 tons)
Dimensions:	45m x 4.4m x 1.3m (147ft 10in x 14ft 6in x 4ft 6in)
Endurance:	3333km (1800nm)
Main armament:	Two 47mm (1.85in) guns; two 355mm (14in) torpedo tubes
Powerplant:	Twin screws, triple expansion engines
Performance:	23.5 knots

Gromkiy

Gromkiy was one of the Russian Type 7 destroyers designed with Italian assistance, something that clearly shows in her lines. As with all pre-World War II designs, the anti-aircraft armament was inadequate, but this was updated during the war. *Gromkiy* was laid down at Leningrad in 1936 and completed in 1939. Her engines developed 48,000hp and oil fuel capacity was 548 tonnes (540 tons), enough for 1529km (826nm) at full speed and 4944km (2670nm) at 19 knots. *Gromkiy* spent her war career in the Arctic, and in November 1941, she was attached to a British naval force (the cruiser *Kenya* and the destroyers *Bedouin* and *Intrepid*) searching for German ships operating off the north coast of Norway. Her principal tasks were escorting coastal convoys, minelaying, and providing fire support for Soviet troops on the Murmansk Front. She survived the war and was discarded in the 1950s.

Country of origin:	Russia
Type:	Destroyer
Launch date:	18 December 1937
Crew:	220
Displacement:	2070 tonnes (2039 tons)
Dimensions:	112.8m x 10.2m x 3.8m (370ft 3in x 33ft 6in x 12ft 6in)
Endurance:	4944km (2670nm)
Main armament:	Four 130mm (5.1in) and two 76mm (3in) guns; six 533mm (21in) torpedo tubes
Powerplant:	Twin screws, turbines
Performance:	36 knots

Gröningen

Completed in September 1956, *Gröningen* was one of of eight Friesland-class post-war destroyers that resembled the light cruisers of the war years. They were among the few destroyers to be built with side armour as well as deck protection. Their armament consisted mainly of conventional dual-purpose guns. These guns had a rate of fire of 50 rounds per minute, which demanded sophisticated automatic ammunition winching and handling systems. Originally, two of the class were installed with eight tubes for anti-submarine torpedoes, but these were removed in 1961. The Friesland-class vessels were never armed with torpedoes, and were among the first destroyers ever to be deployed with no torpedo capability. These ships represented the final development of the gun-armed destroyer, as missiles were on the horizon for this class of vessel.

Country of origin:	Netherlands
Type:	Destroyer
Launch date:	9 January 1954
Crew:	287
Displacement:	3119 tonnes (3070 tons)
Dimensions:	116m x 11.7m x 3.9m (380ft 3in x 38ft 6in x 13ft)
Endurance:	8334km (4500nm)
Main armament:	Four 120mm (4.7in) guns
Powerplant:	Twin-shaft geared turbines
Performance:	36 knots

Grozyashchi

Grozyashchi was an armoured gunboat with a well-balanced design for a small ironclad. The single 228mm (9in) gun was sited forward in a protected mounting beneath the bridge, allowing for a training arc of 100 degrees, while the 152mm (6in) gun was mounted aft in a shield. The ship was fitted with a steel armoured belt extending from the stern to within 9.15m (30ft) of the bow. During World War I, *Grozyashchi* was rearmed with four 152mm (6in) guns, one firing ahead and three aft. Further armour plating was also added. Of *Grozyashchi*'s two sister ships, *Gremyashchi* was mined at Port Arthur on 18 August 1904, while *Otvajni* was scuttled at the same location on 2 January 1905. *Grozyashchi* was scrapped in 1922. The crippling losses sustained in the war of 1904-5 left the Russians short of almost every type of warship except gunboats.

Country of origin:	Russia
Type:	Gunboat
Launch date:	May 1890
Crew:	178
Displacement:	1653 tonnes (1627 tons)
Dimensions:	72.2m x 12.6m x 3.7m (237ft x 41ft 6in x 12ft 2in)
Endurance:	Not known
Main armament:	One 152mm (6in) and one 228mm (9in) gun
Powerplant:	Twin screws, vertical triple expansion engines
Performance:	15 knots

Guadiana

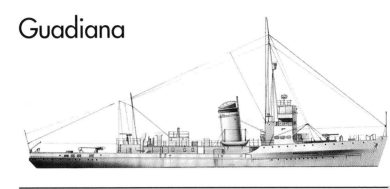

The *Guadiana* was one of four destroyers prefabricated by Yarrow shipbuilders on the Tyne and assembled in Portugal. At the time, the group comprised the largest number of warships to be ordered by the Portuguese Navy for many years. The 102mm (4in) gun was mounted on a platform on the forecastle, with the two twin torpedo mounts located aft on the centreline separated by two small structures, one of which carried a 76mm (3in) gun. The *Guadiana*'s engines developed 11,000hp, and her range at 15 knots was 3033km (1638nm). She was discarded in 1934. Between 1895 and World War II, the Portuguese Government proposed several schemes to increase the size of the navy in defence of its neutrality, and there were even plans to acquire small battleships, but these plans came to nothing mainly because the country's economy could not support a large fleet.

Country of origin:	Portugal
Type:	Destroyer
Launch date:	21 September 1914
Crew:	170
Displacement:	670 tonnes (660 tons)
Dimensions:	73.2m x 7.2m x 2.3m (240ft 2in x 23ft 8in x 7ft 6in)
Endurance:	3040km (1638nm)
Main armament:	One 102mm (4in) and two 76mm (3in) guns; four 457mm (18in) torpedo tubes
Powerplant:	Twin screws, turbines
Performance:	33 knots

Guglielmo Pepe

Designed and built by Ansaldo of Genoa, the *Guglielmo Pepe* was a large and powerful flotilla leader and was one of three boats laid down in 1913. Originally, she was to have been given eight torpedo tubes, but on completion she was fitted with only four. In 1916 she was given two 76mm (3in) anti-aircraft guns, but these were removed in the following year. In 1921 the ship was reclassified as a destroyer and in June 1938 she was transferred to Spain, where she was renamed *Teruel*. She continued to serve until 1947, at which time the Spanish Navy, whose development had stagnated during World War II which was now desperately in need of a modern shipbuilding programme to expand its resources. A programme soon began to replace its pre-war destroyer force with modern, indigenous warships like the Audaz class of the early 1950s.

Country of origin:	Italy
Type:	Destroyer
Launch date:	17 September 1914
Crew:	174
Displacement:	1235 tonnes (1216 tons)
Dimensions:	85m x 8m x 2.8m (278ft 10in x 26ft 3in x 9ft 2in)
Endurance:	2592km (1400nm)
Main armament:	Six 102mm (4in) guns; four 450mm torpedo tubes
Powerplant:	Twin screws, turbines
Performance:	31.5 knots

Gurkha

Launched in 1960, *Gurkha* was one of seven general-purpose frigates in the Tribal class. These vessels were among the first ships to be fully air-conditioned in all crew areas and most working spaces. The standard steam turbine developed 12,500hp, and this could be boosted by a gas turbine which increased output to 20,000hp. The ships were very seaworthy and made good speed even in unfavourable sea states. Of the ships in this class, *Ashanti*, *Eskimo* and *Gurkha* were ordered under the 1955–56 British Navy Estimates, *Nubian* and *Tartar* under the 1956–57 programme, and *Mohawk* and *Zulu* under the 1957–58 programme. The ships were of welded prefabricated construction and were all completed between 1961 and 1964. They were the first frigates designed to carry a helicopter for anti-submarine reconnaissance.

Country of origin:	Britain
Type:	Frigate
Launch date:	11 July 1960
Crew:	253
Displacement:	2743 tonnes (2700 tons)
Dimensions:	109m x 12.8m x 5.3m (360ft x 42ft x 17ft 6in)
Endurance:	7778km (4200nm)
Main armament:	Two 114mm (4.5in) guns; one Limbo three-barrelled anti-submarine mortar
Powerplant:	Single screw, turbine and gas turbine
Performance:	28 knots

Gwin

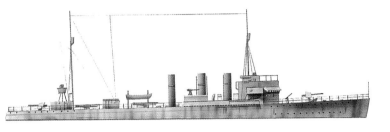

The USS *Gwin*, launched in December 1917, was an early 'flushdecker', many of which served alongside modern counterparts in World War II. She had three funnels and a raised superstructure amidships that carried two of the 102mm (4in) guns. She was sold in 1939. At the time of the Japanese attack on Pearl Harbor in December 1941, of the 171 US destroyers in commission, over one-third were of World War I vintage: the famous 'flushdeckers', of which 272 had been built. Twelve had been lost between the wars and 93 more had been scrapped under the terms of the London Naval Disarmament Treaty of 1930. Another 46 were serving in subsidiary duties, and 50 were transferred to the Royal Navy in 1940. All the Royal Navy's ex-American destroyers were named after towns. The name *Gwin* was later allocated to a light minelayer in 1944.

Country of origin:	USA
Type:	Destroyer
Launch date:	22 December 1917
Crew:	175
Displacement:	1205 tonnes (1187 tons)
Dimensions:	96.2m x 9.1m x 2.7m (315ft 7in x 30ft x 9ft)
Endurance:	2779km (1500nm)
Main armament:	Four 102mm (4in) guns; 12 533mm (21in) torpedo tubes
Powerplant:	Twin screws, turbines
Performance:	32 knots

Habana

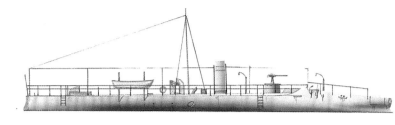

Launched in 1886, *Habana* was built in London by Thorneycroft and was one of 13 first-class boats constructed up to 1887 for the Spanish Navy. Spain had always been in the forefront of naval development, especially in the 1880s, when she possessed a powerful fleet of ironclads that placed her navy sixth in the world. *Habana* carried her machine gun on the conning tower; the two torpedo tubes were mounted in the bow. There is no record of *Habana* being involved in any action during the war with America in 1898, when several gunboats were deployed to Manila and to the Caribbean. The war, which was won decisively by the Americans, destroyed Spain's credibility as a leading naval power and saw the beginning of the USA's rapid rise as a major maritime nation. Two world wars would pass before Spain again became a maritime nation.

Country of origin:	Spain
Type:	Torpedo boat
Launch date:	1886
Crew:	24
Displacement:	68 tonnes (67 tons)
Dimensions:	38.8m x 3.8m x 1.5m (127ft 7in x 12ft 7in x 5ft)
Endurance:	Not known
Main armament:	Two 355mm (14in) torpedo tubes; one machine gun
Powerplant:	Single screw, vertical triple expansion engine
Performance:	24.5 knots

Hachijo

Hachijo and her three sister ships (*Ishigaki*, *Kunashiri* and *Shumushu*) were ordered under the Imperial Japanese Navy's 1937 programme and were designed as general purpose escorts fitted out for coastal patrol, convoy escort, anti-submarine and minesweeping duties. The design proved very satisfactory, and all the later classes of escorts stemmed from it. *Ishigaki* was lost in May 1944; *Shumushu* and *Kunashiri* were surrendered to the Allies at the end of World War II and used to repatriate prisoners. *Shumushu* was handed over to Russia as war reparation, but *Kunashiri* was wrecked in June 1946 when she ran aground on a reef. *Hachijo* was also surrendered, but was in such a bad state of repair that she saw no further service and was scrapped in 1946. In all, very few Japanese vessels survived to be surrendered at the war's end.

Country of origin:	Japan
Type:	Destroyer Escort
Launch date:	10 April 1940
Crew:	Not known
Displacement:	1020 tonnes (1004 tons)
Dimensions:	77.7m x 8.8m x 3m (255ft x 29ft x 9ft 10in)
Endurance:	Not known
Main armament:	Three 120mm (4.7in) guns
Powerplant:	Twin screws, diesel engines
Performance:	19.5 knots

Halifax

Frigates are the most important class of warship in the Canadian Navy, which is an integrated component of the Canadian Armed Forces. H*alifax* is one of 12 frigates of her class, all commissioned between 1992 and 1996. Most have been built by St John Shipbuilding of New Brunswick, who won the competition for the first six of this new class of patrol frigate in 1983. Combat-system design and integration was sub-contracted to Loral Canada; three ships were sub-contracted to Marine Industries Ltd. It was planned to fit a towed integrated active/passive sonar array from 2002 onwards, and there were also plans to convert four of the vessels to the air-defence role from 2002. Five of the class – *Vancouver*, *Regina*, *Calgary*, *Winnipeg* and *Ottawa* – are based in the Pacific. All ships carry either the CH-124A or CH-124B Sea King helicopter.

Country of origin:	Canada
Type:	Frigate
Launch date:	30 May 1988
Crew:	198
Displacement:	4847 tonnes (4770 tons)
Dimensions:	134.7m x 16.4m x 7.1m (441ft 11in x 53ft 9in x 16ft 5in)
Endurance:	15,280km (8246nm)
Main armament:	One 57mm (2.25in) gun; Harpoon SSM; four 324mm (12.75in) torpedo tubes
Powerplant:	Two shafts, two gas turbines, one diesel
Performance:	29 knots

Hamakaze

Hamakaze was the first Japanese destroyer to be fitted with radar. When completed in 1941, she and her 17 sister ships were armed with six 152mm (6in) guns in twin turrets, but between 1943 and 1944, the turret on top of the aft superstructure was removed and replaced by additional anti-aircraft guns. The torpedo tubes were positioned amidships in enclosed quadruple mounts. Hamakaze was involved in almost every Japanese naval operation in the Pacific during World War II, and right from the beginning, she was part of the escort to the aircraft carrier task force that launched the air strike on Pearl Harbor. She was sunk on 7 April 1945, when large numbers of US carrier aircraft attacked a Japanese battle group – including the massive battleship *Yamato* – which was sailing to intercept American forces at Okinawa.

Country of origin:	Japan
Type:	Destroyer
Launch date:	25 November 1940
Crew:	240
Displacement:	2489 tonnes (2450 tons)
Dimensions:	118.5m x 10.8m x 3.7m (388ft 9in x 35ft 5in x 12ft 4in)
Endurance:	8338km (4500nm)
Main armament:	Four 152mm (6in) guns; eight 610mm (24in) torpedo tubes
Powerplant:	Two-shaft geared turbines
Performance:	35.5 knots

Hamayuki

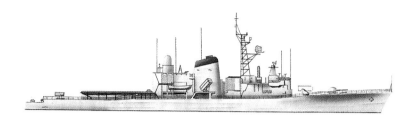

The modern Japanese Navy is a well-handled, efficient fighting force, the core of its strength being submarines, destroyers and frigates. H*amayuki* was a radical departure from previous Japanese anti-submarine destroyer designs. Although the weapons systems are of US origin, the concept and general layout closely resemble the successful French Georges Leygues class. The British propulsion machinery consists of two groups of gas turbines, one set developing 56,780hp, the other 10,680hp. *Hamayuki* is one of 12 guided-missile destroyers of the Hatsuyuki class. *Shirayuki* was the first to be fitted with the Phalanx CIWS, early in 1992, and all the other ships had been retrofitted by 1996. The last three of the class – *Setoyuki*, *Asayuki* and *Shimayuki* – are equipped with the Canadian Beartrap landing aid. All vessels carry the Sikorsky SH-60J Seahawk.

Country of origin:	Japan
Type:	Destroyer
Launch date:	27 May 1982
Crew:	250
Displacement:	3760 tonnes (3700 tons)
Dimensions:	131.7m x 13.7m x 4.2m (432ft x 45ft x 14ft)
Endurance:	9260km (5000nm)
Main armament:	One 76mm (3in) gun; one eight-cell Sea Sparrow launcher; two Phalanx CIWS
Powerplant:	Twin screws, gas turbines
Performance:	30 knots

Hancock

Launched in 1776, *Hancock* was the fastest sailing frigate of her era, and was one of the 13 frigates authorised by Congress in December 1775. By 1777, *Hancock* was in action against British commerce and, in June of that year, she and her fellow frigate *Boston* forced the British frigate *Fox* to surrender. In July, *Hancock* was captured by the British and renamed *Iris*. She served her new owners well until she was captured by the French and used as a cruiser. By 1793, the once-proud ship had become a powder hulk at Toulon, and it was there that she was blown up on 27 August that year, when an Anglo-Spanish expedition captured the harbour and destroyed most of France's Mediterranean Fleet. This was really the beginning of the end for France's aspirations to naval dominance, shattered forever at Trafalgar 12 years later.

Country of origin:	USA
Type:	Frigate
Launch date:	1776
Crew:	350
Displacement:	762 tonnes (750 tons)
Dimensions:	43.8m x 10.8m (144ft x 35ft 6in)
Endurance:	Unlimited, depending on provisions
Main armament:	10 six-pounder, 24 12-pounder guns
Powerplant:	Sail
Performance:	12 knots

Haribing

Haribing was the first of a class of two destroyers – the other being the *Quingdao* – ordered in 1985. Construction was delayed because priority had already been given to warship construction for Thailand, and the vessels were not commissioned until July 1994 and March 1996 respectively. The most notable features are the forward-mounted octuple launcher for the HQ-7 (Crotale) SAM system, improved radar and fire-control systems, and a modern twin 100mm (3.9in) gun which can be elevated to 85 degrees and which fires a 15kg (33lb) shell up to 22km (12nm). *Haribing* is based with the North Sea Fleet at Guzhen Bay, while *Quingdao* is with the East Sea Fleet at Jianggezhuang. The gas turbines for the latter warship were manufactured in the Ukraine. Chinese warships have frequently been criticised for poor-quality construction.

Country of origin:	China
Type:	Destroyer
Launch date:	October 1991
Crew:	230
Displacement:	4267 tonnes (4200 tonnes)
Dimensions:	142.7m x 15.1m x 5.1m (468ft 2in x 49ft 6in x 16ft 8in)
Endurance:	8042km (4340nm)
Main armament:	Two 100mm (3.9in) guns; YJ-1 Eagle Strike SSMs; 324mm (12.75in) torpedo tubes
Powerplant:	Two shafts, two gas turbines, two diesels
Performance:	31 knots

Haruna

Haruna was laid down in March 1970 and completed in 1973. She and her sister ship *Hiei* were intended to serve as command ships for anti-submarine escort groups. They are unusual vessels, with the entire aft part of the ship devoted to operating facilities for the three large Sea King anti-submarine helicopters. They are the only destroyer-sized vessels in the world to carry three such helicopters. The midships section is dominated by the hangar, which occupies the full beam of the vessel and extends forward alongside the single broad funnel. The 127mm (5in) guns are mounted forward and are fully automatic, firing up to 40 rounds per minute. Between 1986 and 1987 *Haruna* underwent a major refit to improve her anti-aircraft defensive system. The Haruna-class vessels were followed into service by the similar Shirane class.

Country of origin:	Japan
Type:	Destroyer
Launch date:	December 1971
Crew:	370
Displacement:	5029 tonnes (4950 tons)
Dimensions:	153m x 17.5m x 5.2m (502ft x 57ft 5in x 17ft)
Endurance:	8894km (4800nm)
Main armament:	Two 127mm (5in) guns; Sea Sparrow missiles
Powerplant:	Twin screws, turbines
Performance:	32 knots

Hatakaze

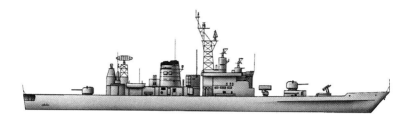

Hatakaze is the lead vessel of a two-ship class, her sister vessel being the *Shimakaze*. Both ships carry a platform for a Sikorsky SH-60J Seahawk helicopter. They are fitted with the Standard SM-1MR surface-to-air missile, which has command guidance and semi-active radar homing out to 46km (25nm) at Mach 2 and a height envelope of 45–18,288m (150-60,000ft). Principal anti-submarine weapon is the Honeywell ASROC Mk112 multiple launcher, which has inertial guidance to 1.6–10km (15.4nm); its payload is the Mk46 Mod 5 torpedo. The ships are also armed with the General Dynamics 20mm(0.7in) Phalanx Mk15 CIWS six-barrelled gun, which fires 3000 rounds per minute and has a range of 1.6km (1 mile). Phalanx is a 'last ditch' air defence weapon, laying down a lethal cone of fire capable of destroying sea-skimming missiles.

Country of origin:	Japan
Type:	Destroyer
Launch date:	9 November 1984
Crew:	260
Displacement:	5588 tonnes (5500 tons)
Dimensions:	150m x 16.4m x 4.8m)
Endurance:	8042km (4342nm)
Main armament:	Two 127mm (5in) guns; Harpoon SSM; ASROC: 324mm (12.75in) Mk46 Neartip torpedoes
Powerplant:	Twin shafts, four gas turbines
Performance:	30 knots

Havock

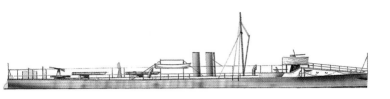

HMS *Havock* was the world's first true destroyer. In 1892 Alfred Yarrow of Tyneside was asked by the Admiralty to prepare an answer to the French torpedo craft then being built: *Havock*, launched in August 1893 and completed in 1894, was his response. Ten watertight bulkheads divided the vessel into 11 compartments. Her 12-pounder gun was mounted on a platform forward, and there were two six-pounders in the waist and one aft. On trials, *Havock* proved to be a very good, fast sea vessel with very little vibration or heel under full helm. She was eventually scrapped in 1912. In years to come, other destroyers would bear the name of their progenitor, and one of them would achieve everlasting fame in battle at Narvik in April 1940, when most of Germany's existing destroyers were annihilated.

Country of origin:	Britain
Type:	Destroyer
Launch date:	12 August 1893
Crew:	68
Displacement:	243.8 tonnes (240 tons)
Dimensions:	54.8m x 5.6m x 3.3m (180ft x 18ft 6in x 11ft)
Endurance:	1482km (800nm)
Main armament:	One 12-pounder and three six-pounder guns; three torpedo tubes
Powerplant:	Twin screws, triple expansion engines
Performance:	26 knots

Hibiki

It is worthy of note that a full decade earlier than the British J class, the Japanese had destroyers in their Fubiki class, which were of a superior specification. This sudden leap in capability was bound to bring problems, as succeeding classes demonstrated. The four Akatsuki-class ships of 1931–33 kept the same arrangement on a slightly shorter hull but reduced the forward funnel to a thick pipe to save topweight. They also featured lightweight masting and a reduction in depth charges. The *Hibiki* of this group was the first all-welded Japanese destroyer; she was also the only Akatsuki-class ship to survive the war. Her X turret was replaced with more light anti-aircraft weapons in 1942, and by the end of the war, she was carrying 28 25mm anti-aircraft cannon. In 1947 she went to the USSR as war booty.

Country of origin:	Japan
Type:	Destroyer
Launch date:	16 June 1932
Crew:	240
Displacement:	2530 tonnes (2490 tons)
Dimensions:	118.45m x 10.8m x 3.76m (388ft 7in x 35ft 4in x 12ft 4in)
Endurance:	9250km (4986nm)
Main armament:	Three twin 127mm (5in) and two twin 25mm (1in) AA guns; two quadruple 610mm (24in) torpedo tubes
Powerplant:	Two sets of geared steam turbines
Performance:	35 knots

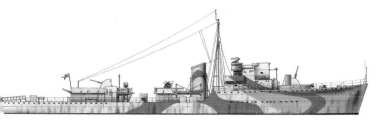

Aware of the shortage of escorts as early as 1938, the British Admiralty designed what was termed a Fast Escort Vessel (FEV) to give convoys both anti-aircraft and anti-submarine coverage without tying down the precious, and, as it turned out, inadequate, fleet destroyers. Rather shortsightedly, there was perceived the need for speed – in order to prosecute sonar contacts more smartly – but not endurance, as the latter requirement was deemed to be met by true escort vessels such as the Flower-class corvettes. To improve them as gun platforms, the Hunt-class ships were fitted initially with active stabilisers as standard. However, their power demands and their poor control systems made them so unpopular that later ships had extra bunker space instead, which considerably improved their endurance. In all, 83 Hunt Types I, II and III -class destroyers were built.

Country of origin:	Britain
Type:	Destroyer
Launch date:	12 December 1939 (HMS *Atherstone*, first unit)
Crew:	170
Displacement:	1107 tonnes (1090 tons)
Dimensions:	85.7m x 9.6m x 2.36m (281ft 3in x 31ft 6in x 7ft 9in)
Endurance:	4626km (2498nm)
Main armament:	Two twin 102mm (4in) guns; two 533mm (21in) torpedo tubes
Powerplant:	Two shafts, geared steam turbines
Performance:	25 knots

Hydra

The Greek Government announced its decision to buy four Meko 200 Mod 3HN frigates from what was then West Germany, on 18 April 1988. The West German Government was to offset the cost of the purchase by supplying tanks and aircraft, whereas US credits contributed to the cost of electronics and weapon systems. The first ship, *Hydra*, was built by Blohm & Voss at Hamburg, with the remainder scheduled to be built by the Hellenic Shipyards at Skaramanga. However, construction of the second vessel, *Spetsai*, was delayed by financial constraints, so some of the construction work was completed in Hamburg. The design closely follows that of the Portuguese Vasco da Gama class. All four ships were commissioned between November 1992 and January 1999, and all four carry the Sikorsky Aegean Hawk ASW helicopter.

Country of origin:	Greece
Type:	Frigate
Launch date:	25 June 1991
Crew:	173
Displacement:	3251 tonnes (3200 tons)
Dimensions:	117m x 14.8m x 4.1m (383ft 11in x 48ft 7in x 13ft 6in)
Endurance:	6591km (3559nm)
Main armament:	One 127mm (5in) DP gun; Harpoon SSM; six 324mm (12.75in) Mk46 torpedoes; Sea Sparrow SAM
Powerplant:	Two shafts, two gas turbines, two diesels
Performance:	31 knots

Impavido

Impavido and her sister ship, *Intrepido*, were the first missile-armed destroyers in the Italian Navy. Derived from the conventional gun-armed Impetuoso-class destroyers, they retained the forward 127mm (5in) twin gun turret, but the after turret was replaced with a US Mk13 launcher for Tartar surface-to-air missiles. The Tartar area defence weapon, similar in concept to Britain's Sea Dart, was developed in response to a 1952 requirement for a weapon capable of engaging targets at all altitudes. The after funnel was made taller to keep exhaust away from the fire-control tracker on top of the aft structure. *Impavido* was fitted with four 76mm (3in) anti-aircraft guns, and anti-submarine capability was provided by two triple torpedo tubes. *Impavido* was modernised between 1976 and 1977, and was stricken on 30 June 1992.

Country of origin:	Italy
Type:	Destroyer
Launch date:	25 May 1962
Crew:	344
Displacement:	4054 tonnes (3990 tons)
Dimensions:	131.3m x 13.7m x 4.4m (430ft 9in x 45ft x 14ft 5in)
Endurance:	9260km (5000nm)
Main armament:	Two 127mm (5in) guns; one Tartar missile launcher
Powerplant:	Twin screws, turbines
Performance:	34 knots

Inhauma

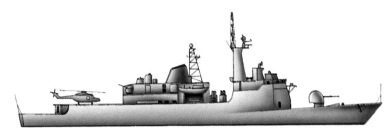

Inhauma is the lead ship of a class of four corvettes designed by the Brazilian Naval Design Office with the assistance of the German privately-owned Marine Technik design company. *Inhauma* was commissioned in December 1989, and the other corvettes between 1991 and 1994. Originally, it had been intended to order a class of 16 ships, but this was reduced to four because of financial considerations. As a country with a long coastline, Brazil has always endeavoured to maintain a substantial navy. Her first dreadnoughts, built in Britain in 1907, came about as a response to the growth of the Argentine Navy, and as a consequence, she had ships of this type in commission even before larger powers such as France, Italy and Russia. Corvettes such as *Inhauma* are ideally suited to the task of defending Brazil's coast.

Country of origin:	Brazil
Type:	Corvette
Launch date:	13 December 1986
Crew:	122
Displacement:	2002 tonnes (1970 tons)
Dimensions:	95.83m x 11.4m x 3.7m (314ft 2in x 37ft 5in x 12ft 1in)
Endurance:	6434km (3474nm)
Main armament:	One 115mm (4.5in) gun; Exocet SSMs; six 324mm (12.75in) torpedo tubes
Powerplant:	Two shafts, one gas turbine, two diesels
Performance:	27 knots

Iroquois

Launched between 1970 and 1971, *Iroquois* and her three sisters – *Athabaskan*, *Algonquin* and *Huron*, all four named after Indian tribes of the Great Lakes region – were designed specifically for anti-submarine warfare operations in Arctic waters, where much naval warfare would have taken place in any East-West conflict. They have the same hull design, dimensions, and basic characteristics as an earlier class of large, general-purpose frigates which had been cancelled in the early 1960s. Properly designated Destroyer Helicopter Escorts (DDH), they carry two Sea King ASW helicopters. They are equipped with anti-rolling tanks to stabilise them at low speed, a pre-wetting system to counter radioactive fallout, and an enclosed citadel from which control of all machinery is exercised. A comprehensive electronics system includes an effective, long-range radar warning device.

Country of origin:	Canada
Type:	Destroyer
Launch date:	28 November 1970
Crew:	246
Displacement:	4267 tonnes (4200 tons)
Dimensions:	129.8m x 15.5m x 4.5m (426ft x 51ft x 15ft)
Endurance:	8338km (4502nm)
Main armament:	One 127mm (5in) gun; one triple A/S mortar
Powerplant:	Twin screw, gas turbines
Performance:	30 knots

Izumrud

**I**zumrud (Emerald) was one of a large group of small anti-submarine frigates built at the rate of three per year, and divided into three sub-groups according to the equipment carried. _Izumrud_ is in the first group. Her twin 57mm (2.25in) gun turret is mounted aft, and the SA-N-4 SAM missiles are mounted forward of the bridge and are fired upward through a circular hatchway in the deck. Two twin, multi-barrel rocket launchers are also fitted in front of the bridge, and twin 533mm (21in) torpedo tubes are mounted amidships. _Izumrud's_ turbines develop 24,000hp, and the diesels produce 16,000hp. Range is 1800km (972nm) at 27 knots and 8550km (4616nm) at 10 knots. _Izumrud_ is intended primarily for inshore anti-submarine patrols, where her principal targets would be small and very quiet diesel-electric boats (SSKs) engaged in special operations.

Country of origin:	Russia
Type:	Frigate
Launch date:	1970
Crew:	250
Displacement:	1219 tonnes (1200 tons)
Dimensions:	72m x 10m x 3.7m (236ft 3in x 32ft 10in x 12ft 2in)
Endurance:	8550km (4608nm)
Main armament:	Two 57mm (2.25in) guns; SAMs
Powerplant:	Triple screws, one gas turbine, two diesel engines
Performance:	27 knots

Jacob van Heemskerck

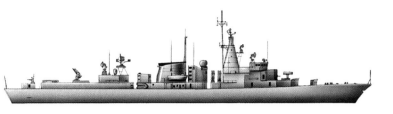

The *Jacob van Heemskerck* is the leader of a two-ship class, the other being the *Witte de With*. Commissioned in 1986, the ships were planned to alternate as the flagship of the Royal Netherlands Navy's 3rd ASW hunter-killer group, assigned to NATO's Channel Command in wartime. The two vessels were originally designed to replace two Kortenaer-class frigates which had been sold to Greece, and were intended to be an air-defence variant. In addition to the Goalkeeper CIWS, they are armed with the Standard and Sea Sparrow SAMs, and are thus capable of providing effective area defence of a task group out to a range of 46km (25nm) with the Standard SM-1MR SAM, the Raytheon Sea Sparrow providing medium-range backup to 14.6km (7.8nm). The Standard missile replaced the Tartar in NATO service.

Country of origin:	Netherlands
Type:	Frigate
Launch date:	5 November 1983
Displacement:	3810 tonnes (3750 tons)
Dimensions:	130.5m x 14.6m x 6.2m (428ft x 47ft 11in x 20ft 4in)
Endurance:	7560km (4082nm)
Main armament:	One 30mm (1.1in) Goalkeeper; two 20mm (0.7in) guns; Harpoon SSM; Standard and Sea Sparrow SAMs; four 324mm (12.75in) torpedo tubes
Powerplant:	Two shafts, four gas turbines
Performance:	30 knots

Jebat

On 31 March 1992, it was announced that a contract had been signed for the construction of two corvettes, subsequently classed as light frigates, between Yarrow Shipbuilders of Glasgow and the Malaysian Navy. The two ships, named *Jebat* and *Lekiu*, were launched between 1994 and 1995 and commissioned in 1998, but delivery dates were delayed because of problems with integrating the weapon system. Basically, the vessels are a GEC Naval Systems Frigate 2000 design with a modern combat data system and automatic machinery control. Missile armament is the Aerospatiale Exocet MM40 Block II sea skimmer and the British Aerospace Vertical Launch Seawolf. Malaysia's long coastline makes it imperative for her to maintain strong patrol forces. As well as three frigates and two corvettes, she has some 40 patrol craft of various types.

Country of origin:	Malaysia
Type:	Frigate
Launch date:	May 1995
Crew:	146
Displacement:	2306 tonnes (2270 tons)
Dimensions:	105.5m x 12.8m x 3.6m (346ft x 42ft x 11ft 9in)
Endurance:	9650km (5208nm)
Main armament:	One 57mm (2.25in) and two 30mm (1.1in) guns; Exocet SSM; Seawolf SAM; six 324mm (12.75in) torpedo tubes
Powerplant:	Two shafts, four diesel engines
Performance:	28 knots

Jianghu class

The first three or four units of what became known as the Jianghu I class were laid down between 1973 and 1974 at Hutung, launched in 1975, and commissioned in 1976. The vessels were a follow-on from the Jiangdong class, the first frigate design to emerge from China after the Cultural Revolution. A second shipyard, the Tungmang at Shanghai, subsequently joined the programme. About 20 ships were built, and one of them (pennant No 544) was modified and redesignated *Jianghu II*, the after part of the ship being rebuilt to take a hangar and flight deck for a single helicopter. Several of the class were expected to be converted, but 544 may have been a one-off helicopter trials ship for the improved Luhu and Jiangwei designs. There is also a Jianghu III class, fitted with improved weaponry and electronics.

Country of origin:	China
Type:	Frigate
Launch date:	1975 (*Chang De*, first unit)
Crew:	195
Displacement:	1900 tonnes (1930 tons)
Dimensions:	103.2m x 10.2m x 3.1m (338ft 7in x 33ft 6in x 10ft 2in)
Endurance:	7408km (4000nm)
Main armament:	Two single 100mm (3.9in) DP and six twin 37mm (1.4in) AA guns; plus anti-ship missiles
Powerplant:	Two shafts, two diesels
Performance:	30 knots

Jianghu III

Based on the Jianghu II, the Jianghu III class reverted to the rounded stack of the first of the class, the Jianghu I, but was armed with twin 57mm (2.25in) DP guns mounted fore and aft plus six twin 37mm anti-aircraft guns, four RBU 1200 ASW rocket launchers, four BMB-2 depth charge projectors and two depth charge racks. The first two units were sold to Egypt in 1984 and 1985 as the *Najim az Zaffer* and the *El Nasser*, and four more to Thailand in 1991-92. Two units are currently in service with the Chinese fleet; the first is the *Huangshi*, commissioned in December 1986, and the other is the *Wuhu*. Two more vessels, one of which is identified as the *Zhoushan* (completed in early 1993) are improved Type IVs. The Types III and IV are referred to as New Missile Frigates. The Type IVs are the first all-enclosed, air conditioned ships to be built in China.

Country of origin:	China
Type:	Frigate
Launch date:	1986 (Huangshi, first unit commisioned)
Crew:	200
Displacement:	1955 tonnes (1924 tons)
Dimensions:	103.2m x 10.8m x 3.1m (338ft 6in x 35ft 3in x 10ft 2in)
Endurance:	6434km (3474nm)
Main armament:	Four 100mm (3.9in) guns; YJ-1 Eagle Strike SSMs; depth charges; AS mortars and mines
Powerplant:	Two shafts, two diesel engines
Performance:	28 knots

Jiangwei class

The programme to construct four Jiangwei I frigates began in 1988, and the ships were commissioned between 1991 and 1994. The vessels are named *Anquing*, *Huainan*, *Huaibei* and *Tongling*, and all are based in the East Sea Fleet at Dinghai. They were followed by three ships of the Jiangwei II class, launched between 1997 and 1998. These vessels have an improved SAM system, updated fire-control radars, and a redistribution of the aft-mounted anti-aircraft guns. They are equipped with a hangar and helicopter platform aft to accommodate one Harbin Z-9A (Dauphin) helicopter for ASW and general-purpose work. A hull-mounted, active search-and-attack medium-frequency Echo Type 5 sonar is fitted. The first of the class began sea trials in early 1998 which was somewhat later than planned, unspecified delays having arisen.

Country of origin:	China
Type:	Frigate
Launch date:	completed December 1991 (*Anqing*. first unit)
Crew:	170
Displacement:	2286 tonnes (2250 tons)
Dimensions:	111.7m x 12.1m x 4.8m (366ft 6in x 39ft 8in x 15ft 8in)
Endurance:	6437km (3472nm)
Main armament:	Two 100mm (3.9in) guns; Eagle Strike or C-802 SSMs; RF-61 SAMs; AS mortars
Powerplant:	Two shafts, two diesel engines
Performance:	25 knots

Kamikaze

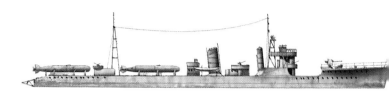

The name Kamikaze means 'Divine Wind', and was first applied to the typhoon that destroyed the fleet of Kubla Khan, sailing to invade Japan in 1281. Ordered between 1921 and 1922, the nine Kamikaze-class destroyers actually formed Group II of the preceding Minekaze class. They were the first destroyers in the Imperial Japanese Navy to be built with a bridge strengthened by steel plating. This gave them a high centre of gravity, which was counterbalanced by an increased displacement and slightly wider beam. The ships of this class had a distinguished record in World War II. In 1944 four were sunk by American submarines and a fifth in an air attack on Truk. *Kamikaze* survived the war and was surrendered at Singapore, but in June 1946, while trying to assist the repatriation ship *Kunashiri*, she became stranded on the same reef and was scrapped where she lay.

Country of origin:	Japan
Type:	Destroyer
Launch date:	25 September 1922
Crew:	148
Displacement:	1676 tonnes (1650 tons)
Dimensions:	102.6m x 9m x 2.89m (336ft 3in x 29ft 6in x 9ft 6in)
Endurance:	6670km (3601nm)
Main armament:	Four 120mm (4.7in) guns; six 533mm (21in) torpedo tubes
Powerplant:	Two shafts, geared steam turbines
Performance:	37.5 knots

Kapitan Saken

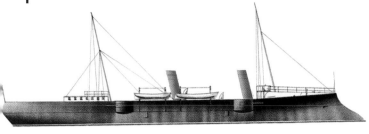

The *Kapitan Saken* was a powerful-looking vessel with twin funnels and a pronounced bow ram. She had two masts, the foremost of which was sited just in front of the forward funnel. Five of the torpedo tubes were in fixed positions: two facing ahead; one on each bow; one in the stern; and with the other two tubes on swivel mounts. Spare torpedoes were housed in racks on the lower deck and moved to the torpedo tubes on railway tracks that ran the whole length of the ship to loading poisitions at the rear of the tubes, an arrangement that saved a great deal of labour. The *Kapitan Saken*'s design was virtually identical to that of the previous torpedo gunboat, *Leitenant Ilin*, except that fewer guns were carried. She was scrapped in 1907. At this time, Russia's gunboats were considered a serious threat by other European navies.

Country of origin:	Russia
Type:	Torpedo gunboat
Launch date:	12 May 1889
Crew:	125
Displacement:	610 tonnes (600 tons)
Dimensions:	64m x 7.3m x 3.3m (210ft x 24ft x 10ft)
Endurance:	Not known
Main armament:	Four 431mm (17in) torpedo tubes; four three-pounder guns
Powerplant:	Twin screws, vertical triple expansion engines
Performance:	18.5 knots

Kashin

Built as the world's first major class of warships to be powered by gas turbines, the Kashin class was produced from 1959 onwards at the Zhdanov shipyard in Leningrad (five units between 1962 and 1966) and at the 61 Kommuna (North) shipyard at Nikolaiev (15 units between 1959 and 1972). In 1972, one of the Nikolaiev-built ships, *Otvzhny*, foundered in the Black Sea following a catastrophic explosion and fire that raged out of control for five hours until the destroyer sank. Over 200 of her crew lost their lives, making this the worst peacetime naval disaster since the end of World War II. The last of the class, *Sderzhanny*, was completed to a revised design designated Kashin II, and three further units were built in the late 1970s for the Indian Navy, named *Rajput*, *Rana* and *Ranjit*. The Kashin class was prolific in all the Soviet Navy's operational areas.

Country of origin:	Russia
Type:	Destroyer
Launch date:	31 December 1960 (*Komsomolets Ukrainy*, first unit)
Crew:	280
Displacement:	4572 tonnes (4500 tons)
Dimensions:	144m x 15.8m x 4.8m (472ft 5in x 51ft 10in x 15ft 9in)
Endurance:	15,750km (8504nm)
Main armament:	Two twin 76mm (3in) guns; 4 533mm (21in) torpedo tubes; SA-N-1 SAMs; ASW rockets
Powerplant:	Two shafts, four gas turbines
Performance:	36 knots

Kaszub

Kaszub's design is based on that of the Russian Grisha class, but with many alterations. Built by the Northern Shipyard in Gdansk, *Kaszub* was to have been followed by a second vessel, but this was cancelled in 1989. However, there are still tentative plans to construct a class of up to seven more ships based on the *Kaszub* hull and carrying specialized equipment for anti-submarine warfare when funds become available. *Kaszub* was commissioned in March 1987 but was not fully fitted out until 1991, when the 76mm (3in) gun was installed. The ship also carries a 23mm (0.9in) gun aft, but there are plans to replace this with a vertical-launch SAM system in due course. *Kaszub* became operational in 1990 and was initially based with the Border Guard, but was transferred to the Polish Navy in 1991. She now exercises regularly with NATO forces in the Baltic.

Country of origin:	Poland
Type:	Frigate
Launch date:	4 October 1986
Crew:	67
Displacement:	1202 tonnes (1183 tons)
Dimensions:	82.3m x 10m x 3.1m (270ft x 32ft 10in x 10ft 2in)
Endurance:	5629km (3038nm)
Main armament:	One 76mm (3in) gun; four 533mm (21in) torpedo tubes
Powerplant:	Two shafts, four diesel engines
Performance:	27 knots

Kelly

Launched in October 1938, HMS *Kelly* was one of a class which marked a considerable change in British destroyer design. The first single-funnelled class this century, the J, K, and I classes adopted the guns and the turrets used in the big vessels of the Tribal class, but mounted on a more easily built hull. The six 119mm (4.7in) Mk XII guns had a maximum elevation of 40 degrees, leaving air defence to the quadruple two-pounder 'pompom' abaft the funnel. This was a weakness that was to be highlighted by the loss early in the war of several vessels, including *Kelly*, to air attack, particularly dive-bombing. By the end of the war, survivors of this class were to mount up to 10 20mm (0.7in) cannon, giving a much more effective air defence. *Kelly* and her sister ship, *Kashmir*, were bombed and sunk by German dive-bombers off Crete on 23 May 1941.

Country of origin:	Britain
Type:	Destroyer
Launch date:	25 October 1938
Crew:	218
Displacement:	1722 tonnes (1695 tons)
Dimensions:	108.7m x 10.9m x 2.75m (356ft 6in x 35ft 9in x 9ft)
Range:	4444km (2400nm)
Main armament:	Six 119mm (4.7in) guns
Powerplant:	Two-shaft geared turbines
Performance:	36 knots

Kidd

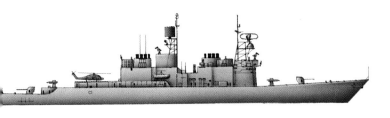

In 1974 the Iranian Government ordered six SAM-equipped versions of the Spruance-class destroyer for service in the Persian Gulf and the Indian Ocean. However, following the revolution in Iran (then Persia), two were cancelled in 1979 while the remaining four under construction were taken over by the US Navy as the Kidd class. These were the world's most powerfully armed, general-purpose destroyers at the time of their commissioning, and because of their origins, they were generally known in the US Navy as the Ayatollah class. The four ships were the *Kidd*, *Callaghan*, *Scott* and *Chandler*. The Kidd-class vessels were optimised for the area defence role, but they also had a powerful surface-to-surface and anti-submarine capability. The principal SAM armament of these powerful warships is the Standard missile.

Country of origin:	USA
Type:	Destroyer
Launch date:	11 August 1979
Crew:	368
Displacement:	9728 tonnes (9574 tons)
Dimensions:	171.6m x 16.8m x 9.1m (563ft x 55ft x 30ft)
Endurance:	14,824km (8004nm)
Main armament:	Two 127mm (5in) DP guns; Harpoon SSM; Standard SAM; six 324mm (12.75in) torpedo tubes
Powerplant:	Two shafts, four gas turbines
Performance:	32 knots

Kongo

The *Kongo* was commissioned in March 1983 and was followed by four more vessels of her class, the *Kirishima*, *Myoko*, and *Choukai*, the latter being commissioned in March 1998. The ships are enlarged and improved versions of the American Arleigh Burke destroyers and are armed with a lightweight version of the Aegis air defence system. As well as providing area air defence for the fleet, the ships also contribute towards the air defence of mainland Japan, standing well out from the Home Islands in the role of air defence picket ships. Although designated as destroyers, the vessels are in fact of cruiser size. Their entry into Japanese Navy service was slowed down by a combination of cost and the reluctance of the US Congress to release Aegis technology. The highly sophisticated Aegis is the US Navy's primary air defence system.

Country of origin:	Japan
Type:	Destroyer
Launch date:	26 September 1991
Crew:	307
Displacement:	9637 tonnes (9485 tons)
Dimensions:	161m x 21m x 10m (528ft 2in x 68ft 11in x 32ft 9in)
Endurance:	7238km (3908nm)
Main armament:	One 127mm (5in) gun; Harpoon SSM; Standard SAM;six 324mm (12.75in) torpedo tubes; vertical launch ASROC
Powerplant:	Two shafts, four gas turbines
Performance:	30 knots

Koni class

Although constructed in the Soviet Union at the Zelenodolsk shipyard on the Black Sea, the Koni class of frigate was intended solely for export, only one unit being retained by the Russians as a crew training ship for the naval personnel from those countries whose navies bought the vessels. There were two distinct sub-classes, the Koni Type II class differing from the Koni Type I class in having the space between the funnel and the aft superstructure occupied by an extra deckhouse believed to contain air-conditioning units for use in tropical climates. Two units sold to Yugoslavia were locally modified to carry SS-N-2B Styx anti-ship cruise missiles. Others were sold to Cuba and the former German Democratic Republic. It appears, however, that sales of the type never reached the level that the Russians had anticipated.

Country of origin:	Russia
Type:	Frigate
Launch date:	completed 1978 (*Delfin*)
Crew:	110
Displacement:	1930 tonnes (1900 tons)
Dimensions:	95m x 12.8m x 4.2m (311ft 8 in x 42ft x 13ft 8in)
Range:	4076km (2200nm)
Main armament:	Two twin 76mm (3in) guns and two twin 30mm(1.1in) guns; SAMs
Powerplant:	Three shafts, two gas turbines and one diesel
Performance:	27 knots

Knox class

The Knox class is similar to the Garcia and Brooke designs from which it is developed, but is slightly larger because of the use of non-pressure fired boilers. It was designed in the early 1960s. The first vessels entered US Navy service in 1969, the last units of the 46-strong class being delivered in 1974. They are specialised ASW ships and have been heavily criticised because of their single propeller and solitary 127mm (5in) gun armament. A five-ship class based on the Knox design but with a Mk22 missile launcher for 16 standard SM-1MR missiles was built for the Spanish Navy. Knox-class frigates have been used over the years to test individual prototype weapon and sensor systems, such as the Phalanx close-range anti-aircraft system. Some units were assigned to the US Naval Reserve Force in the late 1980s as replacements for ageing destroyers.

Country of origin:	USA
Type:	Frigate
Launch date:	19 November 1966
Crew:	283
Displacement:	3939 tonnes (3877 tons)
Dimensions:	133.5m x 14.3m x 4.6m (438ft x 46ft 10in x 15ft)
Endurance:	9260km (5000nm)
Main armament:	One 127mm (5in) DP gun; SAMs; ASW and anti-ship missiles
Powerplant:	Geared steam turbines
Performance:	27 knots

Korietz

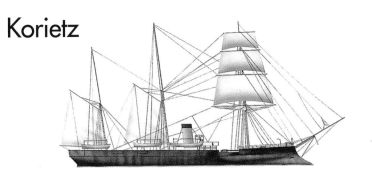

Korietz was laid down in 1885 at Stockholm. She was a barquentine-rigged vessel, with the two 203mm (8in) guns firing forward from sponsons protected by armour shields. The 152mm (6in) guns were mounted aft, and four 107mm (4.2in) weapons were mounted on the broadside. She and her sister *Mandjur* were heavily armed for their size, and ideal for patrol work, although they were considered to be poor sailers, possibly because they carried too great a weight of canvas for their size. Both featured a ram bow, which was much more pronounced in *Korietz* than in her sister ship. On 9 February 1904 *Korietz* was heavily damaged in action with the Japanese armoured cruiser squadron at Port Arthur, and was subsequently scuttled in Korea. The name *Korietz* was later allocated to a vessel of the 1905 Gilyak class.

Country of origin:	Russia
Type:	Gunboat
Launch date:	August 1886
Crew:	179
Displacement:	1290 tonnes (1270 tons)
Dimensions:	66.7m x 10.6m x 3.7m (219ft x 35ft x 12ft 4in)
Endurance:	Not known
Main armament:	One 152mm (6in) and two 203mm (8in) guns
Powerplant:	Twin screws, horizontal compound engines
Performance:	13.3 knots

Krivak II class

In 1970 the first unit of the Krivak I class of large anti-submarine warfare vessel entered service with the Soviet Navy. Built at the Zhdanov shipyard in Leningrad, the Kaliningrad shipyard and the Kamysh-Burun shipyard in Kerch between 1971 and 1982, 21 units of this variant were constructed. In 1976 the Krivak II class, of which 11 were built at Kaliningrad between that year and 1981, was first seen. This differed from the previous class in having single 100mm (3.9in) guns substituted for the twin 76mm (3in) turrets of the earlier version, and a larger variable-depth sonar at the stern. Both classes were re-rated to patrol ship status in the late 1970s, possibly in the light of what some western observers considered to be deficiencies in terms of limited endurance for ASW operations in open waters. Nevertheless, the Krivak IIs caused some consternation in NATO circles when they first appeared.

Country of origin:	Russia
Type:	Frigate
Launch date:	1975 (*Rezvyy*)
Crew:	220
Displacement:	3759 tonnes (3700 tons)
Dimensions:	123.5m x 14m x 4.7m (405ft 2in x 45ft 11in x 15ft 5in)
Endurance:	5188km (2800nm)
Main armament:	Two single 100mm (3.9in) DP guns; SAMs; ASW missiles; eight 533mm (21in) torpedo tubes
Powerplant:	Two shafts, four gas turbines
Performance:	32 knots

Leberecht Maass

The Type 34 or Maass class were the first German destroyers to be built since World War I. Of conventional layout, their only major problem was lack of freeboard, which had disagreeable consequences in heavy seas. All 16 ships were launched between 1937 and 1939. Five were sunk by Royal Navy destroyer forces in the Second Battle of Narvik in April 1943. Of the remainder, *Leberecht Maass* and *Max Schulz* were mined and sunk in the North Sea on 22 February 1940; *Hermann Schoemann* was sunk in Arctic waters by the RN cruiser HMS *Edinburgh* on 2 May 1942; *Bruno Heinemann* was mined and sunk in the English Channel on 25 January 1942; *Friedrich Eckoldt* was sunk in the Barents Sea by the RN cruisers *Jamaica* and *Sheffield* on 31 December 1942; one was broken up post-war in the UK; and two went to the Soviet Union in 1946.

Country of origin:	Germany
Type:	Destroyer
Launch date:	18 August 1935
Crew:	315
Displacement:	3211 tonnes (3160 tons)
Dimensions:	119m x 11.3m x 3.8m (390ft 5in x 37ft 1in x 12ft 6in)
Endurance:	8135km (4393nm)
Main armament:	Five single 127mm (5in) guns; two quadruple 533mm (21in) torpedo tubes; up to 60 mines
Powerplant:	Two-shaft geared turbines
Performance:	30 knots

Lupo

Commissioned between September 1977 and March 1980, and originally described as modified Alpinos, the four ships of the Lupo class – *Lupo, Sagittario, Perseo* and *Orsa* – underwent a mid-life update between 1991 and 1994. This included the installation of a low-altitude CORA SPS-702 search radar, new gyros, and new communications, including SATCOM. Similar vessels were built for Peru (4), Venezuela (6), and Iraq (4), but the Iraqi ships were not delivered because of the international situation and were taken over by the Italian Navy as the Artigliere class. They are the *Artigliere* (Iraqi name *Hittin*), *Aviere* (*Thi Qar*), *Bersagliere* (*Al Yarmouk*) and *Granatiere* (*Al Qadsiya*). The vessels are officially described as Fleet Patrol Ships. Two are based at Augusta and two at Brindisi, and they exercise regularly with units of the US Sixth Fleet.

Country of origin:	Italy
Type:	Frigate
Launch date:	29 July 1976
Crew:	185
Displacement:	2565 tonnes (2525 tons)
Dimensions:	113.2m x 11.3m x 3.7m (371ft 4in x 37ft 1in x 12ft 1in)
Endurance:	6997km (3778nm)
Main armament:	One 127mm (5in) gun; OTO Melara Taseo SSM; Sea Sparrow SAM; six 324mm (12.75in) torpedo tubes, 1 helicopter
Powerplant:	Two shafts, two gas turbines, two diesels
Performance:	35 knots

Lütjens

The three ships of the Lutjens class – *Lütjens*, *Mölders* and *Rommel* – are modified Charles F. Adams class destroyers, fitted out to meet West German requirements. *Mölders* (named after Major Werner Mölders, a leading wartime Luftwaffe ace who was killed in 1941) was completed in March 1984; *Rommel* (named after Field Marshal Erwin Rommel, the 'Desert Fox') in July 1985; and *Lütjens* herself, named after Admiral Günther Lütjens, who went down with the battleship *Bismarck* in May 1941. All three ships underwent a substantial weapons upgrade in the early 1990s. The vessels show some differences from the Charles F. Adams class in general outline, especially in the shape of the funnels. They were expected to have a life of at least 30 years, but *Rommel* was due to be paid off in September 1999.

Country of origin:	USA/Germany
Type:	Destroyer
Launch date:	11 August 1967
Crew:	337
Displacement:	4572 tonnes (4500 tons)
Dimensions:	132.2m x 14.3m x 6.1m (437ft x 47ft x 20ft)
Endurance:	7238km (3908nm)
Main armament:	Two 127mm (5in) guns; Harpoon SSM; Standard SAM; six 324mm (12.75in) torpedo tubes
Powerplant:	Two shafts, two turbines
Performance:	32 knots

Madina class

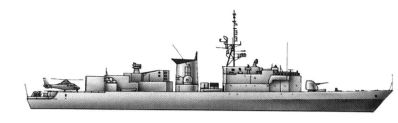

Frigates form the core of Saudi Arabia's navy, which also has some corvettes and fast attack craft armed with missiles. The four frigates of the Madina class – *Madina*, *Hofouf*, *Abha* and *Taif* – were ordered from France by Saudi Arabia in 1980 under a programme called Sawari I. The agreement specified that as well as carrying out the contruction work, France was to provide supplies and technical assistance. The vessels, all of which were delivered between 1985 and 1986, have been progressively upgraded during the 1990s. Work on *Madina* began in December 1995 and was completed in April 1997; work on *Hofouf* started in October 1996 and was completed in 1998. The other two ships were expected to be returned to service between 1999 and 2000. The vessels carry a Dauphin 2 helicopter which can provide mid-course guidance for SSMs.

Country of origin:	France/Saudi Arabia
Type:	Frigate
Launch date:	1997
Crew:	179
Displacement:	2906 tonnes (2870 tons)
Dimensions:	115m x 12.5m x 4.9m (377ft 4in x 41ft x 16ft)
Endurance:	12,867km (6947nm)
Main armament:	One 100mm (3.9in) gun; four 40mm (1.5in) AA; OTO Melara/Matra Otomat SSM; Crotale SAM; four 533mm (21in) torpedo tubes
Powerplant:	Two shafts, four diesel engines
Performance:	30 knots

Maestrale class

The first six Maestrale-class vessels were ordered in 1976 and completed in 1980. All but one (*Grecale*) were built at Rio Trigoso. The Maestrale class is essentially a stretched version of the Lupo design, with fewer weapons and a greater emphasis on anti-submarine warfare. The increase in length and beam over the earlier Lupo ships was to provide for a fixed hangar installation and a variable-depth sonar housing at the stern. The improvements resulted in better seaworthiness and habitability, plus the space required to carry and operate a second light helicopter. However, to compensate for this, the class carries four fewer SSMs, and because of the extra tonnage has suffered a speed reduction of about three knots. There are eight vessels in the class: *Maestrale*, *Grecale*, *Libeccio*, *Schirocco*, *Aliseo*, *Euro*, *Espero* and *Zeffiro*.

Country of origin:	Italy
Type:	Frigate
Launch date:	2 February 1981
Crew:	224
Displacement:	3251 tonnes (3200 tons)
Dimensions:	122.7m x 12.9m x 8.4m (402ft 7in x 42ft 4in x 27ft 7in)
Endurance:	8334km (4500nm)
Main armament:	One 127mm (5in) DP gun; two twin 40mm (1.5in) CIWS; two triple 324mm (12.75in) torpedo tubes
Powerplant:	Two shafts, two gas turbines and two diesels
Performance:	32 knots

MAS 9

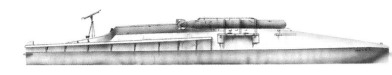

Launched in 1916, *MAS 9* was one of a group of unusual vessels designed for
rapid attack by Engineer Bisio, and built by SVAN in Venice. Total crew for each
vessel numbered eight. The small size of the boats made them very difficult targets
for the enemy, espcially when manouevring at high speed. Torpedoes were carried
one each side amidships, on the whaleback foredeck. One night in December 1917,
MAS 9, commanded by Luigi Rizzo, successfully penetrated Trieste harbour and
sank the Austrian battleship *Wien*. The latter was an elderly second-class battleship,
launched in 1895, which had been used as a gunnery training ship during the early
years of World War I. *MAS 9* was discarded in 1922. Another boat of this class, MAS
15, torpedoed and sank the Austro-Hungarian dreadnought Szent Istvan off
Premuda Island, on 10 June 1918.

Country of origin:	Italy
Type:	Torpedo boat
Launch date:	1916
Crew:	8
Displacement:	16 tonnes (16 tons)
Dimensions:	16m x 2.6m x 1.2m (52ft 6in x 8ft 8in x 4ft)
Endurance:	Not known
Main armament:	One 47mm (1.85in) gun; two 450mm (17.7in) torpedo tubes
Powerplant:	Twin screws, petrol engines
Top speed:	25.2 knots

MEKO 140A16 class

As part of the Argentine Navy's modernization plans, a contract was signed in October 1980 with the German firm, Blohm & Voss, for six MEKO 140A16 ships, to be built under licence at the AFNE shipyard in Rio Santiago, Ensenada, to a light frigate design based on the Portuguese Joao Coutinho class. Known locally as the Espora class, its lead ship, *Espora*, was commissioned into the Argentine Navy in 1983. A trio comprising the *Rosales*, *Spiro* and *Parker* followed in 1985, with a final pair, the *Robinson* and *Seaver*, in 1986 and 1987 respectively. The first three differed from the last three units in initially having only a helicopter landing platform amidships; the others had a telescopic hangar to allow the permanent carriage of a light helicopter. Although designed primarily for use on coastal operations, the class also forms a powerful offensive force.

Country of origin:	Germany/Argentina
Type:	Frigate
Launch date:	23 January 1982 (*Espora*, first unit)
Crew:	93
Displacement:	1727 tonnes (1700 tons)
Dimensions:	91.2m x 12.2m x 3.3m (299ft 2in x 40ft x 10ft 10in)
Endurance:	5559km (3000nm)
Main armament:	One 76mm (2.9in) DP and two 40mm (1.5in) AA guns; two triple 324mm (12.76in) torpedo tubes
Powerplant:	Twin shafts, two diesels
Performance:	27 knots

Minekaze

At the end of World War I, the Japanese applied the concept of first- and second-class destroyers, one being a scaled-up version of the other. Before then, the Japanese either bought or copied British ships, but with the 21-Momi class and 13 Minekaze-class second- and first-class destroyers, they produced something more original, fitting 533mm (21in) torpedo tubes (twins in the Momis and triples in the Minekazes). Both types carried their 120mm (4.72in) guns high on deck-houses and forecastle, enabling them to fight in poor conditions when the weather deck could be swept by water. By World War II standards, the vessels of the Minekaze class were both old and small, and despite their high speed, many fell victim to US submarines. Eight of them were lost in action during World War II. The *Minekaze* was sunk by the submarine USS *Pogy* in the East China Sea on 10 February 1944.

Country of origin:	Japan
Type:	Destroyer
Launch date:	8 February 1919
Crew:	148
Displacement:	1676 tonnes (1650 tons)
Dimensions:	
Endurance:	6657km (3595nm)
Main armament:	Four single 120mm (4.72in) guns; two triple 533mm (21in) torpedo tubes; up to 20 mines
Powerplant:	Two sets of geared steam turbines
Performance:	39 knots

Minsk

During World War I, the Imperial Russian Navy had conducted some outstandingly successful operations with the large, fast destroyer *Novik*. The type was later repeated, but with a reduced displacement. By the early 1930s the Soviet Navy decided that a type of super destroyer would be ideal for raiding operations in the Baltic, and *Minsk* was built between 1932 and 1934 with technical assistance from Italy and France. She saw early action, being flotilla leader of a bombardment force involved in a gun duel with Finnish shore batteries in December 1939, and in August 1941 her gunfire supported the defenders of Tallinn and covered their subsequent retreat to Kronstadt. The *Minsk* was bombed and sunk in a Stuka attack on Kronstadt harbour in September 1941, but was raised and refloated in 1942. She served as a training ship until the early 1960s.

Country of origin:	Russia
Type:	Destroyer
Launch date:	6 November 1935
Crew:	160
Displacement:	2623 tonnes (2582 tons)
Dimensions:	127.5m x 11.7m x 4m (418ft 4in x 38ft 4in x 13ft 4in)
Endurance:	4076km (2200nm)
Main armament:	Five 130mm (5.1in) and two 76mm (3in) guns
Powerplant:	Triple screws, turbines
Performance:	33 knots

Mirka class

Built between 1964 and 1965 at the Kaliningrad shipyard, the nine Mirka I class vessels were followed on the stocks during the latter half of 1965 and 1966 by nine Mirka II class units. The various vessels of the two Mirka classes served only with the Soviet Baltic and Black Sea Fleets, where their task was to search for infiltrating SSKs. The later Mirka II units had the 'Strut Curve' air search radar in place of the 'Slim Net' array of the earlier ships. Almost all units of both classes were retrofitted with dipping sonar in place of the internal depth charge rack on the port side of the stern to improve their ASW capability in their operational areas. This was particularly true in the Baltic, where oceanographic conditions make ASW operations very difficult. The Mirka class had been reduced to five units by 1990, all of which had been laid up or scrapped by 1998.

Country of origin:	Russia
Type:	Frigate
Launch date:	1964 (first unit)
Crew:	98
Displacement:	1168 tonnes (1150 tons)
Dimensions:	82.4m x 9.1m x 3m (270ft 4in x 29ft 11in x 9ft 10in)
Endurance:	6300km (3400nm)
Main armament:	Two twin 76mm (3in) guns; five or 10 533mm (21in) torpedo tubes; ASW rocket launchers
Powerplant:	Two shafts, two gas turbines and two diesels
Performance:	35 knots

Moon

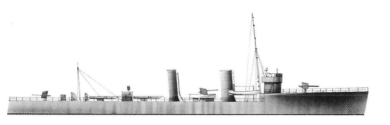

Moon was one of four special boats built by Alfred Yarrow. They formed part of the massive World War I emergency programme which was put in hand in September 1914, in which repeats of the M class were ordered in large numbers. *Moon* and her three sisters had increased length over the rest of the M class, and had raked stems and sloping sterns to improve seakeeping qualities. The central gun was on a raised platform to improve local fire control. There were also two twin mounts for 533mm (21in) torpedo tubes. Construction of the ships was subject to delay because of a shortage of zinc. *Moon* was sold for scrap in 1921. Many of these ships served with the Harwich Force, which made constant forays into the German Bight. At Jutland in May 1916, the British mustered 85 destroyers to the German 72.

Country of origin:	Britain
Type:	Destroyer
Launch date:	23 April 1915
Crew:	160
Displacement:	910 tonnes (895 tons)
Dimensions:	114m x 8m x 2.9m (375ft x 26ft 8in x 9ft 6in)
Endurance:	2594km (1400nm)
Main armament:	Three 102mm (4in) guns
Powerplant:	Twin screws, turbines
Performance:	35 knots

Mourad Rais

Although constructed in the Soviet Union at the Zelenodolsk shipyard on the Black Sea, the Koni class of frigate was intended solely for export, only one unit being retained by the Russians as a crew training ship for the naval personnel from those countries whose navies bought the vessels. Algeria purchased three, named *Mourad Rais*, *Rais Kellik* and *Rais Korfou*. The Libyan Government was also interested in purchasing a number of ex-GDR Koni-class vessels, but the sale was rejected by the German Government. The Libyan vessels underwent minor modifications between 1992 and 1994; all were still active in 1999, the *Rais Korfou* being used for training cruises. There is little doubt that, although the former Soviet Union tried hard to meet the needs of smaller nations with the Koni class of frigate, sales of the class fell a long way short of expectations.

Country of origin:	Russia/Algeria
Type:	Frigate
Launch date:	1978 (*Delfin* completed)
Crew:	130
Displacement:	1930 tonnes (1900 tons)
Dimensions:	95m x 12.8m x 4.2m (311ft 8 in x 42ft x 13ft 8in)
Endurance:	4076km (2200nm)
Main armament:	Two twin 76mm (3in) and two twin 30mm (1.1in) guns; SAMs
Powerplant:	Three shafts, two gas turbines and one diesel
Performance:	27 knots

Murasame

Launched in August 1994 and commissioned in March 1996, *Murasame* is one of a planned class of nine ships, their construction being given added priority because of the Kongo class being reduced to four vessels due to the high cost of the Aegis system installed in them. In fact, *Murasame* somewhat resembles a mini-Kongo-class vessel, with a vertical-launch missile system and a much reduced complement, despite the fact that she is intended to be an enlarged version of the Asagari class. Stealth features are evident in sloping sides and a rounded superstructure. *Murasame*'s sister ships, completed to date, are the *Harusame*, *Yuudachi* and *Kirisame*. The latter was commissioned in March 1999. The other five, as yet unnamed, were scheduled to commission between March 2000 and March 2002 greatly enhancing Japan's maritime capability.

Country of origin:	Japan
Type:	Destroyer
Launch date:	September 1994
Crew:	166
Displacement:	5182 tonnes (5100 tons)
Dimensions:	151m x 17.4m x 5.2m (495ft 5in x 57ft 1in x 17ft 1in)
Endurance:	15,195km (8200nm)
Main armament:	One 76mm (3in) gun; Harpoon SSM; Sea Sparrow SAM; six 324mm (12.75in) torpedo tubes
Powerplant:	Two shafts, four gas turbines
Performance:	30 knots

Nanuchka I class

Classed by the Russians as an MRK, or small rocket ship, the 17 units of the Nanuchka I class were built between 1969 and 1974 at Petrovsky, Leningrad with a modified variant, the Nanuchka II, following on. To western observers, the vessels of the Nanuchka class were classed as coastal missile-corvettes, although the fact that they were often seen quite far from home waters tends to put them more in the light frigate category, especially when the firepower of the class is considered. Later classes of Nanuchkas were exported to several of the Soviet Union's regular customers, including India, Libya and Algeria. The Libyan vessels have occasionally been in confrontation with US naval units in the Mediterranean. On the night of 24/25 March 1986 one, the *Ean Mara*, was sunk by US carrier aircraft; a second was severely damaged in the action.

Country of origin:	Russia
Type:	Frigate
Launch date:	1969 (first unit completed)
Crew:	70
Displacement:	914 tonnes (900 tons)
Dimensions:	59.3m x 12.6m x 2.4m (194ft 7in x 41ft 3in x 7ft 11in)
Endurance:	2779km (1500nm)
Main armament:	Two triple launchers for SS-N-9 Siren anti-ship missiles; one twin 157mm (2.24in) AA or one 76mm (3in) DP gun
Powerplant:	Three shafts, three paired diesels
Performance:	32 knots

Navigatori class

Launched between 1928 and 1930, Italy's Navigatori-class destroyers were produced at a time when high speed was an obsession with the Italians. The vessels of this class were extremely lightly built and their seakeeping left something to be desired, though it was improved later by increasing their freeboard. Eleven of the 12 boats in the class were sunk during World War II. Six of these losses were as a result of direct action by the British and another by a mine; two were sunk in action against the Germans in September 1943; one was scuttled; and the last was sunk in error by an Italian submarine. The *Leone Pancaldo* was sunk twice, the first time by aircraft from HMS *Ark Royal* in July 1940. She was raised, repaired and recommissioned, only to be sunk again (and for good) by air attack off Cape Bon in April 1943.

Country of origin:	Italy
Type:	Destroyer
Launch date:	12 August 1928 (*Nicolo Zeno*, first unit)
Crew:	225
Displacement:	2622 tonnes (2580 tons)
Dimensions:	107.75m x 10.2m x 3.5m (353ft 6in x 33ft 6in x 11ft 6in)
Endurance:	1816km (980nm)
Main armament:	Three twin 120mm (4.72in) and three single 37mm (1.4in) guns; two twin or triple 533mm (21in) torpedo tubes; up to 54 mines
Powerplant	Two sets of geared steam turbines, two shafts
Performance	38 knots

Neustrashimy

There were originally intended to be three frigates in the Neustrashimy class, but the third was launched in July 1993 with only the hull completed, and was scrapped in mid-1997 without any further work being done. *Neustrashimy* was launched in May 1988 and began her sea trials in the Baltic in December 1990, being commissioned in January 1993. The second unit, *Yaroslavl Mudry*, was commissioned in 1998 and may be offered for sale. Both ships were built at Kaliningrad. They are slightly larger than the Krivak class, and each has a helicopter, following the pattern set by Western anti-submarine frigates. The ships have the same propulsion units as the Udaloy II class. Both were assigned to the Baltic Fleet in 1999. Attempts have been made to incorporate stealth features into these vessels, though with what degree of success it is not known.

Country of origin:	Russia
Type:	Frigate
Launch date:	May 1988
Crew:	210
Displacement:	4318 tonnes (4250 tons)
Dimensions:	131.2m x 15.5m x 4.8m (430ft 5in x 50ft 10in x 15ft 9in)
Endurance:	7238km (3908nm)
Main armament:	Combined 30mm (1.1in) gun and SA-N-11 SAM system; fitted for SS-N-25 SSM; SA-N-9 SAM; six 533mm (21in) torpedo tubes; A/S mortars
Powerplant:	Two shafts, four gas turbines
Performance:	30 knots

Nibbio

L aunched in 1878, *Nibbio* was Italy's first torpedo boat. She was built by Thorneycroft, who had already constructed such small, high-speed vessels for Norway, France, Denmark, Sweden and Austria. Her engines developed 250hp, and steam was supplied by a single locomotive boiler. Two torpedoes were carried amidships, and she was also armed with a one-pounder gun. She carried a maximum of 10 crew members. *Nibbio* was commissioned in 1881, and in 1886 she was redesignated IT. She was discarded in 1904, but was later used as a steam boat for general harbour duties and was renumbered PE44. *Nibbio* was not an outstanding craft, but she provided a cadre of Italian Navy personnel with valuable experience in handling boats of her type. The first Italian-built torpedo boat was the *Clio* of 1882.

Country of origin:	Italy
Type:	Torpedo boat
Launch date:	1878
Crew:	10
Displacement:	26 tonnes (25.5 tons)
Dimensions:	24.3m x 3m x 1m (80ft x 9ft 10in x 3ft 3in)
Endurance:	Not known
Main armament:	Two 355mm (14in) torpedo tubes
Powerplant:	Single screw, triple expansion reciprocating engine
Performance:	18 knots

Niels Juel

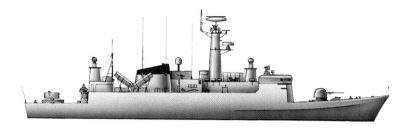

Designed in Britain by Yarrow of Glasgow and built at the Aalborg Vaerft in Denmark, the *Niels Juel* was commissioned in August 1980 and was followed by two other frigates, the *Olfert Fischer* and *Peter Tordenskiold*. The ships underwent a mid-life update between 1996 and 1999; this included the installation of a NATO Sea Sparrow vertical-launch system (VLS) and new communications equipment. The original Plessey air search radar was to be replaced by a modern TRS-3D. Other equipment includes a hull-mounted active search and attack sonar and an Ericsson combat data system; satellite communications equipment can also be fitted aft of the funnel. Like all of Denmark's ocean-going warships, *Niels Juel* is optimised for operations in Arctic waters. The ships are likely to be replaced in the twenty-first century by a new class of multi-role patrol vessel.

Country of origin:	Denmark
Type:	Frigate
Launch date:	17 February 1978
Crew:	94
Displacement:	1341 tonnes (1320 tons)
Dimensions:	84m x 10.3m x 3.1m (275ft 6in x 33ft 9in x 10ft 2in)
Endurance:	4021km (2170nm)
Main armament:	One 76mm (3in) gun; Harpoon SSM; Sea Sparrow SAM; depth charges
Powerplant:	Two shafts, one gas turbine, one diesel
Performance:	28 knots

Niteroi

Of the six ships in the Niteroi class, four (*Niteroi, Defensora, Constituicao* and *Liberal*) were built in the UK by Vosper Thorneycroft Ltd. The other two, *Independencia* and *Uniao*, were built at the Arsenal de Marinha yards in Rio de Janeiro. The ships were based on Vosper's Mk10 frigate design which, fitted with a combined diesel or gas turbine propulsion plant, is considered to be exceptionally economical in terms of manpower when compared with previous warships of this size. The class was being upgraded in the late 1990s, modifications including the replacement of Seacat with the Aspide SAM system. The vessels carry the Westland Super Lynx helicopter, which is armed with the Sea Skua ASM. All are based at Niteroi and form the Brazilian Navy's First Frigate Squadron, which is the Brazilian Navy's premier surface attack unit.

Country of origin:	Brazil
Type:	Frigate
Launch date:	8 February 1974
Crew:	217
Displacement:	3766 tonnes (3707 tons)
Dimensions:	129.2m x 13.5m x 5.5m (424ft x 44ft 2in x 18ft 2in)
Endurance:	8524km (4600nm)
Main armament:	One or two 115mm (4.5in) guns; Exocet SSM; Seacat SAM; Ikara ASW system
Powerplant:	Two shafts, two gas turbines, four diesels
Performance:	30 knots

Oliver Hazard Perry

The USS *Oliver Hazard Perry* was the first of a class of 51 general-purpose frigates designed to escort merchant convoys or amphibious squadrons. Their primary role was to provide area defence of surface forces against attacking aircraft and cruise missiles, with anti-surface warfare as a secondary role. Because of cost considerations, the first 26 ships were not retrofitted to carry two LAMPS III ASW helicopters, as originally planned, but retained the LAMPS I. LAMPS facilities include the Recovery Assistance, Security and Traversing (RAST) system which allows the launch and recovery of the Sikorsky SH-60 helicopters with the ship rolling through 28 degrees and pitching up to 5 degrees. Two ships of this class, the *Stark* and *Samuel B. Roberts*, were damaged in missile attacks while patrolling the Arabian Gulf during the Iraq–Iran war in 1987 and 1988.

Country of origin:	USA
Type:	Frigate
Launch date:	25 September 1976
Crew:	215
Displacement:	3717 tonnes (3658 tons)
Dimensions:	135.6m x 13.7m x 4.5m (445ft x 45ft x 14ft 10in)
Endurance:	10,371km (5600nm)
Main armament:	One 76mm (3in) DP gun; two triple 324mm (12.75in) torpedo tubes; Harpoon SSMs and Standard ASMs
Powerplant:	Single shaft, two gas turbines
Performance:	29 knots

Oslo

The Royal Norwegian Navy's Oslo-class frigates are modifications of the Dealey class of escort destroyers which were built in the USA in the 1950s, with a higher freeboard forward (to suit the sea conditions off Norway) and many European-built sub-systems. The five ships in the class – *Oslo*, *Bergen*, *Trondheim*, *Stavanger* and *Narvik* – were built under the 1960 five-year naval plan, with half the cost borne by the USA. The class underwent modernisation refits in the 1970s, including the fitting of Penguin Mk2 SSMs, a NATO Sea Sparrow launcher and Mk32 ASW self-defence torpedo tubes. During the height of the Cold War, the vessels of the Oslo class provided the only major ASW force in the North Norwegian Sea area. *Oslo* sank while under tow on 24 January 1994 after running aground following a complete engine failure.

Country of origin:	Norway
Type:	Frigate
Launch date:	17 January 1964
Crew:	150
Displacement:	1880 tonnes (1850 tons)
Dimensions:	96.6m x 11.2m x 4.4m (316ft 11in x 36ft 8in x 14ft 5in)
Endurance:	8338km (4500nm)
Main armament:	Two twin 76mm (3in) DP guns; two triple 324mm (12.75in) torpedo tubes; Sea Sparrow SAM; ASW rocket launchers
Powerplant:	Single shaft, geared steam turbines
Performance:	25 knots

PC Type

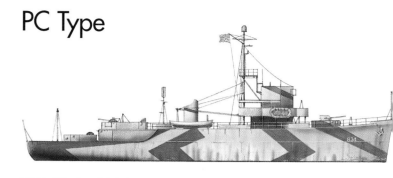

Given the immense length of the seaboards of the United States, together with major Caribbean routes and the Panama Canal, the US Navy had a big problem in protecting its coastal traffic. The vulnerability of shipping not in convoy on the eastern seaboard was ruthlessly exposed by the German U-boat campaign of 1942, but it had been anticipated, in that three prototype 53.26m (174ft 9in) Patrol Craft (PC Type) were completed before the USA's entry into the war. These were slim diesel craft which, although relatively well armed, were restricted by their size to inshore work. A massive building programme was instituted, and over 350 of these craft were built. Fifteen served with the Royal Navy as the Kil class (e.g. *Kilmarnock*). The latter participated in the destruction of the *U-731* off Tangier in May 1944 in the only U-boat sinking credited to the class.

Country of origin:	USA
Type:	Escort
Launch date:	1938 (first unit)
Crew:	100
Displacement:	864 tonnes (850 tons)
Dimensions:	56.24m x 10.05m x 2.89m (184ft 6in x 33ft x 9ft 6in)
Endurance:	6485km (3500nm)
Main armament:	One 76mm (3in) gun; three 40mm (1.5in) and four 20mm (0.7in) AA; depth charges and Hedgehog
Powerplant:	Two shafts, two diesel engines
Performance:	16 knots

Pegaso

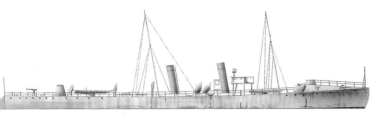

Pegaso was the lead ship of five vessels in a class that eventually increased to 27 units. Their design was very successful, proving strong and seaworthy. *Pegaso* was laid down at Pattison's yard in August 1904, launched a year later and completed in September 1905. Her engines developed 3200hp, and her range at maximum speed was nearly 646km (348nm). She was converted to oil fuel in 1908, and later served in World War I. *Pegaso* was discarded in March 1923; her name, however, was resurrected and given to an escort destroyer of the Orsa class in World War II. The latter vessel was launched in 1938 and scuttled in Pollensa Bay, Majorca, on 11 September 1943, following Italy's armistice with the Allies. The other vessels in the 1905 Pegaso class were *Perseo*, *Procione* and *Pallade*. They were classed as High Seas Torpedo Boats.

Country of origin:	Italy
Type:	Torpedo boat
Launch date:	August 1905
Crew:	50
Displacement:	210 tonnes (207 tons)
Dimensions:	50.3m x 5.3m x 1.7m (165ft 2in x 17ft 5in x 5ft 8in)
Endurance:	2224km (1200nm)
Main armament:	Two 57mm (2.25in) guns; three 450mm (17.7in) torpedo tubes
Powerplant:	Twin screws, vertical triple expansion engines
Performance:	23 knots

Pellicano

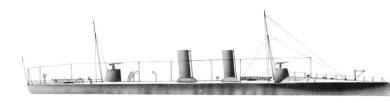

aunched in April 1899, *Pellicano* was commissioned in 1900 as a first-class torpedo boat with a design speed of 25.7 knots, but because of unreliable machinery, this speed was never achieved. Pellicano's vertical triple expansion engines were served by three Blechynden boilers, producing 2740hp. She was an excellent seaboat, however, and served as the prototype for a later group of ocean-going vessels launched between 1905 and 1906. She was discarded in 1920. *Pellicano* and others of her era laid the foundations for Italian torpedo-boat tactics, in which the Italian Navy excelled right up to World War II. Torpedo boats proved ideal vehicles for offensive operations in the Adriatic in World War I, where high speed and manoeuvrability were key factors in combat operations against the Austro-Hungarian fleet.

Country of origin:	Italy
Type:	Torpedo boat
Launch date:	April 1899
Crew:	25
Displacement:	183 tonnes (181 tons)
Dimensions:	48.7m x 5.7m x 1.5m (159ft 10in x 18ft 10in x 5ft)
Endurance:	Not known
Main armament:	Two 37mm (1.5in) guns; two 355mm (14in) torpedo tubes
Performance:	21 knots

Perth

Australia's three Perth-class guided-missile destroyers (the others are the *Hobart* and *Brisbane*) are modified vessels of the American Charles F. Adams class, all commissioned in the mid-1960s. The ships have since undergone several updates; *Perth* was first modernised in 1974 in the USA, when Standard missiles, replacement gun mountings, a new combat data system, and modern radars were fitted. *Hobart* and *Brisbane* were brought up to the same standard in 1978 and 1979 at the Garden Island Dockyard in Sydney. A further upgrade was carried out between 1987 and 1991, all ships receiving the Phalanx CIWS, new search and fire control radars, decoy and ECM equipment, and the new Mk13 missile launcher for the Harpoon SSM. The earlier Ikara ASW system was removed at the same time as these updates were completed.

Country of origin:	USA/Australia
Type:	Destroyer
Launch date:	26 September 1963
Crew:	310
Displacement:	4692 tonnes (4618 tons)
Dimensions:	134.3m x 14.3m x 6.1m (440ft 9in x 47ft 1in x 20ft 1in)
Endurance:	9650km (5210nm)
Main armament:	Two 127mm (5in) guns; Phalanx CIWS; Harpoon SSM; Standard SAM; six 324mm (12.75in) torpedo tubes
Powerplant:	Two shafts, two geared steam turbines
Performance:	30+ knots

Petya class

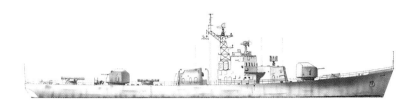

The 18 units of the Petya I class were constructed at the Kaliningrad and Komsomolsk shipyards between 1961 and 1964. From the latter year until 1969 both shipyards switched to building a total of 27 Petya II class units, which differed from their predecessors in having an extra quintuple 606mm (16in) ASW torpedo tube mounting in place of the two aft ASW rocket launchers. From 1973 onwards, eight Petya I vessels were modified to give the 'Petya I (Mod)' sub-class. The conversion involved the addition of a medium-frequency variable-depth sonar in a new raised stern deckhouse. A further three units were converted as trials vessels. During the Cold War, the Petya-class boats were often used in the intelligence-gathering role, shadowing NATO warships during exercises in northern waters, particularly off North Cape and in the north Norwegian Sea.

Country of origin:	Russia
Type:	Frigate
Launch date:	31 December 1970 (first unit completed)
Crew:	98
Displacement:	1168 tonnes (1150 tons)
Dimensions:	81.8m x 9.1m x 2.9m (268ft 5in x 29ft 11in x 9ft 5in)
Endurance:	2779km (1500nm)
Main armament:	Twin 76mm (3in) DP guns; 533mm (21in) mounting for five or 10 AS torpedoes; ASW rocker launchers
Powerplant:	Three shafts, two gas turbines, two diesels
Performance:	33 knots

Prat

The use of British warships is traditional in the Chilean Navy. The Chilean Navy's four ex-Royal Navy County-class destroyers, *Prat* (ex-*Norfolk*), *Cochrane* (ex-*Antrim*), *Latorre* (ex-*Glamorgan*) and *Blanco Encalada* (ex-*Fife)* were transferred from the UK between April 1982 and August 1987, extensive refits being carried out after transfer. All are named after senior officers, but the titles Almirante and Capitan are not used, a practice at variance with that of other Latin American navies. In 1988 *Blanco Encalada* was converted as a helicopter carrier for two Super Pumas, *Cochrane* being similarly converted in 1994. The two remaining vessels serve as flagships. All four ships are fitted with the Israeli Barak I short-range SAM system. The ships differ greatly in appearance, the helicopter carriers having a greatly enlarged flight deck continuing right aft.

Country of origin:	UK/Chile
Type:	Destroyer
Launch date:	16 November 1967
Crew:	470
Displacement:	6299 tonnes (6200 tons)
Dimensions:	158.7m x 16.5m x 6.3m (520ft 6in x 54 ft x 20ft 6in)
Endurance:	5620km (3038nm)
Main armament:	Two 115mm (4.5in) guns; Exocet SSM; Seaslug and Barak SAM; six 324mm (12.75in) torpedo tubes
Powerplant:	Two shafts, two geared steam turbines, four gas turbines
Performance:	30 knots

Rattlesnake

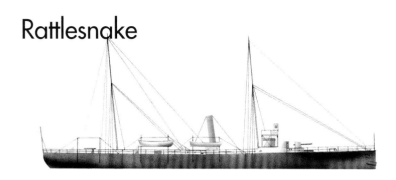

Rattlesnake was one of the world's first torpedo gunboats, and was the first to be commissioned into the Royal Navy. She was the second ship to bear the name Rattlesnake; the first was a Jason-class wooden screw corvette, launched in 1861. She was built to counteract the expanding fleets of torpedo boats then being constructed by many countries – including Russia, with whom there was a threat of war over Afghanistan – and which constituted a serious threat to capital ships. Earlier vessels built for the same purpose, such as the British 1605-tonne (1580-ton) *Scout* and the French 1300-tonne (1280-ton) *Condor*, had proved too large and unwieldy, and so it was decided to build a smaller vessel able to maintain high speed. *Rattlesnake*'s engines developed 2700hp and she had a 19mm (0.75in) thick steel protective deck. She was sold in 1910.

Country of origin:	Britain
Type:	Torpedo gunboat
Launch date:	11 September 1886
Crew:	66
Displacement:	558 tonnes (550 tons)
Dimensions:	60.9m x 7m x 3m (200ft x 23ft x 10ft 4in)
Endurance:	Not known
Main armament:	One 102mm (4in) gun; four 355mm (14in) torpedo tubes
Powerplant:	Twin screws, triple expansion engines
Performance:	19.2 knots

Riga class

Built at the Kaliningrad, Nikolayev and Komsomolsk shipyards, the 64 units – including eight for export – of the Riga class were the design successors to the six slightly older Kola class destroyers. The class proved to be an excellent coastal defence design and followed the Soviet practice in the 1950s of building flush-decked hulls with a sharply raised forecastle. The Rigas were fitted with the Haymarket search radar. Over the years, the vessels of the Riga class constituted one of the larger Soviet warship classes, and numbers were exported. Two went to Bulgaria, five to the former German Deomocratic Republic (one of which was burnt out in an accident soon after being taken over), two went to Finland, and eight to Indonesia. These units have now been scrapped. All Riga-class units still on the Russian inventory, latterly used as training vessels, are now permanently laid up.

Country of origin:	Russia
Type:	Frigate
Launch date:	30 July 1952 (*Gornostay*, first unit)
Crew:	175
Displacement:	1534 tonnes (1510 tons)
Dimensions:	91.5m x 10.1m x 3.2m (300ft 2in x 33ft 1in x 10ft 6in)
Endurance:	4632km (2500nm)
Main armament:	Three single 100mm (3.9in) DP; two twin 37mm (1.4in) or 25mm (1in) AA guns; anti-ship torpedoes; ASW rockets
Powerplant:	Two shafts, geared steam turbines
Performance:	28 knots

River

With the limitations of the Flower-class corvette readily apparent, the British Admiralty produced a design for a larger twin-screw corvette which became known as the River class (the term 'frigate' was not officially reintroduced into the Royal Navy until 1942). Overall they were about 28.3m (93ft) longer than the vessels of the later Flower class, and this made a very great difference in seakeeping, bunker capacity, installed power, and armament. Between 1941 and 1944, some 57 were launched in the UK, 70 in Canada and 11 in Australia. The River class was highly successful, but most of its survivors (seven were sunk in the war) had been scrapped by the mid-1950s. Further River-class vessels, to a slightly modified design, were built by the Americans as the PF type, 21 of which served in the Royal Navy as the Colony class.

Country of origin:	Britain
Type:	Frigate
Launch date:	20 November 1941 (HMS *Rother*, first unit)
Crew:	107
Displacement:	1392 tonnes (1370 tons)
Dimensions:	91.9m x 11.12m x 3.91m (301ft 6in x 36ft 6in x 12ft 10in)
Endurance:	12,945km (6990nm)
Main armament:	Two 102mm (4in) guns; two two-pounders; depth charges
Powerplant:	Two shafts, triple expansion steam engines
Performance	20 knots

Salisbury

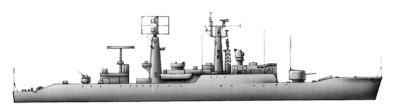

The Bangladesh Navy's sole ex-Salisbury (Type 61) -class frigate was formerly HMS *Llandaff*, completed in April 1958. The Salisbury class was designed primarily for the direction of carrier-borne and shore-based aircraft, but could also serve as a lighter type of destroyer on offensive operations. All ships of the class were named after cathedral cities. *Salisbury* underwent an extended refit in 1962, and *Llandaff* followed in 1966. Four ships of the class were completed; a fifth vessel was to have been named *Exeter*, and a sixth, to have been named *Coventry*, was originally ordered as *Panther* but was completed as the Leander-class frigate *Penelope*. In their fighter direction role, the Salisburys were integrated with the UK air defence system. In Royal Navy service, the obsolete Type 61s were replaced by the Type 21 Amazon-class general-purpose frigates.

Country of origin:	UK/Bangladesh
Type:	Frigate
Launch date:	25 June 1953
Crew:	207
Displacement:	2447 tonnes (2408 tons)
Dimensions:	103.6m x 12.2m x 4.7m (339ft 10in x 40ft x 15ft 6in)
Endurance:	12,056km (6510nm)
Main armament:	Two 115mm (4.5in) guns; two 40mm (1.5in) AA; A/S mortars
Powerplant:	Two shafts, eight diesel engines
Performance:	24 knots

Saumarez

War emergency programmes produced 112 fleet destroyers for the Royal Navy, but only through a great degree of standardisation and reduction of minimum peacetime standards. The two so-called intermediate classes, the eight-gun O and P classes, came first; they were followed by the Q class, the first in a long line of standard groups, based on the very successful J-class design. All the Q class were well received, and eight R-class destroyers were almost identical. With the S class, also of eight, came a modification to the forward lines to reduce spray wetness, a longstanding cause for complaint. They were the first to have 40mm(1.5in) AA guns and a full complement of 20mm (0.7in) Oerlikons. HMS *Saumarez* was launched in November 1942; all the ships in her class survived the war. Damaged by a mine in the Corfu Channel in 1946, *Saumarez* was scrapped in 1950.

Country of origin:	Britain
Type:	Destroyer
Launch date:	20 November 1942
Crew:	225
Displacement:	1758 tonnes (1730 tons)
Dimensions:	109.19m x 10.87m x 2.9m (358ft 3in x 35ft 7in x 9ft 6in)
Endurance:	8690km (4692nm)
Main armament:	Four 119mm (4.7in) guns; two 40mm (0.7in) AA; eight or 12 20mm (0.7in) AA; eight 533mm (21in) torpedo tubes
Powerplant:	Two-shaft geared turbines
Performance:	36 knots

Sokol

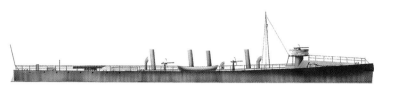

Designed by Yarrow, *Sokol* (Falcon) was Russia's first destroyer, laid down in 1894 and completed in 1895. Her 12-pounder gun was mounted on top of the conning tower, at the end of the turtleback foredeck. Two of the three-pounder guns were placed just aft of the first funnel, with the third gun mounted between the two aft funnels. Her armament was modified during her career, another 12-pounder being added, plus six torpedo tubes. To save weight, nickel steel was used in the construction of the hull and there was some use of aluminium in her fittings. Renamed *Prytki*, she served as a minesweeper in World War I and was scrapped in 1922. Although the Imperial Russian Navy had some excellent destroyers at its disposal during this period, its battle tactics left much to be desired and its crews were poorly trained.

Country of origin:	Russia
Type:	Destroyer
Launch date:	1895
Crew:	54
Displacement:	224 tonnes (220 tons)
Dimensions:	57.9m x 5.6m x 2.2m (190ft x 18ft 6in x 7ft 6in)
Endurance:	1482km (800nm)
Main armament:	Three 3-pounder and one 12-pounder guns; two 380mm (15in) torpedo tubes
Powerplant:	Twin screws, vertical triple expansion engines
Performance:	29 knots

Soldati class

The extensive Soldati-class destroyers, all of which were named after types of soldier (e.g. *Lanciere* after lancer) was the ultimate development of a sequence that began with the four-ship Dardo class of 1930–32. They used deck space very effectively by successfully trunking all boiler uptakes into one substantial funnel casing. Four 120mm (4.72in) guns were carried, but unlike the disposition on British destroyers, they were sited in two twin mountings, one on the forecastle deck and one on the same level atop a house set well aft, saving both deck space and topweight. Slightly smaller than their British counterparts, the Italian ships were more highly powered, being deficient only in torpedoes, weapons the Italians never valued very highly. In fact, their destroyers were used more for minelaying than direct offensive action.

Country of origin:	Italy
Type:	Destroyer
Launch date:	8 August 1937 (*Camicia Nera*, first unit)
Crew:	219
Displacement:	2499 tonnes (2460 tons)
Dimensions:	106.75m x 10.15m x 3.6m (350ft 2in x 33ft 4in x 11ft 10in)
Endurance:	7412km (4000nm)
Main armament:	Four or five 120mm (4.72in) and one 37mm (1.4in) AA guns; two triple 533mm (21in) torpedo tubes; up to 48 mines
Powerplant:	Twin screws, two sets of geared steam turbines
Performance:	39 knots

SP1 or Z40 class

Before World War II, the German Navy was concerned by the potential firepower of France's large destroyers and, perceiving a requirement for ships of their own capable of operating independently, initiated the Spähkreuzer (scout cruiser) or 'SP' concept. At the beginning of World War II, however, the planned number of destroyers was cut back in view of other priorities. Of the five stricken from the Type 36A'programme, three – *Z40* to *Z42* – were reinstated early in 1941 as an enlarged trio, which were to be followed by another with an unspecified hull number. The design passed through several phases before losing favour and being recast into the so-called 'Zerstörer 1941', construction of which was suspended in 1942. The incomplete hulls were broken up at the Germaniawerft, Kiel, in 1943. There is no doubt that these vessels would have been very effective in combat.

Country of origin:	Germany
Type:	Destroyer
Launch date:	not launched
Crew:	321
Displacement:	4613 tonnes (4540 tons)
Dimensions:	152m x 14.6m x 4.6m (498ft 8in x 47ft 11in x 15ft 1in)
Endurance:	22,250km (12,014nm)
Main armament:	Three twin 150mm (5.9in); one twin 88mm (3.46in) DP guns; two quintuple 533mm (21in) torpedo tubes; up to 140 mines
Powerplant:	Three shafts, two sets of geared steam turbines, one diesel
Performance:	36 knots on steam power

Spica

Like its German counterpart, the Italian Navy favoured the construction of small destroyer-type escorts, usually referred to as 'torpedo boats'. Though a long series of related classes had been completed by the mid-1920s, the type had lapsed for a decade before being resumed with the 32-strong Spica class, laid down between 1934 and 1937. The design was influenced by that of the Maestrale class destroyers then completing but, although superficially similar in overall profile, their single funnel lacked the massive trunking of that of the larger ships, serving as it did only one boiler room. Under the wartime construction programme a group of 42 improved Spica vessels was planned; known as the Ariete class, only 16 were laid down. Of the 32 Spica vessels, 23 became war casualties and two were sold to Sweden.

Country of origin:	Italy
Type:	Destroyer escort
Launch date:	11 March 1934
Crew:	116
Displacement:	1036 tonnes (1020 tons)
Dimensions:	83.5m x 8.1m x 2.55m (273ft 11in x 26ft 6in x 8ft 4 in)
Endurance:	6670km (3600nm)
Main armament:	Three 100mm (3.9in) guns; four 450mm (17.7in) torpedo tubes
Powerplant:	Two shafts, geared steam turbines
Performance:	34 knots

Spruance

Built as replacements for the numerous Gearing-class destroyers, the 31 ships of the Spruance class are arguably the most capable anti-submarine warfare vessels ever built. Constructed by the modular assembly technique, whereby large sections of the hull are built in various parts of the shipyard and then welded together on the slipway, these were the first large US warships to employ all gas turbine propulsion. The successful hull design of the Spruance-class destroyers was used, with modifications, on two other classes of US warship, and has reduced rolling and pitching tendencies, thus providing a better weapons platform. All vessels in the Spruance class have undergone major weapons changes over the years. At least nine Spruance-class warships supported the various Battle Groups operating in and around the Gulf in the war of 1991.

Country of origin:	USA
Type:	Torpedo boat
Launch date:	10 November 1973
Crew:	15
Displacement:	31 tonnes (31 tons)
Dimensions:	29m x 3.5m x 0.9m (94ft x 11ft 6in x 3ft)
Endurance:	Not known
Main armament:	None when first completed
Powerplant:	Single screw, vertical compound engine
Performance:	18.2 knots

Stiletto

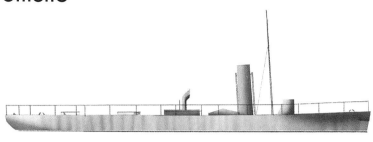

In 1881 the US Advisory Board recommended the construction of a number of torpedo boats of the Herreshoff type for harbour and inshore defence work. However, nothing was done until 1888 when the fast, wooden-hulled yacht *Stiletto* was purchased from the Herreshoff company for experimental trials. Originally she had been laid down as a private speculation at Herreshoff's yard, Bristol, Rhode Island, and had been commissioned in 1887. In 1898 *Stiletto* was given two Howell torpedo tubes, and for the next few years she was engaged in various tactical trials with new types of torpedo. Oil fuel trials in 1897 were unsatisfactory. She was removed from the US Navy List in early 1911, and was sold in July of the same year. There is no doubt that Stiletto played a considerable part in developing valuable tactical procedures for the US Navy.

Country of origin:	USA
Type:	Torpedo boat
Launch date:	1886
Crew:	15
Displacement:	31 tonnes (31 tons)
Dimensions:	29m x 3.5m x 0.9m (95ft x 11ft 6in x 3ft)
Endurance:	Not known
Main armament:	None when first completed
Powerplant:	Single screw, vertical compound engine
Performance:	18.2 knots

Swift

HMS *Swift* was the world's first purpose-built flotilla leader. The design, however, was very ambitious, and the vessel failed to make the contract speed of 36 knots. After many changes to the propeller, and with the funnels heightened, she finally made just over 35 knots, and was eventually accepted into the Royal Navy in 1910, after two years of trials. On 15 October 1914 she had a lucky escape when she was attacked by the German submarine *U9*, which had just sunk the destroyer HMS *Hawke* in the North Sea. Despite being narrowly missed by the submarine's torpedoes, *Swift*'s captain stayed in the area and picked up one officer and 20 men from the *Hawke*. *Swift* later joined the Dover patrol, and on 21 April 1917, she sank the German *TBD G42*, which was part of a force attempting to raid Dover. *Swift* was broken up in 1921.

Country of origin:	Britain
Type:	Flotilla Leader
Launch date:	7 December 1907
Crew:	160
Displacement:	2428 tonnes (2390 tons)
Dimensions:	107.8m x 10.4m x 3.2m (353ft 8in x 34ft 2in x 10ft 6in)
Endurance:	4632km (2500nm)
Main armament:	Four 102mm (4in) guns; two 457mm (18in) torpedo tubes
Powerplant:	Quadruple screws, turbines
Performance:	35 knots

Tachikaze

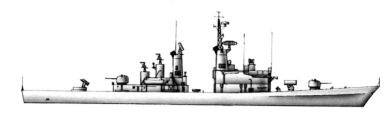

During the early 1970s the Japanese Maritime Self-Defence Force needed to improve its medium-range area-defence SAM capabilities, and thus laid down three Tachikaze-class ships at three-yearly intervals from 1973. The vessels are the *Tachikaze*, *Asakaze* and *Swakaze*, which were commissioned in 1976, 1979, and 1982 respectively. They each carry a single-rail Mk13 launcher for the Standard SM-1MR missile. No helicopter facilities were provided, and ASW armament was confined to ASROC missiles and Mk46 self-defence torpedoes. In order to save on production costs, the class adopted the propulsion plant and machinery of the Haruna class of helicopter-carrying ASW destroyers. In 1999, *Tachikaze* was the flagship of the JMSDF's Escort Force whose vessels provide an important component of the JMSDF's air defence capability.

Country of origin:	Japan
Type:	Destroyer
Launch date:	12 December 1974
Crew:	250
Displacement:	3912 tonnes (3850 tons)
Dimensions:	142m x 14.3m x 4.6m (459ft 4in x 47ft x 15ft 1in)
Endurance:	9265km (5000nm)
Main armament:	Two 127mm (5in) guns; Harpoon SSM; Standard SAM; ASROC; six 324mm (12.75in) torpedo tubes
Powerplant:	Two shafts, two geared steam turbines
Performance:	32 knots

Thetis

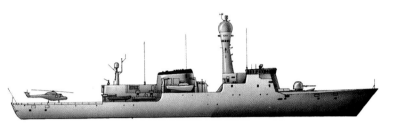

The four frigates of the Thetis class (*Thetis, Triton, Vaedderen, Hvidbjornen*) were all commissioned between 1991 and 1992. Their primary role is fishery protection; *Thetis* is employed for several months every year in carrying out oceanographic and seismological surveys in the Greenland area, a very vital task, as the region is constantly threatened by volcanic activity. The hull is strengthened to enable the vessels to penetrate 1m (3ft 4in-) -thick ice, and efforts have been made to incorporate stealth technology by installing anchor equipment, bollards and winches below the upper deck. The flight deck has been strengthened to permit the operation of Sea King or Merlin helicopters. A rigid inflatable boarding craft is installed alongside the helicopter hangar. There are plans for the installation of a new air search radar and surface-to-air missiles of an unspecified type.

Country of origin:	Denmark
Type:	Frigate
Launch date:	14 July 1989
Crew:	60
Displacement:	3556 tonnes (3500 tons)
Dimensions:	112.5m x 14.4m x 6m (369ft 1in x 47ft 2in x 19ft 8in)
Endurance:	13,672km (7378nm)
Main armament:	One 76mm (3in) gun; one 20mm (0.7in) gun; depth charges
Powerplant:	Single shaft, three diesel engines
Performance:	20.8 knots

Tribal class

Among the finest destroyers ever built for the Royal Navy, the 16 Tribal-class vessels nevertheless seem to have been produced to counter to those being built by potential enemies, rather than to fill any clearly-identifiable role within the fleet. They were regarded as gun-armed super-destroyers, and there was much disagreement over their correct classification. By any standards, they were magnificent-looking ships, their nicely balanced profile in harmony with the high-freeboard hull that was introduced to improve their fighting qualities in poor weather. The class was launched in 1937, but only four of the 16 were still afloat at the end of 1942. All saw a great deal of action, and one, HMS *Cossack*, became famous for rescuing British merchant seamen from the supply ship *Altmark* inside Norwegian territorial waters.

Country of origin:	Britain
Type:	Destroyer
Launch date:	8 June 1937 (HMS *Afridi*. first unit)
Crew:	190
Displacement:	2007 tonnes (1975 tons)
Dimensions:	115.1m x 11.13m x 2.74m (377ft 6in x 36ft 4in x 9ft)
Endurance:	10,523km (5682nm)
Main armament:	Four twin 119mm (4.7in) guns; one quadruple 533mm (21in) torpedo tube mounting
Powerplant:	Two sets of geared steam turbines
Performance:	36 knots

Tromp

The *Tromp* and her sister ship *Jacob van Heemskerck* were interesting in being more 'pocket cruisers' than destroyers. They demonstrated how, at the top of the size scale, the distinction between the two could be blurred. The pair had true destroyer ancestry, however, being classed as leaders. Their design was enlarged, and welding and aluminium were extensively used in order to save weight. An interesting reflection on *Tromp*'s use in the vast Dutch East Indies was the incorporation of a Fokker seaplane. The *Tromp* was completed in August 1938 and deployed to the Far East at the outbreak of war, being extensively damaged during the Japanese invasion of Bali. She survived the war, and took part in the reoccupation of the East Indies in September 1945. The *Heemskerck* served alongside British naval forces in the Indian Ocean and Mediterranean.

Country of origin:	Netherlands
Type:	Destroyer
Launch date:	24 May 1937
Crew:	Not known
Displacement:	4979 tonnes (4900 tons)
Dimensions:	131.9m x 12.41m x 5.41m (432ft 9in x 40ft 9in x 17ft 9in)
Endurance:	Not known
Main armament:	Three twin 150mm (5.9in) and four single 75mm (2.95in) guns.
Powerplant:	Twin shafts, two sets of geared steam turbines
Performance:	32.5 knots

Turbine

Dating from between 1927 and 1928, the eight Turbine-class destroyers were nearly identical with the quartet of Sauro-class boats that preceded them. The major difference was an increase in length of 3m (9.84ft) in the Turbine-class vessels to accommodate more powerful machinery. A feature of both types was a massive armoured 'pillbox' of a conning tower that topped off the enclosed bridge. The four Sauro-class ships were destroyed as part of the hopelessly isolated Red Sea Squadron, and no less than six of the Turbine class were sunk in 1940. The first casualty was the *Espero*, sunk by the Australian cruiser HMAS *Sydney* on 28 June 1940. *Turbine* herself was taken over by the Germans and was destroyed by American aircraft off Salamis in 1944. She was probably the fastest of the class, reaching 39 knots during her trials.

Country of origin:	Italy
Type:	Destroyer
Launch date:	21 April 1927
Crew:	180
Displacement:	1727 tonnes (1700 tons)
Dimensions:	92.65m x 9.2m x 2.9m (304ft 2in x 30ft 2in x 9ft 6in)
Endurance:	3890km (2100nm)
Main armament:	Two twin 120mm (4.7in) guns; six 533mm (21in) torpedo tubes
Powerplant:	Two sets of geared steam turbines
Performance:	36 knots

Type 36A

The Type 36A destroyers were war-built and launched between 1940 and 1942. The initial order for the Type 36As comprised *Z23* to *Z30*; seven more, *Z31* to *Z34* and *Z37* to *Z39* (to a slightly modified design) were later added. These ships, though unnamed, were popularly known as the Narvik class, and spent most of their careers operating in Arctic waters in support of the German battle squadrons stationed in the harbours of northern Norway. Perhaps surprisingly, only six of the 15 Type 36As were lost during the war. Two of the survivors gave the French Navy over a decade of post-war service while another, the *Z38*, was commissioned into the Royal Navy as HMS *Nonsuch* and used for a variety of special trials. *Z37* had a very active war, finally being scuttled at Bordeaux in August 1944 to avoid capture by the advancing Allies.

Country of origin:	Germany
Type:	Destroyer
Launch date:	14 December 1939 (*Z23*, first unit)
Crew:	321
Displacement:	3658 tonnes (3600 tons)
Dimensions:	127m x 12m x 3.9m (416ft 7in x 39ft 5in x 12ft 9in)
Endurance:	10,935km (5904nm)
Main armament:	Three single and one twin 150mm (5.9in) guns; two quadruple 533mm (21in) torpedo tube mountings; up to 60 mines
Powerplant:	Twin shafts, two sets of geared steam turbines
Performance:	36 knots

Type 82 and Type 42

Used during the Falklands War, the Type 82-class destroyer HMS *Bristol* was originally to have been the lead ship of four vessels designed to act as area defence escorts for the new CVA-01-class of British aircraft carriers. These and the other three Type 82s were cancelled. With the cancellation of the planned aircraft carriers in the mid-1960s, a Naval Staff Requirement was issued for a small fleet escort to provide area defence. This resulted in the Type 42-class design, which suffered considerably during gestation from constraints placed on the dimensions as a result of Treasury cost-cutting. The ships lacked any close-range air defence system, had reduced endurance, and a short forecastle which resulted in a very wet forward section. The main armament included the Sea Dart SAM system, which proved to be a very effective area defence in the Falklands and the Gulf.

(Specification referes to Type 42)	
Country of origin:	Britain
Type:	Destroyer
Launch date:	30 June 1969
Crew:	300–312
Displacement:	4851 tonnes (4775 tons)
Dimensions:	141m x 14.9m x 508m (463ft x 48ft x 19ft)
Endurance:	5188km (2800nm)
Main armament:	One 114mm (4.5in) gun; helicopter-launched Mk44 torpedoes; two triple mounts for Mk46 AS torpedoes; one Sea Dart SAM launcher
Powerplant:	Twin screw, gas turbines
Performance:	30 knots

Type F2000

Although optimised for anti-submarine warfare in the world's leading navies, frigates tend to be used as general purpose 'workhorse' vessels in smaller navies. Only those that serve wealthier countries have the benefit of custom-built ships. France has proved extremely adept at exporting naval hardware to Middle East countries. A good example of this is Saudi Arabia, which purchased Type F2000 class frigates from France in the 1980s. In terms of capability and equipment, these vessels, at the time of their delivery, could out-perform many of the frigates in service with NATO and the Warsaw Pact, with particular regard to their state-of-the-art electronic equipment. The weapon systems are predominantly French in origin, although the SSMs are the Franco-Italian Otomat rather than the Exocet. A Dauphin helicopter is carried for ASW work.

Country of origin:	France/Saudi Arabia
Type:	Frigate
Launch date:	23 April 1983
Crew:	179
Displacement:	2652 tonnes (2610 tons)
Dimensions:	115m x 12.5m x 4.7m (377ft 4in x 41ft x 15ft 5in)
Endurance:	9265km (5000nm)
Main armament:	One 100mm (3.9in) DP and two 40mm (1.5in) AA guns; Otomat SSMs; Crotale SAMs; four 533mm (21in) and two 324mm (12.75in) torpedo tubes
Powerplant:	Twin shafts, four diesel engines
Performance:	30 knots

Udaloy

The Udaloy class of large anti-submarine-warfare destroyers was originally designated BalCom 3 (Baltic Combatant No 3) by NATO. The original seven ships, all operational by 1987, were *Udaloy*, *Vitse Admiral Kulakov*, *Marshal Vasilievsky*, *Admiral Zakorov*, *Admiral Spiridinov*, *Admiral Tributs* and *Marshal Shaposhnikov*. *Udaloy* herself achieved Initial Operational Capability (IOC) in 1981. The vessels of the Udaloy class are similar to the US Spruance-class destroyers, even to the use of gas turbine propulsion. Each Udaloy can carry two Ka-27 Helix helicopters, and they were the first Russian destroyers to have this capability. All Udaloy units were built at either the Yantar shipyard in Kaliningrad or the Zhdanov shipyard in Leningrad (St Petersburg). The vessels are reported to be extremely capable in their designed role.

Country of origin:	Russia
Type:	Destroyer
Launch date:	5 February 1980
Crew:	300
Displacement:	8332 tonnes (8200 tons)
Dimensions:	162m x 19.3m x 6.2m (531ft 6in x 63ft 4in x 20ft 4in)
Endurance:	23,162km (12,500nm)
Main armament:	Two 100mm (3.9in) guns; SS-N-14 ASW missiles; SA-N-9 SAMs; eight 533mm (21in) torpedo tubes
Powerplant:	Two shafts, four gas turbines
Performance:	34 knots

Ugolini Vivaldi

The *Ugolini Vivaldi* was one of a group of powerful destroyers authorised in 1926 and laid down between 1927 and 1928. Slightly smaller than their French counterparts, the Chacal class, the Italian vessels carried the same armament and were several knots faster. Some vessels in the class achieved considerable speeds; *Alvise da Mosto*, for example, developed 70,000hp and reached 45 knots. *Ugolini Vivaldi* served throughout the war until the Italian armistice of September 1943, when she set out from Castellamare with the destroyer *Da Noli* to surrender. As the two vessels passed through the Straits of Bonifacio, they came under fire from German shore batteries. *Da Noli* was sunk by mines and *Ugolini Vivaldi*, heavily damaged by shellfire, sank a few hours later after being targeted by German air attack.

Country of origin:	Italy
Type:	Destroyer
Launch date:	9 January 1929
Crew:	225
Displacement:	2621 tonnes (2580 tons)
Dimensions:	107.3m x 10.2m x 3.4m (352ft x 33ft 6in x 11ft 2in)
Endurance:	6485km (3500nm)
Main armament:	Six 120mm (4.7in) guns
Powerplant:	Twin screws, turbines
Performance:	38 knots

Ulsan

The nine Ulsan-class frigates of the Republic of Korea Navy were commissioned between 1981 and 1993, the last being the *Chung Ju*. Together with the *Che Ju*, this vessel conducted the South Korean Navy's first ever deployment to European waters during a four-month tour from September 1991 to January 1992. The last four vessels of the class feature a built-up gun platform aft and have a different combination of search, target indication and navigation radars from the others. Three of the class have a shore datalink and act as local area command ships to control attack craft engaged in coastal protection duties. The last five vessels are equipped with a Ferranti combat data system; others have been fitted with the Litton Systems Link 11. These warships were monitoring North Korean naval movements as tension increased toward the end of the 1990s.

Country of origin:	Republic of Korea
Type:	Frigate
Launch date:	8 April 1980
Crew:	150
Displacement:	2215 tonnes (2180 tons)
Dimensions:	102m x 11.5m x 3.5m (334ft 7in x 37ft 8in x 11ft 6in)
Endurance:	6434km (3474nm)
Main armament:	Two 76mm (3in) guns; Harpoon SSM; six 324mm (12.75in) torpedo tubes; depth charges
Powerplant:	Two shafts, two gas turbines, two diesels
Performance:	34 knots

Uragan

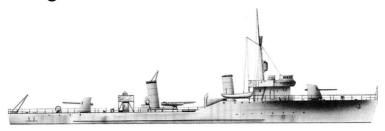

U*ragan* (Hurricane) was laid down in 1927, the lead ship in the Soviet Navy's first new major construction programme. Eighteen ships were ordered but only 12 were laid down, with the remaining six being held over for five years. Their engines developed 6300hp, and design speed, which was never attained, was 29 knots. Additional anti-aircraft armament was added before World War II, and complement was increased from 70 to 108 to service and man the extra weaponry. All ships of the class served during the war, mainly in the Baltic and Black sea theatres, where they were used as troop and supply transports. Both the Black Sea and the Baltic saw bitter naval skirmishing during the war. Many survived the conflict, including *Uragan*; she served as a training ship for many years after the war, being discarded in 1959.

Country of origin:	Russia
Type:	Torpedo boat
Launch date:	1929
Crew:	70
Displacement:	629 tonnes 619 tons
Dimensions:	71.5m x 7.4m x 2.6m (234ft 7in x 24ft 9in x 8ft 6in)
Endurance:	1524km (1500nm)
Main armament:	Three 102mm (4in) guns
Powerplant:	Twin screws, turbines
Performance:	24 knots

Van Speijk

aid down in June 1964, the Van Speijk was one of five frigates built for the Royal Netherlands Navy in the mid-1960s, the others being the *Tjerk Hiddes, Van Galen, Van Nes, Evertsen* and *Isaac Sweers*. Although in general the ships were based on the design of the British Improved Type 12 Leander class, a number of modifications were carried out in order to meet the requirements of the Netherlands Naval Staff, and equipment of Dutch manufacture was installed wherever possible. This resulted in a number of changes in the ships' superstructure when compared with the Leanders. To avoid delaying their entry into service, in some cases the ships were fitted with equipment that was already available but rather less than modern, being retrofitted with new gear at a later date. The ships replaced the frigates of the Van Amstel class (former US DEs).

Country of origin:	Netherlands
Type:	Frigate
Launch date:	5 March 1965
Crew:	251
Displacement:	2896 tonnes (2850 tons)
Dimensions:	113.46m x 12.5m x 5.5m (372ft x 41ft x 18ft)
Endurance:	8042km (4340nm)
Main armament:	Two 114mm (4.5in) guns; Seacat SAMs; Limbo AS mortar
Powerplant:	Twin screws, geared turbines
Performance:	28.5 knots

Viborg

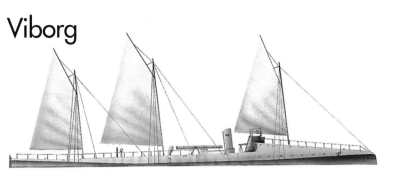

Viborg was the largest torpedo boat of her period. She was built at Thompson's Yard, Clydebank, Scotland, the company being specialists in the construction of this type of vessel. Two 37mm (1.5in) revolving Hotchkiss cannon were placed forward, abreast of the funnels. The third torpedo tube was on a trainable mount abaft the twin funnels, which were mounted side by side. The forward part of the boat's turtle deck was thickly plated in front of the conning tower. After *Viborg*, which was discarded in 1910, the Imperial Russian Navy turned increasingly to German and French shipyards for its gunboats; the next two classes, Abo and Yalta (nine boats in all) were built at the German yard of Schichau, while the following Izmail class was built by Normand. After the revolution, the Russians sought help from the Italians.

Country of origin:	Russia
Type:	Torpedo boat
Launch date:	1886
Crew:	21
Displacement:	169 tonnes (166 tons)
Dimensions:	43.4m x 5m x 2m (142ft 6in x 17ft x 7ft)
Endurance:	Not known
Main armament:	Three 381mm (15in) torpedo tubes
Powerplant:	Twin screws, vertical compound engines
Performance:	20 knots

Victoria

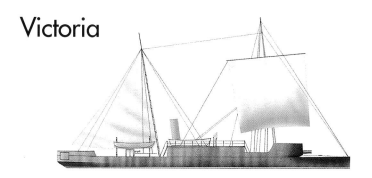

During the 1880s, Britain's Australian colony began to build up a sizeable navy for local defence. As Australia had no suitable construction facilities, the new additions were built in Britain. *Victoria* was a steel-hulled vessel armed with a single 254mm (10in) gun mounted forward behind a raised bulwark. The entire vessel had to be turned in order to train the gun on its target. Engines developed 800hp and coal supply was 91 tonnes (90 tons). Although relatively small, vessels such as *Victoria* proved a useful deterrent against raiding cruisers, which could not afford to run the risk of being damaged so far from their home ports, and whose activities were hampered by a lack of coaling facilities. Setting these up was a major drain on the resources of the European naval powers. *Victoria* was sold in 1896.

Country of origin:	Australia
Type:	Gunboat
Launch date:	1884
Crew:	20
Displacement:	538 tonnes (530 tons)
Dimensions:	42.6m x 8.2m x 3.3m (140ft x 27ft x 11ft)
Endurance:	Not known
Main armament:	One 254mm (10in) gun
Powerplant:	Twin screws, compound engines
Performance:	12 knots

Vincenzo Gioberti

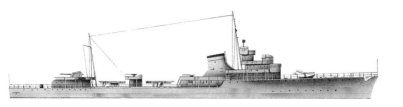

Launched in September 1936, *Vincenzo Gioberti* was one unit in a class of four vessels that were repeats of the Maestrale class, but which had increased power. The 120mm (4.7in) guns were in twin mounts, one forward and one aft on the raised superstructure. Six 533mm (21in) torpedo tubes were mounted on triple carriages down the centreline. The class also had eight 13.2mm (5.2in) weapons, later replaced by 20mm (0.8in) anti-aircraft guns. *Vincenzo Gioberti* was laid down by Odero Terni-Orlando of Livorno (Leghorn) in January 1936, and was completed in October 1937. She was torpedoed and sunk by the British submarine *Simoon* on 9 August 1943. The other vessels in the class were the *Vittorio Alfieri*, *Giosue Carducci* and *Alfredo Oriani*; the latter served in the French Navy after the war as the *d'Estaing*, and was retired in 1954.

Country of origin:	Italy
Type:	Destroyer
Launch date:	19 September 1936
Crew:	207
Displacement:	2326 tonnes (2290 tons)
Dimensions:	106.7m x 10m x 3.4m (350ft x 33ft 4in x 11ft 3in)
Endurance:	4074km (2200nm)
Main armament:	Four 120mm (4.7in) guns; six 533mm (21in) torpedo tubes
Powerplant:	Twin-shaft geared turbines
Performance:	39 knots

Vincenzo Giordano Orsini

Vincenzo Giordano Orsini was one of a quartet of fast destroyers of the Sirtori class, which were improved versions of the Pilo class. A higher-calibre gun armament was now carried, plus twin torpedo mountings. The engines developed 15,000hp, and endurance at 14 knots was 3800km (2051nm) or 760km (410nm) at 29 knots. All vessels in the class were reclassified as torpedo boats in 1929. On 8 April 1941 *Orsini* was scuttled at Massawa, Eritrea, together with other torpedo boats and many merchant vessels, shortly before British forces entered the port. Another vessel in the class, *Giovanni Acerbi*, was destroyed by RAF bombing at Massawa on 4 April 1941. Of the two remaining vessels, *Giuseppe Sirtori* was damaged by German bombs and scuttled in September 1943, while *Francesco Stocco* was sunk by German bombs at the same time.

Country of origin:	Italy
Type:	Destroyer
Launch date:	23 April 1917
Crew:	98
Displacement:	864 tonnes (850 tons)
Dimensions:	73.5m x 7.3m x 2.8m (241ft x 24ft x 9ft)
Endurance:	3800km (20451nm)
Main armament:	Six 102mm (4in) guns; four 500mm (17.7in) torpedo tubes
Powerplant:	Twin screws, turbines
Performance:	33.6 knots

Viper

Launched in September 1899, *Viper* was the world's first turbine driven warship. The principle of the turbine had been known for centuries, but it was not until the 1880s that Charles Parsons succeeded in making practical use of a steam turbine. In fact, he proved the concept in dramatic style by sailing his steam turbine-powered prototype, *Turbinia*, at full speed between the rows of warships anchored for Queen Victoria's Diamond Naval Review at Spithead in 1897. None of the picket boats or duty torpedo boats that set off in pursuit were able to catch her. *Viper* had eight screws on four shafts, and on a three-hour trial she developed 1041hp and achieved 33.9 knots. She had not been in service long when she ran aground in a thick mist off the Channel Islands in August 1901. A similar vessel, *Cobra*, built by Armstrong, was also lost in 1901.

Country of origin:	Britain
Type:	Destroyer
Launch date:	6 September 1899
Crew:	65
Displacement:	350 tonnes (344 tons)
Dimensions:	64m x 6.4m x 3.8m (210ft 3in x 21ft x 12ft 6in)
Endurance:	Not known
Main armament:	One 12-pounder gun; two 457mm (18in) torpedo tubes
Powerplant:	Eight screws, turbines
Performance:	37 knots

Vulcan

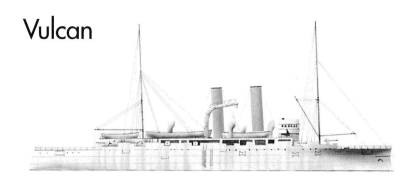

Vulcan was the world's first purpose-built torpedo depot ship. She was designed to accompany the main fleet and launch her squadron of six second-class torpedo boats at the first suitable opportunity. Her boats were normally stowed on cross-trees on the upper deck, aft of the two funnels. They were launched and retrieved by two large goose-necked cranes in the centre of the hull. She could also act as a depot and resupply ship to other torpedo boats as the situation required. She had a full-length armoured deck, 64mm (2.5in) thick on the flat, and 128mm (5in) thick on the slopes and engine hatches. Her engines developed 12,000hp from four double-ended boilers, and a further boiler provided steam to power machinery in the vessel's repair shop. *Vulcan* became a training hulk, renamed *Defiance III*, in 1931, and was eventually broken up in 1955.

Country of origin:	Britain
Type:	Torpedo Depot Ship
Launch date:	13 June 1889
Crew:	432
Displacement:	6705 tonnes (6000 tons)
Dimensions:	113.6m x 17.6m x 6.7m (373ft x 58ft x 22ft)
Endurance:	Not known
Main armament:	Eight 120mm (4.7in) guns
Powerplant:	Twin screws, triple expansion engines
Performance:	20 knots

Walker

Instantly recognisable through their two thick and thin funnels, the V-class and W class-destroyers served the Royal Navy well for over a century. Stemming from five new half-leaders ordered in 1916 to counter rumoured German construction, the class introduced superfiring guns both forward and aft, and featured extra length and freeboard for improved seaworthiness. Once proved, the design was extended by 25 V class and then 25 W class. Most were cancelled with the Armistice, but the survivors formed the backbone of the fleet destroyer strength between the wars, and entered their second war in 1939. HMS *Walker* was one of the most successful of all U-boat hunters. She sank the *U99* (Lt Cdr Kretschmer) on 17 March 1941 and participated in the destruction of *U100* (Lt Cdr Schepke), after its ramming by HMS *Vanoc*. *Walker* was scrapped at Troon, Scotland, in March 1946.

Country of origin:	Britain
Type:	Destroyer
Launch date:	29 November 1917
Crew:	134
Displacement:	1529 tonnes (1505 tons)
Dimensions:	95.1m x 8.99m x 3.28m (312ft x 29ft 6in x 10ft 9in)
Endurance:	6426km (3470nm)
Main armament:	Four 119mm (4.7in) and one 76mm (3in) guns; six 533mm (21in) torpedo tubes
Powerplant:	Two shafts, two sets of geared steam turbines
Performance:	34 knots

Weapon class

Hard wartime experience had exposed the limitations of fleet destroyers as anti-submarine platforms. Nevertheless, the fleet still required a fast anti-submarine screen of ships that could not only protect themselves but also contribute to the AA defences of a task group, allowing the carrier's aircraft complement to be devoted to offensive, rather than defensive operations. It was for these reasons that the Weapon-class destroyers came into being. The choice of the high-angle 102mm (4in) gun for the main battery was logical, its 14kg (31lb) projectile enabling fast hand-working even up to the maximum elevation of 80 degrees. Only two twin mountings ould be shipped, however, as the hull length was limited by available building berths. Close-in AA protection was provided by two twin stablised 40mm (1.5in) mountings aft, with single guns flanking the bridge structure.

Country of origin:	Britain
Type:	Destroyer
Launch date:	12 June 1945 (HMS *Battleaxe*, first unit)
Crew:	255
Displacement:	2870 tonnes (2825 tons)
Dimensions:	111.2m x 11.58m x 3.2m (365ft x 38ft x 10ft 6in)
Endurance:	4447km (2400nm)
Main armament:	Two 102mm (4in) DP guns; two quintuple 533mm (21in) torpedo tube mountings
Powerplant:	Two shafts, two sets of geared steam turbines
Performance:	35 knots

Wielingen

The Belgian Navy has three Wielingen-class frigates (*Wielingen*, *Westdiep* and *Wandelaar*), all commissioned in the late 1970s. Designed by the Belgian Navy and built in Belgian yards, the ships are compact and well-armed. Plans to install a CIWS were abandoned in 1993, but the Sea Sparrow SAM system has been updated. In addition, the vessels' WM25 surface search/fire control radar is being updated to improve electronic counter-countermeasures (ECCM). New sonars have been installed from 1998. The ships are likely to remain in service well into the twenty-first century; two are operational at any one time, a third being laid up on a rotational basis. The Belgian Navy's principal area of operations within the NATO framework is the English Channel and the North Sea, and the Wielingens are capable of operating in the aircraft direction role.

Country of origin:	Belgium
Type:	Frigate
Launch date:	30 March 1976
Crew:	159
Displacement:	2469 tonnes (2430 tons)
Dimensions:	106.4m x 12.3m x 5.6m (349ft x 40ft 4in x 18ft 5in)
Endurance:	9650km (5186nm)
Main armament:	One 100mm (3.9in) gun; Exocet SSM; Sea Sparrow SAM; two 533mm (21in) torpedo tubes
Powerplant:	Two shafts, one gas turbine, two diesels
Performance:	26 knots

Wilmington

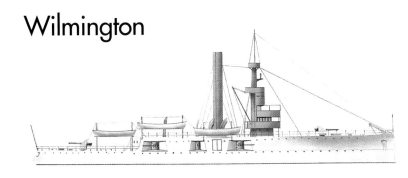

Wilmington was laid down in 1894 and completed in May 1897. She and her sister *Helena* were patrol gunboats for use in the waters around Florida. They had one tall funnel and the hull cut down to form a long poop. Two of the 102mm (4in) guns were mounted on the foredeck, with two more mounted aft and two on each broadside behind 38mm (1.5in) armour. The ships had a shallower draught than other US gunboats, making them ideal for river work. *Wilmington*'s engines developed 1900hp. She saw service in the 1898 war with Spain, later serving as a training ship, but she was retained on the Navy List along with other former combatant vessels that were unclassified but were kept as relics, for use as training ships or adapted for other duties. *Wilmington* was renamed *Dover* and she was allocated the number IX.30. She was scuttled in 1947.

Country of origin:	USA
Type:	Gunboat
Launch date:	19 October 1895
Crew:	80
Displacement:	1716 tonnes (1689 tons)
Dimensions:	76.4m x 12.4m x 2.7m (250ft 9in x 41ft x 9ft)
Endurance:	Not known
Main armament:	Eight 102mm (4in) guns
Powerplant:	Twin screws, triple expansion engines
Performance:	12 knots

Yubari

The Yubari class of frigate is basically an improved and enlarged variant of the Ishikari design, authorised between 1977 and 1978. The greater length and beam improved the seaworthiness and reduced the internal space constrictions of the earlier design. The original number of units to be built was three, but this was reduced to two (*Yubari* and *Yubetsu*) when the Japanese Government deleted funds from the naval budget in the early 1980s. Although not heavily armed and having no helicopter facilities, the vessels of the Yurabi class are ideal for use in the waters around Japan, where they are able to operate under shore-based air cover. Most of their weapons, sensors and machinery have been built under licence from foreign manufacturers. It was originally planned to fit Phalanx, but this is no longer likely.

Country of origin:	Japan
Type:	Frigate
Launch date:	22 February 1982
Crew:	95
Displacement:	1717 tonnes (1690 tons)
Dimensions:	91m x 10.8m x 3.6m (298ft 6in x 35ft 5in x 11ft 10in)
Endurance:	7412km (4002nm)
Main armament:	One 76mm (3in) gun; Harpoon SSM; six 324mm (12.75in) torpedo tubes; A/S mortars
Powerplant:	Two shafts, one gas turbine, one diesel
Performance:	25 knots

Yukikaze

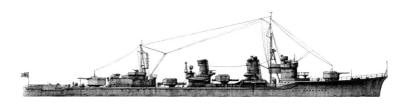

Completed in 1956, *Yukikaze* (Snow Wind) and her sister ship *Harukaze* (Spring Wind) were authorized under the 1953 fiscal year programme and were the first destroyer-hulled vessels to be built in Japan since World War II. Electric welding was extensively used in their hull construction; another novelty was the development and usage of high tension steel in the main hull and of light alloy in the superstructure. Nearly all the armament was supplied by the USA and was modified in March 1959, when homing torpedo tubes were mounted and depth charge equipment correspondingly reduced. *Harukaze* was built at Ngasaki and *Yukizake* at Kobe, both by the Mitsubishi company. The other Japanese destroyer classes in service at this time were named Cloud, Moon, Rain, River, Thunder, Twilight and Rain.

Country of origin:	Japan
Type:	Destroyer
Launch date:	20 August 1955
Crew:	240
Displacement:	2378 tonnes (2340 tons)
Dimensions:	106m x 10.5m x 3.7m (347ft 8in x 34ft 6in x 12ft)
Endurance:	9636km (5203nm)
Main armament:	Three 127mm (5in) DP guns; eight 40mm (1.5in) AA; A/S mortars
Powerplant:	Two shafts, geared steam turbines
Performance:	30 knots

Z37

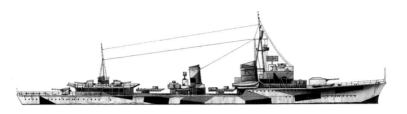

The German destroyer *Z37* was one of seven modified Type 36A boats, popularly known as Narviks because they spent most of their operational careers in Arctic waters. The Z-class destroyers were formidable fighting ships, but between 1943 and 1944, were no match for the weight of Allied air power directed against them, even though their AA armament was constantly increased. Three were sunk by air attack, and several severely damaged. Like most German equipment, their quality was of limited value against overwhelming odds. Attacking them was a risky business; on 28 March 1943, four Z-class boats, including *Z37*, were escorting the Italian blockade runner *Pietro Orseleo* on her voyage from the Gironde to Japan when they beat off an attack by a strike wing of RAF Beaufighter torpedo-bombers and shot down five aircraft. *Z37* was scuttled at Bordeaux in August 1944.

Country of origin:	Germany
Type:	Destroyer
Launch date:	24 February 1941
Crew:	321
Displacement:	3658 tonnes (3600 tons)
Dimensions:	127m x 12m x 3.9m (416ft 7in x 39ft 5in x 12ft 10in)
Endurance:	10,935km (5904nm)
Main armament:	Four 150mm (5.9in) guns; two quadruple 533mm (21in) torpedo tubes
Powerplant:	Two shafts, geared steam turbines
Performance:	36 knots

Zieten

Designed and built by the Thames Ironworks, London, *Zieten* was Germany's first major torpedo vessel. An elegant ship with a clipper bow, she had a very good speed for her day. Thanks to her good qualities as a seaboat, and the number of torpedo reloads she was able to carry (10 rounds), she would probably have given a good account of herself in action, despite her lack of guns. She was initially armed with one submerged torpedo tube at bow and stern. Later, six 50mm (1.95in) guns were added, making her an effective torpedo gunboat. From 1899 she served as a fishery protection vessel, and in 1914 she became a coastal patrol ship, a duty which she shared with the old torpedo boats *D3*, *T61*, *T62* and the sloop *Schwalbe*. She was scrapped in 1921. Nearly all subsequent classes of German torpedo boats were built by Schichau.

Country of origin:	Germany
Type:	Torpedo gunboat
Launch date:	9 March 1876
Crew:	94
Displacement:	1170 tonnes (1152 tons)
Dimensions:	79.4m x 8.5m x 4.6m (260ft 6in x 28ft x 15ft 2in)
Endurance:	Not known
Main armament:	Two 380mm (15in) torpedo tubes
Powerplant:	Twin screws, horizontal compound engines
Performance:	16 knots

Index

Page numbers in **bold** refer to main entries

318